# A WORLD OF SALADS

D1490006

HOLT, RINEHART AND WINSTON

NEW YORK

# A WORLD OF
# SALADS

R O S A L I E   S W E D L I N

First published in 1981 by Holt, Rinehart and Winston,
383 Madison Avenue, New York, New York 10017.

Library of Congress Cataloging in Publication Data
Swedlin, Rosalie.
A world of salads.
Includes index.
1.  Salads.  2.  Cookery, International.  I.  Title.
TX740.S93   1981      641.8'3      80–18134
ISBN Hardbound: 0–03–053391–0
ISBN Paperback: 0–03–059191–0

Published in Great Britain in a slightly different version
under the title *World of Salads* by Elm Tree Books/Hamish Hamilton Ltd.

Designer: Amy Hill
Illustrations by Pamela Dowson
Printed in the United States of America

Grateful acknowledgement is made for permission
to quote from the following:
*The Artist's Cookbook*, published by the Museum of
Modern Art, New York. Copyright © 1977 by
Madeleine Conway and Nancy Kirk.
*Good Things* by Jane Grigson, copyright © 1979
by Jane Grigson. Used by kind permission
of David Higham Associates Ltd., London.

# CONTENTS

# ACKNOWLEDGMENTS

AMONG THE MANY PEOPLE who encouraged this neophyte act of authorship, I am particularly grateful to June Hall and Kate Dunning, the first editors who showed faith in, and commissioned, this book; and to Jennifer Josephy, whose sharp eye for detail and commonsense approach transformed my manuscript into a useful kitchen companion.

I also wish to thank my colleagues at Anthony Sheil Associates, who sampled the salads, and my family, who encouraged my writing and research, especially my mother.

# INTRODUCTION

I HAVE ALWAYS BEEN FASCINATED by the endless possibilities of salads. While, as Gertrude Stein might have said, a roast chicken is a roast chicken is a roast chicken on almost any dinner table in the country, a salad is a highly unpredictable combination of cold vegetables and herbs—and a multitude of other ingredients including meats, fish, pasta, beans, cheese, eggs, and rice—which may be chopped, sliced, diced, boiled, blanched, shredded, grated, mashed, or puréed, and dressed in an equally various and unpredictable fashion.

Although salads were known to many of the civilizations of the ancient world, the first recipe to be written in English was recorded in 1390 by Richard II's master chef; and the first major contribution to the discussion of salads in the English language was John Evelyn's *Acetaria,* published in 1699. "Sallets in general," he wrote, "consist of certain esculent Plants and Herbs, improv'd by Culture, Industry and Art of the Gard'ner; Or, as others say, they are a composition of Edule Plants and Roots of several kinds, to be eaten Raw or Green, Blanch'd or Candied; simple, and serfe, or intermingl'd with others according to the season." And for their composition he recommended a balance of ingredients which should "fall into their places, like the *Notes* in *Music,* in which there should be nothing harsh or grating."

Both Evelyn and his contemporary, Gervase Markham, author of *The English Housewife,* divided salads into three groupings: simple, compounded, and those to decorate the table. Markham added a fourth group by combining those "both for use and adornation."

The French classical repertoire includes two kinds of salad: the simple salad, a bowl of tossed greens or another single vegetable, served sometimes as an accompaniment to the main course, but mainly afterward, for the purpose of refreshing the palate, and the combination salad, a separate and special course, most often served as an hors d'oeuvre or as a meal in itself. Also in this second category are the crudités, a selection of raw (*cru*) vegetables served as a first-course salad.

Our own salad repertoire includes some indigenous recipes learned by the early settlers from the native North American Indians and the Aztecs, Mayans, and Incas of Central and South America, as well as the imported dishes of the Europeans, Asians, and Africans who emigrated here.

Colonial gardens and markets offered a splendid selection of greens. William Byrd, a prominent Southern landowner and contemporary of John Evelyn, recorded several dozen varieties of salad greens in his *Natural History of Virginia,* and Thomas Jefferson, a passionate gardener himself, noted in the diaries of his White House years the availability of tomatoes, parsley, radishes, cucumbers, sorrel, cabbage, and celery, and, of course, lettuce.

However, our main salad heritage from the eighteenth and nineteenth centuries consists primarily of pickled, marinated, and "wilted" dishes: salads used chiefly as relishes with other foods. Fresh salads, as we know them today, have become a central feature of our diet thanks to refrigerated transport, sophisticated growing methods, and a better understanding of nutrition. A splendid assortment of fresh salad ingredients can now be purchased all year round in almost every part of the country. The increased importance of salads in our diet can be easily seen in the proliferation of salad bars and salad restaurants from coast to coast. Salads have a great appeal to anyone concerned about keeping slim and eating nutritiously. In addition they are easy to prepare and provide a meal that is as pleasing to the eye as to the palate.

These and many other reasons have made the salad a prominent feature of our national cuisine. Some of our favorite creations (Waldorf salad, Delmonico salad, chef salad, and so on) have achieved great popularity in other countries, while our own interest in traditional and exotic cuisines from foreign lands continues to increase. A growing American food sophistication now means that such previously rare delights as *caponata, baba ghanoush, céleri rémoulade,* and *horiatiki salata* have become familiar items. For those who have tasted these flavorful creations, a wedge of iceberg lettuce smothered in artificially flavored bottled dressing can never pass for salad again.

# GREEN SALADS

*Bibb Lettuce*

*Cos Romaine*

FOR MOST PEOPLE, a salad means lettuce. And why not? Lettuce has been cultivated for food since the earliest civilizations.

Our modern word *lettuce* derives from the Latin *lactuca,* but lettuce was known to the Greeks as *tridax* and features in Herodotus' accounts of the feasts served to Persian kings in the sixth century B.C. Throughout the ancient world, the green salad appeared as a standard feature on the banquet menu. The Hebrews served watercress and lettuce with just a sprinkling of salt, the Greeks dressed their salads with honey and oil, and the Romans prepared a more elaborate dish with oil, spices, hard-boiled eggs, and other garnishes.

The many varieties of lettuce cultivated today are descended from a wild, prickly lettuce of Asian origin. During the reign of Elizabeth I, lettuce was introduced to England; it proved so popular that within thirty years no fewer than eight varieties existed, and it became an important early crop in the American colonies.

Admired for its delicate taste and colorful adornment of the dinner table, lettuce has been equally appreciated as a rich and freely available source of vitamins and minerals, and as a useful aid to digestion. The Roman physician

1

Galen praised it for curing the stomach disorders of his youth, and in old age he claimed that it brought him a good night's sleep. In the sixteenth century, *Gerard's Herball* advised readers that "lettuce cooleth the heate of the stomache, called the heart-burning and helpeth it when it is troubled with choller."

Perhaps it was the medicinal virtues of lettuce that prompted the still-unresolved question as to when during the meal a green salad should be served. In the first century A.D., the Roman poet Martial recorded his confusion when the Emperor Domitian changed the well-established custom of serving the salad course last: "How comes it that this food which our ancestors ate only as a desert is now the first that is put before us?" The answer, appropriate even today, is that the salad is such a versatile dish it can be served whenever it best enhances the rest of the meal—as a first course or an hors d'oeuvre; with the main dish; before the cheese; with the cheese; or as a whole meal in itself!

My own preference, if the main dish is a roast or rich casserole, is to serve a green salad either as a first course or following the entrée with some cheese. However, for suppers, light luncheons, and summer meals, a green salad makes a suitable and refreshing accompaniment to the main course.

The perfect salad begins with the choice of greens. A basic salad can be made from one, or a combination of greens—primarily lettuce—which complement each other in color, texture, and flavor.

The four most popular varieties of salad greens generally available in American markets are: Boston or butterhead lettuce, iceberg, romaine, and curly endive and broad-leafed endive (escarole). Many other greens are also available seasonally in the markets (and don't forget the greens that can be picked wild—these tasty plants add wonderful variety and distinctive flavor to the salad bowl whenever they are in season).

Here is a basic selection:

*Arugula* is the Italian-American name for this pungent, peppery salad green grown originally in southern Europe. It is available from Italian and other specialty food stores, but should be used moderately as a seasoning for the salad bowl, since it can be quite bitter. It is also known as rocket, roquette, rugula, or ruchetta.

*Belgian endive,* often found in seed catalogs as witloof chicory, was discovered in 1850 by the chief gardener of the Belgian Horticultural Society, who noticed that some chicory plants in his dark basement would form hard, white salad cones if some leaves were pressed around them. At its best between May and October, this lovely, delicate vegetable is almost always very expensive. It need not be washed before using; just remove any bruised outer leaves and wipe the rest gently with a damp paper towel.

*Bibb,* a kind of butterhead lettuce, is much prized for its crisp, pungent flavor. Characterized by soft, dark-green leaves, it needs careful rinsing to clean properly. Limestone is a particular type of Bibb lettuce grown mainly in the limestone soil of Kentucky and Indiana.

*Boston lettuce* is another butterhead green with loosely packed, pale-green, pliable leaves. Available through most of the year, it makes an excellent all-purpose lettuce but should be washed carefully to prevent the delicate inner leaves from bruising.

*Chinese cabbage,* originally grown in eastern Asia and northern China, is long, crisp, and heavy; it is similar in shape to a romaine lettuce but much more densely packed. It has a wonderfully juicy, crisp, fresh taste, and its sturdy leaves will stand up to some of the heavier dressings we Americans like on our salads.

*Cress,* the most popular of which, garden cress, is usually grown together with the delicate white mustard plant, makes a fresh, distinctive garnish for salads. It can be grown easily from seeds on damp blotting paper and is also becoming more widely available in supermarkets.

*Curly endive,* sometimes called chicory, is a bushy green plant with tough, feathery leaves and a sharp, bitter flavor. A rich source of vitamins B and C and minerals, its main season is winter. Many people prefer to mix the strong-tasting chicory leaves with other, milder greens. I think it is delicious on its own with a mustard vinaigrette or *à la Périgord,* with walnut oil dressing, a garnishing of sliced hard-boiled eggs, and a *chapon.*

*Dandelion greens*—the young, fresh leaves—are a wonderful, free treat for the salad bowl. Their thin, arrow-shaped leaves have a sharp, bitter flavor that can be reduced by blanching, that is, covering the plant with an inverted flower pot for several days before using. Long appreciated for medicinal purposes, these greens are rich in iron, minerals, and vitamins A and C.

*Escarole,* known also as broad-leafed endive and Batavia, is similar to curly endive, but its taste is less bitter and its leaves broader and fan-shaped. The center is pale and yellowish; the edges and outer leaves turn dark green.

*Fiddlehead ferns* have been popular in America since colonial times. These tender green plants, with tips that curl like the head of a violin, usually grow in moist soil along streams in woody areas. Gather when the heads are still tightly curled, and eat, lightly steamed, as soon as possible.

*Iceberg* has its many detractors—"I think all iceberg lettuces should be put into the Atlantic Ocean with the other icebergs," wrote Dione Lucas—but its crisp, pale, tightly packed leaves are ideal with heavy dressings such as Roquefort, thousand island, or green goddess. Most iceberg lettuce comes from California and Arizona and is available throughout the year.

*Leaf lettuce,* of which Salad Bowl, Green Ice, and Oakleaf are popular varieties, is a delicate, loose-leaf lettuce that does not form heads. Its soft-textured leaves provide a pleasant contrast when mixed with coarser greens like romaine and curly endive. Leaf lettuces wilt quickly and should not be stored for too long. Ruby, Bronze, and Redleaf lettuces have lovely decorative red-tinged leaves.

*Purslane,* sometimes considered a troublesome garden weed, has an acidic flavor, soft, fleshy leaves, and plenty of calcium, vitamin C, and iron.

*Radicchio* is a type of chicory grown in the northeastern Veneto region of

Italy. A red variety called Rosso di Treviso, with deep-rose-colored leaves and sturdy white veins, is sometimes available from Italian food stores during the winter months. The wonderfully distinctive flavor of radiccio's cabbagelike leaves is enhanced by a freshly made garlic-and-mustard vinaigrette.

*Romaine* has crisp, long leaves and a strong, sharp flavor. The outer dark-green leaves are often too coarse for salads, but they should be saved as decorative lining for platters. Usually available throughout the year, it is the basic lettuce of such popular creations as Caesar and Delmonico salads.

*Sorrel,* both wild and cultivated, has a heavenly lemony flavor. Wood and mountain sorrel are the most acidic, French sorrel the mildest. It is available in markets in late spring and early summer, and can also be easily grown in the garden. Use young, tender leaves for salads.

*Spinach* leaves are now widely accepted and very popular salad greens. Wash thoroughly to remove the sand that tends to cling to the leaves. Delicious with so many things, spinach leaves are especially good combined with sliced raw mushrooms, hard-boiled egg, and crumbled bacon or grated Parmesan cheese.

*Watercress* has been used as both a food and a medicine for more than two thousand years. The Greek general Xenophon included it in his soldiers' diet, and it is still appreciated as a rich source of iodine and vitamin C. Its peppery, spicy taste combines well with many other greens. Watercress perishes easily and should be used within two days of purchase. Sort out the bad sprigs immediately, wash the rest, drain, and store in a plastic bag in the refrigerator.

When selecting salad ingredients, always look for fresh, crisp greens. These should be washed carefully ahead of time so that the leaves are absolutely dry when placed in the salad bowl (accumulated water will dilute the flavor of the dressing and cause the leaves to wilt). Tightly packed greens—romaine, iceberg, Belgian endive, and so on—can be left intact when washing; however, loose-leaf lettuces, which tend to accumulate dirt at their centers, should be carefully separated before washing and storing.

There are several good ways to wash greens. Some people soak the greens in cold, lightly salted water (which is meant to kill any possible germs or bugs); or you can simply rinse leaves under a cold, running tap. Yet another method involves cutting a core out of the center of the lettuce and running water into the hollow with enough force to split the head apart, forcing the dirt from the center.

After washing, gently tear or cut the leaves into appropriately sized pieces (according to your recipe), remove any bruised or wilted leaves, shake, and allow excess water to drain by placing leaves in a lettuce basket, colander, or sieve. There are now several mechanical salad spinners on the market, which operate by centrifugal force. These are wonderful for preparing last-minute salads, when quick drying is essential.

To crisp and store lettuce, place the leaves between layers of paper toweling or cloth towels; then gently roll or fold the towels and place in a plastic bag or directly in the salad compartment of the refrigerator. Make sure the temperature is not too low, or the lettuce will become translucent and wilt.

In spite of much that has been said against the wooden salad bowl—for example, oil and garlic turn the wood rancid, and washing leaves a wet wood taste—I still believe it is the ideal bowl for a tossed salad. A large, deep bowl made of unvarnished wood is least likely to bruise the leaves, and its depth makes for easy tossing and requires less dressing. Do make sure to clean a wooden bowl with warm soapy water after each use, drying it immediately with a cloth towel—otherwise it will indeed become rancid.

With glass, Lucite, and ceramic bowls there is positively no danger of lingering aftertastes from previous dressings, and glass and Lucite bowls have the added advantage of showing off your mixture of greens from top to bottom.

A green salad should not be dressed until just before serving, but the dressing can be prepared well in advance in a separate dish or actually mixed in the bowl in which the salad will be served. With the latter method, the greens can be piled loosely on top of the dressing and allowed to stand in the refrigerator until just before serving. Sometimes the dressing is made *on* the salad: the oil is poured on first and the leaves carefully tossed until they glisten; then the other ingredients are added and the salad is tossed lightly once again. I recommend this method only to experienced salad-makers, since it is not so easy to correct a mistake.

In general, the bowl should be no more than half full and the leaves should be tossed just enough times so that they glisten with oil.

No salad is complete without a suitable garnish. This need be no more than a sprinkling of fresh herbs or something that adds color, a seasonal touch, or a subtle accent of flavor. The following list may be used for inspiration, but developing your own favorite garnishes is part of the aesthetic pleasure in salad making.

# GARNISHES FOR GREEN SALADS

## VEGETABLES

Artichoke hearts, canned or freshly cooked
Diced avocado
Pickled beets
Shredded cabbage
Shredded carrots
Cucumber slices
Fennel bulbs, sliced
Garbanzo beans (chick-peas), canned or cooked
Thinly sliced green pepper rings
Thinly sliced leeks

Sliced raw mushrooms
Thinly sliced onion rings
Palm hearts, cut into thin strips
Cooked green peas

Chopped pimiento or red pepper
Radish slices
Chopped shallots or scallions
Cherry tomatoes or tomato wedges

## FRESH HERBS

Basil
Chives
Coriander leaves
Dill leaves

Fennel leaves
Mint
Parsley

## FRUITS

Thin slices of unpeeled apple or pear
Finely chopped dried fruits—dates,
    figs, apricots, etc.
Sections of fresh grapefruit, orange,
    or tangerine

Seedless green grapes
Orange or lemon zest
Pomegranate seeds
Raisins or currants

## FLOWERS

*use lemon juice rather than vinegar dressing
if flowers are used for garnish*

Yellow and white chrysanthemum
    flowers
Marigold petals

Nasturtium leaves and flowers
Rose petals
Violet flowers

## MISCELLANEOUS

Chopped anchovies
Crisp bacon bits
Capers
Crumbled blue, Roquefort, or feta
    cheese
Grated Parmesan cheese
Croutons

Hard-boiled egg slices
Chopped or slivered nuts
Olives
Minced spicy sausage
Toasted sesame seeds
Thinly sliced water chestnuts

# GREEN SALAD WITH EGG SAUCE

*Serves 4*

This recipe, from Mrs. Alma McKee, formerly cook to H.M. Queen Elizabeth II, was a favorite at royal picnics.

½ teaspoon dry mustard
2 tablespoons wine vinegar
Pinch of sugar
4 hard-boiled eggs
2 raw egg yolks

½ cup light cream
Salt and freshly ground pepper
1 large head Boston, romaine, or
   iceberg lettuce
1 small bunch fresh chives, chopped

Mix mustard with the vinegar and sugar to form a smooth paste. Sieve the hard-boiled egg yolks into a small bowl and slowly add the raw egg yolks, lightly beaten, and half the cream. When smooth, add the vinaigrette paste, stirring all the time. Finish by adding this mixture to the remaining cream, and season with salt and pepper to taste. Chop the egg whites and set aside.

To make the salad, break the washed and well-dried lettuce into small pieces and add the chives. Pour on the dressing, toss, and garnish with the chopped hard-boiled egg whites.

*Note:* A richer variation of the recipe, called Normandy Lettuce Salad, requires 2 fresh egg yolks, ½ cup heavy cream or sour cream, and 3 tablespoons vinegar. Blend until smooth, then pour over lettuce and serve.

# ZELENA SALATA SA KISELIM MLEKOM

### YUGOSLAVIAN GREEN SALAD WITH YOGURT DRESSING

*Serves 6*

2 heads romaine lettuce
1 cup yogurt
Pinch of sugar

Salt and freshly ground pepper
2–3 tablespoons olive oil

Wash lettuce thoroughly, removing any outer bruised leaves, and tear remainder into small pieces. Drain and dry well before putting leaves into the salad bowl. To the yogurt, add sugar, salt and pepper to taste, and gradually stir in oil. Pour mixture over salad, and toss leaves gently until they glisten with dressing. Chill and serve.

# SALADE VERTE AUX ANCHOIS

### GREEN SALAD WITH ANCHOVIES

*Serves 5–6*

½ head romaine lettuce
½ head escarole
1 head Belgian endive
1 tablespoon chopped fresh parsley

2 teaspoons chopped fresh tarragon
4/5 cup mayonnaise
8 anchovy fillets, chopped

Wash the romaine and escarole, removing any bruised outer leaves. Drain and allow to dry thoroughly. Clean endive with a damp paper towel. Each of the greens should be broken into similar bite-size pieces.

In the bottom of a large salad bowl put the parsley, tarragon, mayonnaise, and anchovies. Stir well. Add the greens on top of dressing and toss gently until all the leaves are covered. Serve cold.

# SALADE QUERCYNOISE

### FRENCH CHICORY SALAD

*Serves 4*

The Dordogne is the largest walnut-growing region of France, and walnut oil is traditionally used in the preparation of salad dressings. The walnuts themselves, when not cracked for oil, are sun-dried in the autumn on slats of wood and stored for winter and early-spring use.

1 head chicory
6 tablespoons walnut oil
2 tablespoons wine vinegar
Salt and freshly ground pepper to taste

1 *chapon* (see note)
12 walnuts, roughly chopped
2 hard-boiled eggs, sliced (optional)

The lettuce should be very thoroughly washed (chicory collects a lot of dirt at its center), then broken into pieces and shaken dry in a lettuce basket. Wrap lettuce in a dish towel, pat dry, and place in the refrigerator to crisp. The dressing is made by slowly adding the oil to the vinegar, salt, and pepper.

Place the *chapon* in the bottom of a wooden salad bowl. Add the chicory, walnuts, and sliced hard-boiled eggs, if desired. Pour over dressing and toss gently.

*Note:* A *chapon* is a slice of French bread toasted and rubbed on both sides with a piece of cut garlic.

## ANTOINE'S SALADE DES CHAMPS

*Serves 4–5*

Antoine Alciatore opened his New Orleans restaurant in 1840. Many of his dishes—pompano en papilotte, pommes soufflés, oysters à la Rockefeller—became world-renowned favorites. This delicate salad was specially created at Antoine's for the Chevaliers du Tastevin.

1 large bunch watercress
3 heads Belgian endive
1 large pink-fleshed grapefruit
¼ teaspoon dry mustard
4 tablespoons olive oil

1 tablespoon white wine vinegar
Dash of Tabasco or chili sauce
Dash of Worcestershire sauce
Salt and freshly ground pepper

Wash the watercress and remove any damaged stalks. Drain off excess moisture and allow to dry. Wipe the endive with a damp paper towel and remove any bruised leaves. Cut off the bottoms of the endive and separate into individual leaves. Place in a wooden salad bowl and add the watercress.

Cut the grapefruit in half and remove the pits. With a serrated knife, separate the segments and add to the salad.

Prepare the dressing from the remaining ingredients, pour over salad, and toss gently. Serve immediately.

## DELMONICO SALAD

*Serves 4–5*

This salad was created at one of New York's smartest turn-of-the-century restaurants.

1 large head romaine lettuce or
   escarole
6–8 tablespoons olive oil
2 tablespoons vinegar
2 tablespoons cream
2–3 tablespoons crumbled Roquefort
   cheese

Freshly ground pepper
Tabasco sauce
1 hard-boiled egg, finely chopped
2 strips of bacon, cooked, drained,
   and crumbled
Handful of garlic-flavored croutons
   (optional)

Wash and drain the lettuce. If using romaine, break the leaves in half; the leaves of escarole need only be separated from the core. Place the leaves in a dish towel, gently fold, and place in the refrigerator to crisp until ready to use.

To prepare dressing, combine the olive oil, vinegar, cream, and crumbled cheese in a small bowl and whisk until smooth. Add freshly ground pepper and Tabasco to taste, followed by the egg and bacon.

Arrange the lettuce in a salad bowl and pour on dressing just before serving. Garlic-flavored croutons make an excellent garnish.

## SALADE DE PISSENLITS AU LARD

### FRENCH DANDELION SALAD

*Serves 4–6*

Food writer Waverley Root claims this to be the "only indisputably local dish" of the Champagne region. It is also very popular in the American South.

| | |
|---|---|
| 1 pound fresh young dandelion leaves | 1 teaspoon butter |
| 1 clove garlic, peeled and halved | Freshly ground pepper |
| 1 tablespoon wine vinegar | 1 hard-boiled egg yolk, crumbled |
| ½ pound fatty, unsmoked bacon, cut into small pieces | |

Wash the dandelion leaves thoroughly to remove dirt and any traces of chemical spray. Sort through the leaves and remove any brown or bruised bits. Drain and dry on paper towels or a clean dish towel.

Rub a large wooden bowl with the garlic and add the dandelion leaves. Sprinkle with vinegar and toss several times.

Soften the bacon in a frying pan with the butter over low heat for about 10 minutes. Pour the entire contents of the pan over the leaves and toss. Add freshly ground pepper to taste, toss again, and garnish with crumbled egg yolk. Serve at once.

## CAESAR SALAD

*Serves 6*

This American classic, created in Tijuana in the 1920s by restaurateur Caesar Cardini, is now an international favorite. Most recipes for Caesar salad call for anchovies, but according to Julia Child, who consulted Caesar's daughter on the ingredients in the original recipe, Caesar never used anchovies, only anchovy-flavored Worcestershire sauce.

Ms. Child also discovered Caesar's method for making croutons—well worth the extra effort: "Cut homemade-type unsweetened white bread into half-inch dice and dry out in the oven, basting them as they brown with olive oil in which you have steeped fresh crushed garlic for several days."

The following recipe uses one egg, instead of the two recommended by Rosa Cardini, and if you do have a passion for anchovies, eliminate the Worcestershire sauce from the dressing and add 6–8 anchovy fillets, drained and finely chopped, to your salad. A dishonor, perhaps, to the memory of Caesar Cardini, the anchovies are nonetheless undeniably delicious in combination with the dressing and Parmesan cheese!

2 heads romaine lettuce
8 slices white bread, crusts removed
  and cut into small dice
12 tablespoons olive oil
2–3 cloves garlic, crushed
2 tablespoons fresh lemon juice

Salt and freshly ground pepper
1 egg, boiled for exactly 1 minute
Worcestershire sauce or 6–8 anchovy
  fillets
1 ounce freshly grated Parmesan
  cheese

Wash the lettuce and discard any bruised leaves. Remove the leaves gently from the stalks and break into pieces 4–5 inches long. Drain and dry well. Wrap loosely in a clean dish towel and refrigerate until ready to use.

The croutons can be made Caesar's way or more quickly by sautéing the diced bread in 4 tablespoons of olive oil with the crushed garlic. Turn frequently to avoid burning and remove when the bread is a delicate brown color. Drain on paper towels.

Just before serving, place the lettuce leaves in a large wooden or glass bowl. Put the remaining ingredients in small individual bowls to be brought to the table with the lettuce. Chill large, flat dinner plates on which the salad will be served.

First, pour on the remaining 8 tablespoons of olive oil and toss well so that each leaf is thoroughly coated. Next, add the lemon juice, a sprinkling of salt, and several grinds of black pepper. Now break the egg into the salad, add a few drops of Worcestershire sauce or the anchovies, and toss well again, making sure to get down to the leaves at the bottom of the bowl. Sprinkle on the cheese, add the croutons, and toss once or twice more. Serve on the chilled plates.

## FLEMISH ENDIVE SALAD

*Serves 4–6*

½ pound thickly sliced bacon
Oil for frying bacon
6 Belgian endive
2 hard-boiled eggs, finely chopped

½ cup olive oil
⅛ cup white wine vinegar
Salt and freshly ground pepper
2 tablespoons chopped fresh parsley

To reduce the saltiness of the bacon, cut each slice into small pieces and place these in boiling water for approximately 5 minutes. Drain the bacon on paper towels and, when thoroughly dry, fry the pieces in a little oil until crisp.

Wipe the endive with a damp cloth and remove any bruised leaves. Cut each head into pieces approximately ½ inch long, place in a glass salad bowl, and add the chopped egg.

Make the dressing with the olive oil, vinegar, salt, and pepper. Pour over the salad and garnish with the bacon and parsley. Toss thoroughly and serve immediately.

*Note:* This salad can also be made quite successfully with watercress instead of Belgian endive, or use both for an attractive blend of flavors and color.

# SALADE D'ENDIVES À L'ORANGE

### ENDIVE SALAD WITH ORANGE DRESSING

*Serves 4–6*

6 Belgian endives
Juice of 2 oranges
4 tablespoons olive oil
Salt and freshly ground black pepper

Lemon juice (optional)
Parsley or mint, chopped
Slivers of orange peel

Remove any bruised leaves from the endive heads and wipe with a damp paper towel. Cook them whole in gently simmering water for 15–20 minutes, or until tender. Drain carefully and allow to cool completely. The dressing is made by combining the juice of the oranges with the olive oil, salt, and pepper. (If the oranges are very sweet, add a dash of lemon juice to taste.) Arrange the endives on a flat dish, pour on dressing, and garnish generously with chopped parsley or mint and a sprinkling of orange peel slivers. Serve chilled.

# DRESSINGS AND DIPS

THE DRESSING IS THE CROWNING GLORY of a salad: it should enhance the flavor of the salad's components, complement the other foods with which it is to be served, and refresh the palate with its mildly piquant taste.

The classic worldwide favorite is vinaigrette—a basic combination of oil and vinegar, salt, and freshly ground pepper, varying in proportions to accommodate regional and personal preferences. Variations on this standard theme include ingredients such as dry mustard, garlic, sugar, chopped herbs, shallots, Dijon mustard, cream, eggs, and crumbled cheese. Often, too, lemon juice is used to soften the flavor, in combination with, or in place of, vinegar.

Before considering the preparation techniques and different types of dressings, a few words about the basic constituents.

## OIL

"SMOOTH, LIGHT AND PLEASANT upon the tongue," wrote John Evelyn of the perfect salad oil. Naturally he meant olive oil, long the acknowledged

Western favorite for dressing salads. But other plants yield oils of equal character and equal appeal.

Historically, flax and radish seeds provided oil for the Egyptians; the Greeks extracted oil from walnuts and opium poppies; while the richest earliest sources of oil for most Asian peoples were probably the soybean and the coconut. Groundnut (peanut) corn, and sunflower are the traditional oils of Central and South America; and in West Africa the deep-orange palm oil is most widely used, along with oils extracted from peanuts, sesame, and corn.

Even where olive oil is widely available, many cooks prefer oils with blander taste and less aroma. The lightest of all oils is safflower oil, an almost colorless oil with a very low cholesterol count. Other types recommended by the health-conscious and by natural-food advocates are sunflower, sesame (*not* the dark Oriental variety), peanut, and corn oils.

The ancient civilizations of the eastern Mediterranean that cultivated the olive discovered the versatility of the oil it yielded. They used the first-pressing oil for cooking; the second, for skin ointments, hair dressings, and medicines; and further pressings as fuel for lighting and heat. Today *la première pression à froid,* the first-pressing oil, extracted from the finest-quality olives and crushed without application of heat, is the connoisseur's most coveted dressing oil.

The flavor, character, and quality of olive oil are affected as much by the country of origin as they are by the methods of extraction, harvesting, and the degree of ripeness of the fruit when picked. The French oils—gold, fruity, and light in color—are generally the most expensive.

Of the other Mediterranean varieties commonly available—Greek, Spanish, and Italian—I prefer the Greek and Sicilian oils. They are not at all like the delicate French *huiles vierges.* Robust, thick, dark green, and strongly aromatic, they are far more distinctive than the rather bland oils generally found in supermarkets. They make excellent dressings for all but the most delicate of salads.

Walnut oil, a product of the Périgord and Burgundy regions of France, adds a unique, aromatic flavor to salads. It can be difficult to obtain, however, and is expensive. A less expensive domestic variety can be purchased at health-food stores. Walnut oil substituted for olive oil in mayonnaise makes a distinctive *céleri rémoulade,* Waldorf salad, or dressing for any chicken salad.


# VINEGAR


THE MEASURE OF VINEGAR in a classic vinaigrette tests the real expertise of the salad dresser. The basic formula in the traditional repertoires calls for three parts oil to one part vinegar, but many great cooks insist on more oil in the mixture. Equally, the palates of different nationalities dictate different proportions of vinegar to oil, as the recipes in this book amply illustrate.

Red or white wine vinegar is most often used, although cider vinegar—a favorite of natural-food devotees—is an acceptable substitute. Generally, malt vinegar is too tart for dressing but will do if no other vinegar is available. Distilled vinegar is best saved for pickling vegetables, and rice vinegar, a delicate white Japanese variety, should be used in greater quantity than most vinegars to achieve a proper balance of piquancy.

The best wine vinegars are imported from Orléans in France, many with added herbs and spices. Flavored and aromatic vinegars can also be made quite easily at home.

The simplest method is to steep the washed and dried herbs in vinegar (approximately 4–6 ounces herbs to 4 cups white wine vinegar) in a large, tightly sealed jar. Store, away from direct light, for about 6–8 weeks. Then strain the vinegar into smaller bottles containing 2 or 3 sprigs of fresh leaves and cork or seal securely. In the spring and summer, try this method with tarragon, thyme, mint, basil, or chervil.

Another homemade technique requires boiling the vinegar. Use white wine or cider vinegar, approximately 4 cups to every 4–6 ounces fresh herbs. Place the washed and dried leaves in the bottom of a heatproof jar and crush lightly with a wooden spoon to release the flavor. Pour in the boiling vinegar and leave to cool. Seal tightly and store in a cool spot, away from direct light for 10 days to 2 weeks. Every now and then, invert the jar and replace right side up again. Taste to check the flavor, and when ready, strain into smaller jars. Cork or seal securely and label for future use.

For a tasty garlic vinegar, peel and halve about a dozen cloves. Place these in a large heatproof jar and pour in approximately 4 cups boiling cider vinegar. Cover and leave at room temperature for 24 hours. Then discard the garlic, strain the vinegar into smaller bottles, cover, and label.

For an unusually pretty *fin de siècle* vinegar—lovely for dressing fruit salads —place 2 cups of tightly packed, cleaned rose petals in a large jar. In a saucepan over low heat dissolve ⅓ cup sugar with 2 cups white distilled vinegar. Remove from the heat and leave to cool. Pour over the rose petals, cover with a tight-fitting lid, and allow to stand in a cool, dark place for 3–4 weeks. Remove the rose petals and strain the liquid into a clean jar. Cork and label for future use.

Leftover wine can also be used to make an excellent wine vinegar. Mix equal quantities of wine with a cider vinegar (try 2 cups of each to start), a couple of peeled and halved garlic cloves, 3 sprigs of fresh tarragon, a few peppercorns and a pinch—if desired—of dried basil or oregano. Pour into a bottle with a tight-fitting lid and store in a cool place for 2 weeks or so. Strain and use for dressing salads.

# THE SEASONINGS

SALT AND PEPPER are the basic seasonings for vinaigrette, although some people prefer to leave the addition of salt to each individual eater. Pepper, mainly black, should always be freshly ground from the peppermill.

Peppermills come in all shapes and sizes. Choose one with a good stainless-steel or aluminum mechanism for adjusting the size of the grind. Salt mills are also widely sold, but most people happily use the traditional open dish. Fill it with sea salt, which has none of the chemical additives commonly found in ordinary table salt.

Mustard, sugar, and garlic are the commonly used optional constituents in the standard vinaigrette. Both dry mustard and prepared mustard (the French varieties, such as Dijon or Pommery mustard, are better choices than the less interesting American mustards) are suitable for salad dressings.

Sugar, to many, is a heresy, but it seems to be well liked by those who find even the slightest hint of vinegar too acidic. Garlic, on the other hand, is widely favored around the globe, but its advocates disagree on the methods by which it is incorporated into the dressing.

There are many ways of adding a garlic flavor to salads. Rub a cut clove along the sides of the bowl; steep a peeled clove in the oil for an hour or so, and remove just before dressing the salad; or, as the French do, rub a piece of stale bread or toast with a cut clove, then place it in the bottom of the salad bowl and toss with the chosen greens and dressing. Sometimes a clove is put through a press or pounded with some salt in a mortar—this method makes a much stronger dressing, well suited to cold vegetable salads.

To avoid the persistence of a garlic smell on a knife or chopping board, sprinkle salt on the board, then cut the clove in the salt; and to avoid odor on the hands, rinse them first with *cold* water after handling garlic.

Herbs can transform a simple vinaigrette into a seasonal delight. When available, always use fresh herbs—two or three carefully chosen to complement your salad greens. Generally, 1–2 tablespoons of finely chopped fresh herbs is the right amount for every 8 tablespoons of dressing, but if dried herbs are substituted, use only one-third the amount. Dried herbs are sometimes soaked to restore their flavor before they are added to a recipe, but crushing them between the fingers as they are added to the oil can work just as well. Whereas fresh herbs may be sprinkled directly onto the salad, dried herbs should be added to the oil well before the salad is dressed.

Since there is an extensive literature on cooking with herbs, I have omitted a detailed description of the many herbs that can be used in salads, but the following list includes various possibilities to invite experimentation and personal research:

## THE BASICS

*Chervil* is warm and spicy, with a slight aniseed flavor. It is somewhat like a mild parsley, and popular with the French for making vinaigrette.

*Chives* are used for a mild onion flavor; they are available frozen or dried, and are among the easiest herbs to grow.

*Dill* is popular in northern and central Europe; it is especially tasty with cucumber and radish salads.

*Sweet marjoram,* a relative of oregano, has a slightly milder, though similar, sweet spicy flavor.

*Mint,* one of the oldest culinary herbs, is used widely in Middle Eastern cooking. Because mint is easy to grow, it is worth experimenting with different kinds.

*Parsley,* the universal herb, is easy to grow and a rich source of vitamin C. The curly variety is most commonly available, but the flat-leafed Italian variety has greater flavor.

*Sweet basil* grows profusely throughout southern France, Greece, and Italy, where this fragrant herb is widely used in cooking.

*Summer savory,* similar to thyme but more delicate, is a very versatile herb.

*Tarragon* adds a delicate but distinctive flavor to all sorts of foods. The French variety is the one to look for.

*Thyme* is a strong-flavored herb native to southern Europe.

## OTHER HERBS

*Angelica* is most commonly eaten as a candied preserve; the stems may be chopped and added to salads.

*Balm* has distinctive lemon-scented leaves. When adding chopped balm leaves to salad, use slightly less vinegar or lemon juice in the dressing.

*Caraway seeds* add a spiciness to cabbage salads and also act as a digestive aid. The fresh green leaves are also good for salads.

*Celery seeds* are the small, aromatic seeds of the celery plant and are excellent in dressings.

*Coriander* leaves (also known as cilantro or Chinese parsley) are popular in Indian and Middle Eastern recipes; the seeds are used for poaching vegetables *à la Grecque,* in ratatouille, and in many African and Asian recipes.

*Fennel* leaves may be substituted for parsley. This vegetable is a great favorite in France and Italy. The seeds are used for broths *à la Grecque* and in various Eastern salad recipes.

*Lovage* has peppery, celery-flavored leaves that may be chopped and added sparingly to salads.

*Oregano* is stronger than sweet marjoram, to which it is related; it is used extensively in Mediterranean cooking.

# VINAIGRETTES

## BASIC VINAIGRETTE
*Makes ½ cup*

2 tablespoons wine vinegar
6–8 tablespoons olive oil

Salt and freshly ground pepper
1 ice cube (optional)

Place the vinegar in a small bowl and gradually add the olive oil, beating with a fork or whisk until the mixture thickens. Season to taste with salt and pepper. An ice cube added to the mixing bowl will produce a creamier dressing, but be sure to remove it once the desired consistency is achieved.

## VINAIGRETTE À LA MOUTARDE

Add ¼ teaspoon dry mustard or 1 scant teaspoon French mustard to the salt and vinegar in the basic recipe. Stir well before blending with olive oil.

## VINAIGRETTE AUX FINES HERBES

Add 2 tablespoons chopped fresh herbs to the basic dressing. Choose from tarragon, parsley, basil, marjoram, chives, thyme, or mint.

## CAPER DRESSING

To the basic vinaigrette, add 1 teaspoon chopped capers, plus 1 peeled clove of garlic, finely minced. Prepare well in advance so that the oil has time to absorb the flavors.

## CURRY DRESSING

Add ½ teaspoon curry powder and 1 teaspoon finely chopped shallots to the vinegar and salt, then proceed as for basic vinaigrette.

# VINAIGRETTE AU CITRON

Crush a peeled clove of garlic with a pinch of salt and pound to a pulp. Place in a small bowl and stir in 1 tablespoon lemon juice, 1 tablespoon white wine vinegar, and ¼ teaspoon dry mustard. Blend until smooth. Gradually add the olive oil, beating with a fork or whisk until the mixture thickens. Season with salt, freshly ground pepper, and a sprinkling of freshly chopped herbs.

# CHOPPED VEGETABLE VINAIGRETTE

A delicious dressing for seafood salads, cold artichokes, and crudités.

2 small firm tomatoes, peeled and
  finely chopped
1 small green pepper, finely chopped
1 clove garlic, minced
2 small shallots, finely chopped
1 tablespoon capers, chopped

8–9 tablespoons olive oil
2–3 tablespoons lemon juice, freshly
  squeezed and strained
1 teaspoon chopped fresh tarragon
  leaves
Salt and freshly ground pepper

Place all the ingredients in a jar with a tight-fitting lid. Shake well and chill for at least an hour. Before serving, correct the seasoning with more salt or pepper.

# LOW-CALORIE VINAIGRETTE

Homemade stock is substituted here for the usual quantity of olive oil, the calorie demon in salad dressings.

5 tablespoons vegetable stock
1 tablespoon olive oil
1 clove garlic, peeled
½ teaspoon finely chopped fresh
  tarragon
½ teaspoon finely chopped fresh basil

1 teaspoon finely chopped fresh
  parsley
1 tablespoon white wine vinegar
2 teaspoons lemon juice
Salt and freshly ground pepper

Pour the stock into a small bowl and gradually whisk in the olive oil. Add the garlic and herbs and allow to marinate for several hours. Remove the garlic and add the vinegar and lemon juice, beating with a fork to blend thoroughly. Season to taste with salt and pepper and whisk again before serving.

## VINAIGRETTE À L'OEUF

Dressing made with a raw egg yolk has a glossy, adhering quality that combines nicely with cooked vegetable salads if added while the vegetables are still lukewarm.

Break the egg yolk into a small bowl and combine with a pinch of salt and 1 teaspoon French mustard. Gradually stir in vinegar to form a smooth paste. Then slowly add the olive oil, beating with a fork or whisk until the mixture thickens.

## MAYONNAISE MASTER RECIPE

*Makes approximately 1¼ cups*

This recipe can be made with either a hand or electric beater.

| | |
|---|---|
| 2 egg yolks | Lemon juice and/or wine vinegar |
| ½ teaspoon dry mustard | 1 cup olive oil |
| ½ teaspoon salt | Freshly ground pepper |

With a wire whisk or fork, beat the egg yolks for 2 minutes, or until smooth and pastelike in consistency. (If using an electric beater, set it to the speed used for whipping cream.) Add the dry mustard, salt, and 1 teaspoon lemon juice or vinegar. Beat for another minute.

Begin adding oil slowly, *drop by drop,* while beating continuously. When approximately ½ cup of the oil has been added and thoroughly absorbed, the beating can stop. When resumed, the beating should alternate with additions of oil (less caution is necessary at this stage, and larger quantities of oil can be added each time) and more lemon juice or vinegar (1 teaspoon at a time) if the mixture becomes too thick.

When all the oil has been added, adjust the seasoning with a pinch or two of salt, if desired, and a few grinds of pepper. If the mayonnaise is not to be used immediately, add 1 tablespoon of boiling water as a protection against curdling. If the correct texture has been achieved, the sauce should be thick enough to cut with a knife!

### WAYS TO DEAL WITH CURDLED MAYONNAISE

Here are five remedies for mayonnaise which has separated. As you become more expert, your eye will be the best judge as to which cure is appropriate each time.

1. While beating with a fork or wire whisk, add ½ teaspoon boiling or very hot water.
2. In a clean bowl, break an egg yolk and beat lightly with a few drops of hot water or lemon juice. Gradually add spoonfuls of the curdled mayonnaise, beating after each addition.
3. In a clean bowl, beat 1 egg yolk with a few drops of oil until very thick. Gradually add the curdled mayonnaise, beating continuously.
4. In a clean bowl, put 1 tablespoon Dijon (or a similar prepared mustard), plus 1 teaspoon of the curdled mayonnaise. Beat until well blended; then slowly, one teaspoonful at a time, add more of the mayonnaise until it again emulsifies. The remaining curdled mayonnaise can then be added to the fresh mixture in larger quantities.
5. Stir the curdled mixture with an electric beater (or in a blender) at very high speed for several seconds.

## STORAGE

Mayonnaise will store well in the refrigerator, in a tightly covered jar, for up to 1 week. Before stirring or serving, allow it to stand at room temperature for at least 2 hours.

# SPEEDY WHOLE-EGG MAYONNAISE

*Makes approximately 1¼ cups*

The use of a whole egg in this quick blender method prevents the mixture from becoming too thick before all the oil is added. If a larger quantity is required, only extra egg yolks are necessary. Increase the oil and other ingredients in proportion (see page 20).

1 egg
¼ teaspoon dry mustard
½ teaspoon salt
1 tablespoon (or more, if required)
  lemon juice or wine vinegar

1 cup olive or salad oil
Freshly ground pepper

Place the egg, mustard, and salt in the blender jar. Cover and blend at high speed for 30 seconds. Add 1 tablespoon of lemon juice or vinegar, cover, and blend for another 15 seconds. Uncover the jar, continue to blend at high speed, and gradually add the oil, drop by drop. When half the quantity has been added, the mixture will begin to thicken. Continue adding oil until the mixture is

21

thick enough to almost stop the action of the blades. Stop the machine and, with a rubber scraper, push all the mayonnaise from the sides into the center of the jar. Cover and blend for a few seconds at high speed. Turn the mayonnaise into a serving bowl or storage jar, and correct the seasoning with additional salt and freshly ground pepper.

## GREEN MAYONNAISE

*Makes 1½ cups*

You can substitute any combination of chopped fresh herbs for the greens listed below. There should be 8 tablespoons in all.

3 tablespoons chopped fresh spinach
  or watercress
2 tablespoons chopped fresh chives,
  basil, or chervil

3 tablespoons chopped fresh parsley
1 cup mayonnaise
Pinch of nutmeg (optional)

Blanch the herbs in a small quantity of boiling water for 1–2 minutes. Drain, rinse with cold water, and pat dry with a cloth. Press through a sieve or purée in an electric food processor or blender, remove any remaining excess liquid, and blend into the mayonnaise, adding nutmeg if you wish.
  Serve with eggs, fish, cooked or raw vegetables.

## RUSSIAN MAYONNAISE

To 1 cup mayonnaise add 3 tablespoons tomato catsup (or, for spicier taste, 2 tablespoons catsup and 1 tablespoon chili sauce); 3 tablespoons red caviar (or red lumpfish roe); 1 tablespoon finely grated onion; 2 heaping tablespoons sour cream, and some freshly cut dill. Blend thoroughly.

## LEMON MAYONNAISE

This is best made by the quick blender method (see page 21). Use 2 table-spoons grated lemon rind to each cup of mayonnaise. Add to the egg yolk mixture *before* the oil is added.

## ANCHOVY MAYONNAISE

To 1 cup mayonnaise add 4–5 finely chopped anchovy fillets, 1 tablespoon finely chopped chives, and 1–2 teaspoons fresh lemon juice, to taste. Blend thoroughly and serve with egg dishes and cold vegetables.

## HORSERADISH MAYONNAISE

Another excellent variation for eggs and seafood. Add 1–2 tablespoons lemon juice to 1 cup mayonnaise, then blend in 2 tablespoons freshly grated horseradish. Serve at once.

## CURRY MAYONNAISE

Use approximately 1 teaspoon curry powder to each cup of mayonnaise. Blend the powder into the egg yolk mixture *before* the oil is added. If a stronger curry flavor is desired, add additional powder to a little mayonnaise in a separate dish. When well blended, add this to the main mixture. Excellent with hard-boiled eggs and raw or parboiled cauliflower.

## PIMIENTO MAYONNAISE

Chop 2 canned pimientos which have been thoroughly drained, and pass through a sieve to purée. Add to 1 cup mayonnaise, along with 1 clove garlic, crushed, and a few drops of lemon juice, to taste. Grind in some fresh pepper and serve with poached fish and cold egg dishes.

## CREAMY MAYONNAISE

To 1 cup slightly chilled blender mayonnaise (made with a whole egg), add approximately ⅓ cup whipped cream. Gently fold the cream into the mayonnaise, add salt and pepper to taste, and serve.

# AÏOLI

*Makes approximately 1⅓ cups*

This famous French garlic mayonnaise from Provence is traditionally served with cold fish and boiled potatoes. It is excellent with crudités and, as with ordinary mayonnaise, can be stored for a week in the refrigerator in a tightly sealed jar.

3–4 cloves garlic
½ teaspoon salt
2 egg yolks

1 tablespoon lemon juice
1 cup olive oil
Freshly ground pepper

Peel the garlic and mash with the salt in a mortar. Add the egg yolks and beat with a wire whisk until smooth. Add the lemon juice and beat for a few seconds more. Gradually add the oil, drop by drop, until the mixture becomes smooth and thickens. When approximately half the oil has been added, the rest can be incorporated at a faster rate; if the mixture becomes too thick, add a few extra drops of lemon juice or warm water.

Pour into a serving dish and adjust seasoning with freshly ground pepper and extra salt, if desired.

# THOUSAND ISLAND DRESSING

*Makes approximately 1⅓ cups*

1 cup mayonnaise
4 tablespoons catsup or chili sauce
2 tablespoons finely chopped pimiento-stuffed olives
2 tablespoons finely chopped green pepper

1 tablespoon finely chopped fresh chives or scallions
1 hard-boiled egg, finely chopped
1 tablespoon finely chopped fresh parsley

Put the mayonnaise into a mixing bowl and add all the remaining ingredients, folding in gently with a wooden spoon. When well blended, cover and chill for at least an hour before using. If stored in a tightly sealed jar in the refrigerator, this dressing will keep well for up to a week.

## SAUCE RÉMOULADE

*Makes approximately 1¼ cups*

1 cup mayonnaise
1 tablespoon chopped capers
2 teaspoons chopped gherkins

2 teaspoons chopped parsley
1 teaspoon anchovy paste (optional)

Blend the mayonnaise with the other ingredients, adding anchovy paste if desired. Serve with seafood or cold vegetables.

# SOUR-CREAM DRESSINGS

COMMERCIALLY BOUGHT SOUR CREAM can be used as a base for dressings. Sweetened with sugar or honey, fruit juices, or fruit purées, and served well chilled, it makes a refreshing accompaniment to a variety of fruit salads. It also combines well with mayonnaise, herbs, spices, crumbled cheeses, and crunchy chopped vegetables. If a more liquid consistency is preferred, thin the sour cream with heavy cream, lemon juice, or cider vinegar.

## BASIC SOUR-CREAM DRESSING

*Makes approximately 1¼ cups*

Use a selection of freshly chopped seasonal herbs. For fruit salads, you might try chopped mint; eggs, tomatoes, and peppers taste delicious with basil and oregano.

3 tablespoons cider vinegar
1–2 tablespoons sugar
½ teaspoon salt

Freshly ground pepper
1 cup sour cream
Chopped seasonal herbs

Beat the vinegar, sugar, salt, and pepper until well blended. Fold in the sour cream, stir, and add herbs to taste.

25

## ROQUEFORT SOUR-CREAM DRESSING

*Makes approximately 1⅓ cups*

2 tablespoons cider vinegar
½ teaspoon dry mustard
1 teaspoon finely chopped shallots

1 cup sour cream
2 ounces Roquefort or blue cheese
Salt and freshly ground pepper

Combine the vinegar, mustard, and shallots and add to the sour cream, stirring to blend well. Crumble the cheese into this mixture, stir again, and season to taste with salt and pepper. Chill before serving.

## COOKED SOUR-CREAM DRESSING

*Makes approximately 1⅓ cups*

1 cup sour cream
2 egg yolks, well beaten
3 tablespoons tarragon vinegar
2–3 teaspoons confectioners' sugar

1 teaspoon salt
1 teaspoon dry mustard
½ teaspoon celery salt
½ teaspoon paprika

In the top of a double boiler, away from the heat, beat the sour cream with the egg yolks. Gradually add the vinegar. Stir in the sugar, salt, and spices. Place over simmering water (the upper section should not touch the water) and whip until creamy smooth. Turn into a serving dish and chill until ready to serve.

## IRISH SOUR-CREAM DRESSING

*Makes approximately 1½ cups*

2 hard-boiled eggs
1 teaspoon dry mustard
1–2 teaspoons sugar
2–3 teaspoons malt vinegar

1 cup sour cream
⅓ cup light cream
Salt and freshly ground pepper

"Rice" the eggs by passing them through a sieve, and pound them together with the mustard and 1 teaspoon sugar until well blended. Gradually add the vinegar while stirring with a wooden spoon. Continue stirring and slowly add the creams. Blend well and season with salt and pepper. Add additional sugar, if desired. Chill until ready to serve.

## GREEN GODDESS DRESSING

*Makes approximately 3½ cups*

A popular favorite for serving with seafood and vegetable salads, this famous dressing was created at the Palace Hotel, San Francisco, in honor of the actor George Arliss for his performance in a play called *The Green Goddess.*

2 tablespoons finely chopped fresh
   chives or 1 tablespoon dried
1 clove garlic, minced
5 tablespoons finely chopped fresh
   parsley
1 tablespoon finely chopped scallions
5–6 anchovy fillets, rinsed, drained,
   and chopped

2 cups sour cream
1 cup mayonnaise
1 tablespoon lemon juice
3 tablespoons tarragon vinegar
Salt and freshly ground pepper

Place the chives, garlic, parsley, scallions, and anchovy fillets in a mixing bowl. Add the sour cream and mayonnaise, and gently stir. Season with lemon juice and vinegar. Stir and add salt and pepper to taste. Cover and chill for at least 2 hours. Just before serving, stir again.

## SOUR-CREAM VERTE

*Makes approximately 1½ cups*

A simple mixture of chopped herbs and finely chopped green vegetables to garnish a salad of hearty greens (cabbage, spinach, romaine, watercress). A sprinkling of well-cooked, crumbled bacon makes a crisp, pleasant garnish for this fragrant dressing.

2 teaspoons freshly squeezed lime
   juice
1 cup sour cream
Salt
Pinch of white pepper
1 teaspoon finely chopped fresh
   parsley

1–2 tablespoons finely chopped fresh
   dill
3 scallions, finely chopped
   (including 2 inches of green tops)
3 tablespoons finely chopped green
   pepper

Mix the lime juice with the sour cream and season to taste with salt and white pepper. Add the remaining ingredients. Mix well and chill for several hours to allow the flavors to penetrate the sour cream.

## FRUITED SOUR CREAM

A purée of fresh fruit pulp—approximately ½ cup fruit to 1 cup sour cream —makes a delicious dressing for fresh fruit salads. Add sugar according to taste and the natural sweetness of the puréed fruit.

## SOUR CREAM AND HONEY DRESSING FOR FRUIT SALADS

Add 2 tablespoons honey (Hymettus or other dark-golden honeys mix best) to 1 cup sour cream; adjust the balance to taste and according to the other ingredients to be added.

## ORANGE RIND DRESSING

To the Sour Cream and Honey Dressing (preceding) add 1 teaspoon grated orange rind, plus 2–3 tablespoons fresh orange juice.

## COCONUT DRESSING

An excellent accompaniment to tropical fruit salads.
  Soften 5 tablespoons freshly grated coconut in 2–3 teaspoons lemon juice, and fold into Sour Cream and Honey Dressing (above).

## MINTED SOUR CREAM

Wonderful with summer berries, melons, and sliced peaches.
  Use slightly less honey (1–1½ tablespoons) than in the Sour Cream and Honey Dressing (above), plus 1 tablespoon crème de menthe and 1 table-spoon finely chopped fresh mint. Mix well before serving.

# OTHER DRESSINGS

## ROQUEFORT DRESSING

*Makes approximately ½ cup*

Roquefort is so expensive that you may wish to substitute blue cheese in this recipe.

2 ounces Roquefort cheese
2 tablespoons heavy cream (more, if desired)
1 teaspoon Worcestershire sauce

4 tablespoons olive oil
1 tablespoon white wine vinegar
½ teaspoon finely grated onion

Mash the cheese with a wooden spoon until smooth and pasty by gradually adding the cream and Worcestershire sauce. In a separate bowl, blend the oil and vinegar. Add this vinaigrette, along with the grated onion, to the cheese mixture. Blend well, add additional cream if desired, and chill until ready to serve.

## BACON DRESSING

This recipe must be prepared *immediately* before serving. Have the selection of greens washed, dried, and arranged in the salad bowl, reading for tossing once the dressing is added.

4 slices bacon, cut into small pieces
4 teaspoons lemon juice
Salt and freshly ground pepper

Sauté the bacon in a small frying pan. When the pieces are cooked but still tender, pour the entire contents of the pan onto the lettuce. Return the pan to a low heat and add the lemon juice, stirring for several seconds until warm. Add this to the salad and toss well with salt and freshly ground pepper to taste.

## CREAM DRESSING I

*Makes approximately ½ cup*

½ teaspoon salt
½ teaspoon finely ground white
  pepper

4 teaspoons white wine vinegar
6 tablespoons heavy cream
2 tablespoons light vegetable oil

Combine the salt, pepper, vinegar, and cream in a small bowl and beat with a fork or wire whisk for 20–30 seconds, or until the mixture achieves a foamy consistency. Gradually add the oil and continue mixing. Correct the seasoning and chill until ready to serve.

## CREAM DRESSING II

*Makes approximately ½ cup*

½ teaspoon Dijon mustard
1 teaspoon sugar (or less, to taste)
2 teaspoons tarragon vinegar
½ clove garlic, crushed (optional)

1 hard-boiled egg yolk, mashed
½ cup cream
1–2 tablespoons chopped fresh
  tarragon and chives

In a small bowl, combine the mustard, sugar, vinegar, garlic (if desired), and mashed egg yolk. Beat with a fork until creamy smooth, then gradually add the cream, stirring constantly, until all ingredients are well blended. Chill, and just before serving, stir in the fresh herbs.

*Note:* If the vinegar curdles the cream, add a few drops of milk or water to the dressing.

## LOW-CALORIE RUSSIAN DRESSING

*Makes approximately 1⅓ cups*

Each tablespoon of this dressing contains 12 calories.

1 cup cottage cheese
1 tablespoon lemon juice
4 tablespoons tomato juice
Salt and freshly ground pepper

Dash of Worcestershire sauce
1 small gherkin, finely chopped
1 hard-boiled egg, finely chopped

Place the cottage cheese and lemon juice in an electric blender and mix at high speed for 10 seconds. Add the tomato juice and blend at low speed until the mixture is creamy smooth. Season to taste with salt, pepper, and Worcestershire sauce. Chill for a couple of hours, and just before serving stir in the chopped gherkin and chopped egg.

## LOW-CALORIE BUTTERMILK DRESSING

*Makes approximately 1⅓ cups*

This dressing, if kept refrigerated in a tightly sealed jar, will last for at least a week. Each tablespoon contains about 10 calories.

| | |
|---|---|
| 1 cup buttermilk | 1 teaspoon salt |
| 4 tablespoons cider vinegar | ½ teaspoon ground white pepper |
| 1 tablespoon light salad oil | |

Place all ingredients in a jar with a tight-fitting lid. Shake well and chill until ready to serve.

## ORIENTAL SALAD DRESSING

*Makes ½ cup*

This and the following recipe both make delicious dressings for salads composed of fresh Chinese cabbage, bean sprouts, chopped water chestnuts, and bamboo shoots. They are also delicious with white or red cabbage and with iceberg lettuce.

| | |
|---|---|
| 1 tablespoon toasted sesame seeds | 2 tablespoons rice wine vinegar |
| 4 tablespoons light soy sauce | 1 teaspoon Chinese mustard, dissolved |
| 2 tablespoons Oriental sesame oil | in 1 teaspoon water |

Toast the sesame seeds in a roasting pan under the broiler or in a deep-frying pan over low heat. Shake occasionally and remove from heat when seeds begin to pop.

Place all the liquid ingredients in a small jar with a tight-fitting lid. Shake well and chill. Just before serving, add the sesame seeds to the mixture, shake again, and pour over the salad.

## ORIENTAL DRESSING WITH CHOPPED PEANUTS

*Makes approximately ¾ cup*

5 tablespoons peanut oil
3 tablespoons plus 1 teaspoon rice
  wine vinegar
1 tablespoon sugar
3 scallions, thinly sliced including
  3 inches green stem

3 tablespoons shelled and chopped
  roasted peanuts
2 tablespoons toasted sesame seeds
  (see preceding recipe)

Place the oil, vinegar, sugar, and scallions in a jar with a tight-fitting lid. Shake well and chill. Just before serving, add the chopped peanuts and sesame seeds, cover, shake again, and pour over the salad.

## POPPY-SEED DRESSING

*Makes approximately ½ cup*

Poppy seeds were a popular crop with the early Shakers. Mennonite cooks developed a dressing of poppy seeds for citrus fruit salads and red cabbage salads. Here is one version of this popular recipe.

½ teaspoon dry mustard
2 tablespoons lemon juice
1 tablespoon sugar
½ teaspoon grated onion

6 tablespoons sunflower oil
Salt
1 teaspoon poppy seeds

In a small bowl, blend the mustard with the lemon juice and sugar. Add the grated union and gradually stir in the oil. Season to taste with salt and toss in the poppy seeds. Pour immediately onto fruit salads and allow to macerate and chill before serving. For lettuce salads, dress and toss just before serving.

*Note:* Orange juice may be used in place of lemon juice, or try a mixture of the two.

## PARTY POPPY-SEED DRESSING

*Makes approximately 1 cup*

A "spiked" dressing for bowls of buffet fruit salads. Try an assortment of tropical fruits—melons, mangoes, citrus, pineapple, and so on.

2 tablespoons white wine vinegar
2 tablespoons freshly squeezed lime
  juice
½ teaspoon dry mustard
½ teaspoon grated onion
2 tablespoons sugar

2 tablespoons honey
½ cup sunflower oil
Salt to taste
2 tablespoons bourbon whiskey
2 tablespoons poppy seeds

Place the vinegar, lime juice, and dry mustard in a small saucepan and stir with a fork or wire whisk until smooth. Add the grated onion, sugar, honey, oil, and salt. Stir this mixture over moderate heat until it begins to boil; reduce the heat and simmer, while stirring, to dissolve the sugar and salt.

Remove from the heat and add the bourbon and poppy seeds. Stir and cool to room temperature before serving. Spoon some of the dressing onto the fruit and serve the rest in a sauceboat.

## HONEY CREAM DRESSING FOR FRUITS

*Makes approximately 2 cups*

2 eggs
½ cup honey
½ cup lemon juice

½ cup orange juice
½ cup heavy cream, whipped
2 teaspoons grated orange rind

Beat the eggs in a small saucepan and stir in the honey, lemon juice, and orange juice. Place the saucepan over low heat and cook, stirring constantly, until the mixture coats the back of a spoon. Remove from heat and cool to room temperature. Fold in the whipped cream and orange rind. Chill for a couple of hours and serve in a sauceboat with fresh fruit salads.

## DIPS FOR CRUDITÉS

CRUDITÉS MAKE ONE OF THE SIMPLEST mixed salads. They are frequently served at cocktail parties or as an hors d'oeuvre in pieces that can be eaten with the fingers and dipped into a creamy dressing or pâté. Arrange a dish with a selection of raw vegetables such as carrot and celery sticks, cauliflower florets, button mushrooms, watercress, strips of turnip or celeriac, and cherry tomatoes. Serve with one of the puréed salads (see index); one of the "dips" following; or a mayonnaise blended with herbs, anchovy paste, or curry.

As an hors d'oeuvre, crudités may be shredded into julienne strips—try cabbage, celeriac, and zucchini—and arranged around a mound of watercress, button mushrooms, or cauliflower florets. Dress generously with a strongly flavored garlic or herb vinaigrette.

Whichever way you choose to serve them, crudités should be crisp, fresh, and slightly chilled.

# KUAH LADA

### SPICY MALAYSIAN DRESSING

*Makes approximately ⅓ cup*

This should be used sparingly, more as a condiment than a dressing. Serve it with crudités or shrimp.

| | |
|---|---|
| 2 red chili peppers | 1 tablespoon vinegar |
| 1 clove garlic, crushed | 2 tablespoons water |
| ½ teaspoon salt | Pinch of sugar |

Red chili peppers are a favorite spice in Malaysia. Traditionally, this dressing is prepared by pounding the peppers with the garlic and salt to a pasty consistency. It is much quicker to deseed and chop the peppers (see page 95) and blend them with the other ingredients in a blender until a puréelike mixture is achieved.

# BAGNA CAUDA

### ITALIAN GARLIC AND ANCHOVY DRESSING

*Makes approximately 1 cup*

Not strictly a salad dressing, this sauce is served as a "hot bath" for a variety of raw vegetables in the Piedmont region of Italy. The white Alba truffle is the essential (though expensive) ingredient for making this dressing in the truly authentic manner. The sauce should be brought to the table in the pot in which it has been cooked and kept warm on top of a table burner or hot plate.

⅓ cup olive oil
¼ pound butter
A few leaves of fresh basil, chopped
2–3 cloves garlic, finely chopped

6–7 anchovy fillets, chopped
Pinch of salt
1 small white truffle (optional)

Place 1 tablespoon each of oil and butter in a small frying pan over low heat. While this heats, put the remaining oil and butter in a small earthenware pot (or in the top of a double boiler) over simmering water. Add the basil and garlic to the frying pan and cook until the garlic softens. Add the anchovy fillets and cook, stirring regularly, until they dissolve to a paste. Add salt, stir, and transfer these ingredients to the pot of oil and butter.

The white truffle, if available, should be grated into thin slivers and added to the sauce just before it is brought to the table.

## NAM PRIK PAK

### RAW VEGETABLES WITH THAI HOT SAUCE

*Nam prik* is a hot, spicy sauce served throughout Thailand in many varieties and accompanying many different types of food. In *Far Eastern Cookery,* Robin Howe describes its presentation as "a cross between the French hors d'oeuvre and a salad served with a pungent sauce." It is usually eaten, he goes on to say,

> with everyone sitting around the table or on the floor, with a plate of rice in front of each person. A bowl of *nam prik* is placed in the centre of the table with all the side dishes around it. The food is eaten with a little of the *nam prik,* followed by a spoonful or handful of the rice. Each one selects the item of food he likes and the combinations can be made by placing different bits of food on a lettuce leaf, adding a few drops of the *nam prik* sauce, then folding the leaf into a bite-size package. This is placed whole in the mouth.

*Nam prik pak* should include a large selection of vegetables and flowers, varying in size, color, texture, and taste. In Thailand, there would most certainly be slices of tart green mango, but if mangoes are out of season, use a crisp, tart cooking apple.

For a really authentic *nam prik, blachan* (dried shrimp cake) and fish sauce should be used, but shrimp or anchovy paste can be substituted for *blachan* and soy sauce for fish sauce. Dried shrimp are available, as are the other Oriental ingredients, from specialty grocery stores.

You may vary these quantities according to taste; no two Thai cooks make *nam prik* the same way.

6 dried shrimp, pounded
2–3 cloves garlic
1 teaspoon *blachan,* roasted in foil, or 1 teaspoon shrimp or anchovy paste
Chili peppers, seeded and chopped (see page 95), to taste

Juice of 1 lime or lemon, freshly squeezed
2 teaspoons sugar
2 teaspoons fish sauce or soy sauce

Place all the ingredients in a blender and mix until a fairly smooth sauce is formed (bits of garlic and chili should still be visible). Serve the sauce in a bowl, set amid a large platter of raw vegetables.

## ROQUEFORT DIP

¼ pound Roquefort or blue cheese
8 ounces cream cheese
1–2 tablespoons cream
Dash of Tabasco sauce

Dash of Worcestershire sauce
3 scallions, chopped, including 2 inches of green stem

Allow the cheese to soften at room temperature. Crumble with a fork and blend with the cream cheese, adding as much cream as is required to achieve the correct "dip" consistency. Season with Tabasco and Worcestershire sauces and fold in all but 1 teaspoon of the chopped scallions. Chill until ready to serve and sprinkle with the remaining scallions.

## SOUR CREAM, BACON, AND HORSERADISH DIP

1 cup sour cream
1 tablespoon freshly grated horseradish
3 slices bacon, cooked until crisp, and crumbled

1 teaspoon Worcestershire sauce
2 scallions, finely chopped (optional)

Blend the sour cream, horseradish, and bacon with the Worcestershire sauce. If desired, add the scallions. Chill.

## COTTAGE CHEESE WITH CHOPPED HERBS
## AND VEGETABLES

1 carrot, finely chopped
2–3 large scallions, finely chopped,
   including 2 inches of green stem
½ small green pepper, finely chopped
½ small red pepper, finely chopped
1 tablespoon chopped fresh chives

1 tablespoon finely chopped fresh
   parsley
1 cup cottage cheese
Salt and freshly ground pepper
Paprika

Mix the chopped vegetables and herbs with the cottage cheese and season to taste with salt and pepper. Chill and sprinkle with paprika just before serving.

*Note:* For a spicier dip, add 1 large clove of garlic, finely minced, or 1 chopped chili pepper (see page 95).

# SINGLE-VEGETABLE SALADS (A TO Z)

THE RECIPES FOR SALADS in this section are largely based on one main ingredient, a boon for the shopper who likes to buy on impulse the best seasonal bargains available.

A wide range of recipes is included from all over the world for vegetables that can usually be bought fresh at some time during the year. Fresh ingredients are always best, but where it is possible to substitute frozen or canned varieties, I have given appropriate quantities.

The brief introductions contain bits of historical information, folklore, and anecdotes about each vegetable, as well as useful tips for preparation and storage. For a truly comprehensive and delightful survey of the vegetable kingdom, I recommend *Jane Grigson's Vegetable Book* (Atheneum, 1979).

# ARTICHOKES (GLOBE)

THESE BEAUTIFUL, flowerlike vegetables are now available most of the year, with large domestic supplies coming from California and imported varieties from the Mediterranean, where the artichoke originated.

The ancient Romans considered artichokes a delicacy and devised tasty ways for preserving the hearts in vinegar and brine. Catherine de Medici adored them and may well have been responsible for popularizing the artichoke in France. Perhaps the speed with which it found favor in the sixteenth century was due as much to its purported aphrodisiac powers as to its distinctive taste.

The most delicate of the varieties available today is the small Florence artichoke, rarely seen in the United States, which can be boiled and eaten whole. The ubiquitous California variety we generally find in our supermarkets weighs between 10 and 12 ounces and has smooth, closely clinging leaves, a roundish head, and a green or purplish green color.

Cold boiled artichokes, served with vinaigrette or stuffed, make an excellent first course. To prepare for cooking, cut off the stem and remove the small leaves at the base of the artichoke. With a sharp knife, slice off 1 inch from the top of the center cone of leaves and trim the base so that the artichoke will stand upright. Trim the outer, pointed leaves with scissors and immerse the artichoke in acidulated water (water with 1 tablespoon of lemon juice or vinegar added) to avoid discoloration until ready to use.

The prepared artichokes should be dropped into a large pan of lightly salted boiling water. Bring the water quickly back to the boil, reduce the heat, cover, leaving a small aperture for steam to escape, and boil gently for approximately 40 minutes. The artichokes are ready if the bottoms feel tender when pierced with a fork. Remove from the water and drain, upside down, in a colander.

If you wish to remove the choke before serving—unnecessary, but an attractive way of presenting the artichoke—gently spread the outer leaves so you can reach into the center. Pull out the tender, pale-leaved cone in one piece, scrape off the hairy growth that covers the top of the heart, and remove the choke gently with a spoon. Sprinkle the exposed heart with a few drops of lemon juice, and salt and pepper, if desired. Replace the cone of leaves upside down in the hollow now formed.

The *fond d'artichaut* is the delicate bottom with the innermost leaves still adhering to it but the choke removed. Artichoke bottoms can be purchased in cans and used individually as a beautiful, tasty base for chopped vegetables or mixtures of seafood dressed with mayonnaise or vinaigrette.

## ARTICHAUTS À LA PROVENCE

*Serves 6*

6 small young artichokes
2 lemons, halved
2 medium-size onions, sliced into
    rings
2 tablespoons finely chopped fresh
    parsley
1 sprig fresh thyme, or ½ teaspoon
    dried thyme

3 cloves garlic, crushed
1 bay leaf
¾ cup light olive oil
1 tablespoon lemon juice
Salt and freshly ground pepper
Parsley sprigs

Prepare the artichokes for cooking as described above. Fill a large saucepan with salted water, add the halved lemons, and bring to the boil. Add the artichokes and simmer gently for 20–25 minutes. Remove and drain, upside down, in a colander.

Place the artichokes in a heavy enamel or cast-iron sauté pan and add the onions, chopped parsley, thyme, garlic, and bay leaf. Sprinkle with the olive oil, add about ½ cup water, and cook, partially covered, over medium heat for 10 minutes, or until the artichokes are very tender. Remove the artichokes with a slotted spoon and arrange them in a deep serving dish. Add some of the cooked onion rings. Strain the cooking oil and combine with 1 tablespoon lemon juice, freshly ground pepper, and salt, to taste. Pour over the artichokes and garnish with parsley sprigs.

# ASPARAGUS

THE ASPARAGUS is a member of the lily-of-the-valley family, originating in the eastern Mediterranean, where it still grows wild today. In the United States, most cultivated varieties are grown in California, Michigan, Washington, and New Jersey. Asparagus is one of the earliest spring vegetables. Supplies may arrive in the markets in mid-February, but peak quantities and cheaper-priced vegetables are available from April through June.

When choosing asparagus, look for firm, straight stalks with well-formed and tightly closed tips. They should be used as soon as possible after purchase, but if they must be kept for several days, wrap the butt ends in a damp cloth or paper towel and store in the refrigerator. Before cooking, rinse the stalks in cold running water and snap off the woody ends.

## ASPARAGUS VINAIGRETTE

*Serves 3–4*

One of the simplest and loveliest ways to serve cold asparagus.

| | |
|---|---|
| 1 large bunch asparagus | Salt and freshly ground pepper to |
| 6–8 tablespoons olive oil | taste |
| Juice of 1 lemon or 2 tablespoons | Pinch of sugar |
| white wine vinegar | Pinch of grated nutmeg |

Trim the lower ends of the stalks and tie the asparagus into loose bundles. Stand them upright in a deep pan and pour boiling water over them, leaving the tips uncovered. Cover the pan, and boil gently for 5–10 minutes, or until tender. Drain and then refresh by rinsing them with cold water. Drain again and arrange the stalks on a serving platter.

Combine the rest of the ingredients and pour the dressing over the asparagus.

## ASPARAGUS AND HARD-BOILED EGG SALAD

*Serves 4*

This very attractive salad, with its colorful contrasts, should be served with a bowl of mayonnaise or vinaigrette.

| | |
|---|---|
| 1 large bunch asparagus | 4 firm tomatoes |
| 1 head Boston lettuce | 2 pieces of pimiento |
| Oil | Salt and freshly ground pepper |
| Vinegar | Parsley |
| 4 hard-boiled eggs | |

Prepare the asparagus according to the recipe for Asparagus Vinaigrette (see preceding recipe).

Remove damaged leaves from the outside of the lettuce. Wash and drain the remaining head. Place the largest leaves around a large, flat platter. Separate the tender, light-colored leaves from the heart and place them in the middle of the dish. Dress lightly with oil and vinegar.

Place the cooked asparagus, separated into 4 equal bunches, in a circular fashion around the platter. In the quarter sections created place the hard-boiled eggs and tomatoes, sliced into halves.

Cut the pimiento into thin strips and wrap one strip around each bunch of asparagus. Place additional pimiento strips in crisscross fashion on top of the eggs. Season with salt and pepper and garnish generously with parsley.

## SALATA DE SPARANGHEL

RUMANIAN ASPARAGUS SALAD

*Serves 3–4*

| | |
|---|---|
| 1 large bunch asparagus | 1 tablespoon white wine vinegar |
| 3 hard-boiled eggs | 1 tablespoon capers |
| Salt and freshly ground pepper | Finely chopped fresh parsley |
| 2 tablespoons olive oil | |

Prepare the asparagus according to the preceding recipe for Asparagus Vinaigrette. Arrange the asparagus stalks on a shallow serving platter. Mash the hard-boiled egg yolks and add salt and pepper to taste. Gradually stir in the oil until the mixture is well blended, then add the vinegar, and finally, the capers. (For a thinner sauce, add either more vinegar or a little sour cream.) Pour the sauce over the asparagus, then sprinkle with chopped parsley and egg whites, finely chopped or cut into slivers. Chill and serve.

## AVOCADO

THE AVOCADO PEAR, a fruit, is generally prepared and eaten as an hors d'oeuvre or salad. Its origins are probably in tropical America. There is a story that Spanish conquistadors in Mexico observed the Aztecs enjoying a strange green fruit that they called *ahuacatl*. The natives explained that this meant "testicle," and that the fruit was so named because it was capable of exciting intense sexual passion.

Cultivation of the avocado on the North American mainland began in 1833 when horticulturist Henry Perrine planted a crop in Miami. At first they were served only in exclusive clubs and dining rooms. Chef Charley Ranhofer introduced the "alligator pear," as it became known, to New York's chic diners at Delmonico's restaurant. By the 1920s, California was producing large supplies for domestic consumption, which is where (along with Florida) our chief supplies are still grown.

Avocados have a smooth, creamy texture, a distinctive nutty flavor, and rich protein content. When buying avocados for immediate use, choose those that feel slightly soft when light pressure is applied and appear free of bruises or black marks. Ready-to-eat avocados can be stored uncut in the refrigerator for 4–7 days. Avocados can also be bought hard, then ripened on a sunny windowsill. Once cut in half and destoned, the flesh should be sprinkled with

lemon juice to avoid discoloration, especially if it is not to be immediately consumed.

A delicious way of serving the avocado as an hors d'oeuvre is to stuff the cavity left by the stone with a specially prepared filling, a fragrant herbal vinaigrette, or a rich, creamy dressing (see index). The following recipes illustrate a few of the many fillings that may be used. Experiment with your own combinations.

## AVOCADOS WITH SHELLFISH

*Serves 4*

| | |
|---|---|
| 9 sprigs fresh parsley | 2 large, ripe avocados |
| 4 sprigs fresh tarragon | 2 teaspoons lemon juice |
| 2 ounces spinach | 6 ounces cooked crabmeat, lobster, |
| 1–1¼ cups mayonnaise | or shrimp |
| 2 tablespoons heavy cream | 4 large lettuce leaves |
| Salt and freshly ground pepper | |

Cook 5 sprigs of the parsley, the tarragon, and the spinach in a small quantity of boiling salted water until just tender (5–8 minutes). Drain well and purée in a sieve or electric blender. Gently fold the greens into the mayonnaise, add the cream, and season with salt and pepper to taste. All this should be done very close to serving time.

Cut the avocados in half, destone, and lightly sprinkle with lemon juice. Gently remove some of the pulp to enlarge the cavity. Mix the shellfish with the tarragon mayonnaise and pile equal portions of the mixture in the centers of the halved pears. Place a small sprig of parsley on each and serve on individual plates lined with a lettuce leaf.

## AVOCADOS WITH HAM AND CHEESE FILLING

*Serves 4*

| | |
|---|---|
| ½ cup cottage cheese | 1 tablespoon sour cream |
| 2 ounces cooked ham, cut into small dice | Salt and freshly ground pepper |
| | 2 large ripe avocados |
| 1 teaspoon finely chopped fresh chives | 1 ounce flaked toasted almonds |
| 2 teaspoons lemon juice | |

43

Mix the cottage cheese with the ham, chives, lemon juice, and sour cream. Season with salt and pepper, and chill for at least 1 hour. Cut the avocados in half, destone, and sprinkle with lemon juice. Gently remove some of the pulp to enlarge the cavity. Fill the centers with the cottage cheese mixture, sprinkle with the almonds, and serve immediately.

## STUFFED AND SLICED AVOCADOS

### Serves 4

2 large ripe but firm avocados
2 teaspoons lemon juice
3 ounces cream cheese, at room
    temperature
2 tablespoons light cream
2 teaspoons mayonnaise
1 teaspoon finely chopped fresh chives

1½ tablespoons chopped walnuts
1 tablespoon destoned and chopped
    black olives
Salt and freshly ground pepper
Large lettuce leaves
Fresh grapefruit sections (optional)

Cut the avocados in half, destone, and peel. Scoop out approximately 1 tablespoon of flesh from each half to enlarge the cavity. Sprinkle lightly with lemon juice and set aside.

To prepare filling, mix together the cream cheese, cream, mayonnaise, chives, walnuts, and olives. Blend thoroughly and season with salt and pepper to taste.

Fill the centers with this mixture and replace the halves together. Enclose carefully in aluminum foil or plastic wrap and chill for several hours. When ready to serve, unwrap the avocados and cut into thick crosswise slices. Place the slices on a large platter lined with lettuce leaves, and garnish with grapefruit sections, if desired.

## AQUACATE CON COLIFLOR

### MEXICAN AVOCADO AND CAULIFLOWER SALAD

### Serves 4

1 medium-size cauliflower
2 tablespoons wine vinegar
Salt and freshly ground pepper
4 small very ripe avocados

2 ounces ground almonds
½–1 teaspoon ground nutmeg
6 red radishes, thinly sliced

Wash and trim the cauliflower, removing outer leaves and the hard stalk. Cut into florets and cook in boiling salted water for just 5 minutes. Drain and cool. Sprinkle with vinegar and a dash of salt and pepper, and set aside in a large bowl.

Cut the avocados in half, destone, and remove flesh. Mix the flesh with the ground almonds and nutmeg, salt, and pepper to taste. Add this mixture to the cauliflower and blend gently. Chill and serve on a round platter, garnished with radish slices.

# BAMBOO SHOOTS

THE TENDER SHOOTS of young bamboo cane, collected before they appear above ground, are an essential ingredient in Chinese cooking and can be purchased fresh from Oriental food stores. Although canned bamboo shoots are an acceptable substitute for most recipes, they lack the crispness of freshly cooked shoots and are therefore less suitable for salads.

## BAMBOO SHOOT SALAD

### *Serves 4–6*

1 fresh bamboo shoot or two 8-ounce
  cans bamboo shoots
2 small red peppers, seeded and
  thinly sliced

1–2 tablespoons white wine vinegar
2 tablespoons *mirin* or dry sherry
½ teaspoon salt
1–2 tablespoons sugar

Fresh bamboo shoots should be cleaned, sliced into julienne strips, and gently boiled for several minutes, until tender but still crisp. Drain and place in a large glass bowl with the red pepper slices. Canned shoots need only be drained and then sliced into julienne strips.

In a small saucepan, mix the remaining ingredients. Heat until the sugar has completely dissolved and adjust the seasoning with either more vinegar or more sugar. Remove from the heat and pour over the bamboo shoots and peppers. Toss to cover all ingredients with dressing, and chill, tossing occasionally, for several hours before serving.

# BEANS

FRESH BEANS, including French beans, runner beans, lima, and broad beans, make wonderful salads.

The broad bean originated in North Africa and the Near East, but it has long been grown on our continent as well. Today most supplies come from the Pacific Northeast, Michigan, and Wisconsin. There are many varieties, such as Windsor, Scotch, fava, and horse beans (some of which grow up to 18 inches long). Fresh broad beans are best eaten small and young, when both the pod and bean are tender. They can be cooked or served raw as a crudité with a bowl of salt.

What the broad bean is to the European diner, the lima is to the American; neither bean has ever shared equal popularity with the other on the same continent, despite their similarities. Peak supplies of fresh beans are in the markets between May and October. Recipes for broad beans are suitable for lima beans. (For additional dried bean recipes see pages 135–42.)

Runner beans were originally grown in Mexico. When picked young, they make fine salads, but older beans become tough and tasteless.

Green beans, particularly the thin, French variety, are the best salad bean. Try snap beans, the wide, flat Italian Romano bean, or the yellow wax bean—featured in German dishes like *Bohnenkraut*.

The French *haricots verts vinaigrette* is one of the simplest and most delicious of bean salads. Beans for salads should be cooked *al dente*—5–8 minutes in boiling salted water—until they are barely tender.

## INSALATA DI FAGIOLINI

### ITALIAN GREEN BEAN SALAD

*Serves 4–5*

1½ pounds green beans
Lettuce leaves
4 tablespoons olive oil
2 tablespoons white wine vinegar
1 teaspoon finely chopped fresh
 parsley

1 clove garlic, finely chopped
Salt and freshly ground pepper
1 large onion, thinly sliced
1 hard-boiled egg, chopped
2 ounces freshly grated Parmesan
 cheese

Wash, trim, and cut the beans in half. Cook in boiling, salted water for 5–8 minutes. Drain and set aside. While the beans are cooling, prepare the salad bowl by lining it with a few crisp lettuce leaves. Combine the oil, vinegar, parsley, chopped garlic, salt, and pepper. Pour over beans and add sliced onion. Mix lightly and chill. Just before serving, arrange the beans on the lettuce base and sprinkle with the chopped egg and grated cheese.

## GREEN BEAN SALAD

*Serves 3–4*

| | |
|---|---|
| 1 pound green beans | 1 small onion, finely chopped |
| 1 clove garlic | 4–5 tablespoons light olive oil |
| 2 teaspoons salt | 2 slices bacon, well cooked and |
| 1 tablespoon lemon juice | drained (optional) |

Wash and top and tail the beans. Cook in boiling salted water until just tender (5–8 minutes). Drain and place in a serving bowl.

Crush the garlic with the salt. Add lemon juice, chopped onion, and oil. Mix well and pour over the beans while still warm. If desired, chopped bacon makes a delicious garnish.

*Note:* For *Bohnensalat,* a favorite German recipe, substitute vinegar for lemon juice in approximately the same proportions as above. A sprinkling of herbs— dill, tarragon, oregano—may be added, and yellow beans substituted for French beans.

## INSALATA ALLA MACEDONE I

### ITALIAN MIXED-BEAN SALAD

*Serves 6–8*

| | |
|---|---|
| ½ pound haricot or small white beans | 6–8 tablespoons olive oil |
| Salt | 2 tablespoons lemon juice |
| 1 pound cooked fresh or frozen peas | Freshly ground pepper |
| 2 pounds fresh green beans | Chopped fresh parsley |
| 2–3 pieces canned pimiento, or 2 | Chopped fresh chives |
| small red peppers, finely chopped | |

Soak the haricot beans for about 2 hours. Drain and cook in enough gently boiling water to cover for 45 minutes, or until tender but not mushy. Add 1–2 teaspoons salt to beans during last 10 minutes of cooking.

Both peas and green beans should be cooked separately in boiling salted water for 5–8 minutes.

Drain the vegetables well and place in a large glass or ceramic bowl. Add the chopped pimientos or peppers.

Combine the oil, lemon juice, salt and pepper to taste, parsley, and chives. Mix well and pour over the salad. Stir ingredients until thoroughly coated with dressing. Garnish with additional parsley and chives.

## INSALATA ALLA MACEDONE II

This blend of ingredients is as colorful and tasty as the preceding mixture. Following the same basic procedures as above, substitute for the haricot beans ¼ cup pine nuts gently sautéed in oil until golden brown, then drained; for the green peas, one medium Bermuda onion, finely chopped; and for the lemon juice 1 tablespoon vinegar.

## BROAD BEAN SALAD

*Serves 4*

2 pounds fresh broad beans or lima
   beans
1 large clove garlic
4 slices bacon, well cooked, drained,
   and crumbled

3 tablespoons olive oil
1 tablespoon lemon juice
1 tablespoon chopped fresh basil
Salt and freshly ground pepper

Shell the beans and cook in gently boiling salted water until just tender, 8–10 minutes. Drain and set aside to cool. Cut the clove of garlic in half and rub it all over the inside of a salad bowl. Add the beans and bacon. Combine oil, lemon juice, most of the basil, salt, and pepper. Mix well and pour over the beans. Chill, and just before serving sprinkle remaining chopped basil over the top.

## FAVE ALLA ROMANO

### ITALIAN BROAD BEAN SALAD

*Serves 4–6*

3 pounds broad beans
5 tablespoons light olive oil
1 large onion, finely chopped
1 sprig fresh sage, chopped, or 1
   teaspoon dried

2 teaspoons tomato purée
Chopped fresh parsley

Shell the beans. In a medium-size saucepan heat 3 tablespoons of the olive oil and cook the chopped onion on low heat until nearly tender but still firm. Add the sage, tomato purée, and the beans. Pour on boiling water to cover and continue cooking at a fast boil until the liquid has reduced by half.

Serve cold with a sprinkling of parsley and the remaining 2 tablespoons olive oil.

# BEETS

THE EDIBLE ROOT OF *Beta vulgaris* was virtually unknown to the ancients. The Greeks cultivated the vegetable only for its leaves, and for many centuries the Romans used the root strictly for medicinal purposes. Today we do the opposite: the vitamin-rich tops are often discarded, although they could be cooked as a tasty dish on their own or even added to the salad bowl.

Beets play an important role in the cuisine of Slavic peoples, and pickled beet salad is to the Scandinavians what coleslaw is to the Americans. Beets are grown in many states and are generally available all year round. Peak supplies come to the markets between June and October.

Never cut into beets before cooking or the lovely red pigment will end up in the cooking liquid. Cook in boiling water until tender when pierced with a fork.

## SYLTEDE RØDBEDER

### DANISH PICKLED BEETS

*Serves 6*

½ cup cider or wine vinegar
¼ cup sugar
1 teaspoon salt
¼ teaspoon freshly ground pepper

2 pounds beets, cooked, peeled, and
   thinly sliced
2 teaspoons caraway seeds (optional)

In a large saucepan, combine the vinegar, sugar, salt, and pepper with ½ cup water. Bring to a fast boil, stirring occasionally, then remove from the heat and cool. Place the beets in a deep bowl and pour the dressing over them. Sprinkle with caraway seeds if you like, and chill for 12 hours, occasionally turning the beets in the dressing. Drain off some of the liquid before serving.

## RUSSIAN-STYLE PICKLED BEETS
## WITH WALNUT SAUCE

*Serves 6–8*

2 pounds beets  
1 cup wine vinegar  
Salt  
3 tablespoons sugar  
6 peppercorns  
5 whole cloves  

1 bay leaf  
¾ cup shelled walnuts  
2–3 cloves garlic  
1 teaspoon ground coriander  
Cayenne pepper  
Lettuce leaves  

If the beets are purchased with the tops still on, cut them off, leaving 1 inch of stem. (Save the tops to cook as a green vegetable.) Wash the beets but do not peel them. Place in a large saucepan and pour on boiling water to half cover. Cook covered over medium heat for 45 minutes, or until tender but still firm (adding more water if necessary).

Drain the beets, reserving 1 cup of the liquid. Plunge the beets immediately into cold water. When cool enough to handle, peel and cut into thick slices. Place in a glass storage jar.

In a saucepan, combine most of the reserved liquid with the vinegar, 1 teaspoon salt, sugar, peppercorns, cloves, and bay leaf. Bring to a boil. Pour the liquid over the beets to cover completely. Seal the jar and store in the refrigerator for at least 24 hours before serving.

To make walnut sauce, combine the walnuts with the garlic, coriander, and cayenne and pound with a mortar and pestle to a smooth paste. Adding 1 teaspoon of beet liquid at a time, stir the paste until it attains the consistency of a thick sauce. Adjust the seasoning.

Take about half the prepared quantity of pickled beets and chop into thick dice. Mix with the sauce and toss gently. Serve on a bed of crisp lettuce leaves. Pickled beets will keep well in a tightly sealed jar for several weeks.

## REMOLACHA

SPANISH BEET SALAD

*Serves 6–8*

1½ pounds beets  
1 pound cold boiled potatoes  
4 large scallions  
4 sprigs parsley, finely chopped  

3 tablespoons olive oil  
1 tablespoon wine vinegar  
Salt and freshly ground pepper

Wash and scrub the beets. Cut off tops, leaving 1-inch stems. Cook in boiling water for 45 minutes, or until tender but still firm. Drain and plunge immediately into cold water. When cool enough to handle, peel and slice thinly. Slice potatoes into pieces of similar size.

Chop the scallions coarsely and place all three ingredients in a salad bowl. Combine parsley, oil, vinegar, and salt and pepper to taste. Pour this dressing over the vegetables and toss gently.

*Note:* Another variation is made with mayonnaise rather than vinaigrette. Prepare the beets and potatoes as in the first recipe, but instead of scallions use 4–5 shallots that have been boiled for 3–5 minutes and coarsely chopped. Add 4–5 finely chopped anchovy fillets, a dash of cayenne pepper, and enough mayonnaise to bind the ingredients.

# BROCCOLI

BROCCOLI IS ACTUALLY a type of cauliflower, cultivated originally from a wild cabbage. It was eaten by the Greeks and Romans more than two thousand years ago, but was virtually unknown in America until the 1920s, when the enterprising d'Arrigo brothers of Northern California began a nationwide promotion for the vegetable.

There are many varieties of broccoli, but the green sprouting kind is the best for salads. Broccoli is available throughout the year. Added to a mixed green salad, its dark florets provide an eye-pleasing accompaniment to the paler shades of lettuce leaves. Cooking time should be very carefully monitored so that the flowery heads do not become mushy.

## BROCCOLI VINAIGRETTE

*Serves 4–6*

2 bunches young, crisp broccoli
½ cup olive oil
4 tablespoons lemon juice
1 tablespoon chopped parsley
1 tablespoon chopped fresh chives
   or 1 teaspoon dried

½ tablespoon chopped fresh tarragon
   or 1 teaspoon dried
1 teaspoon grated lemon rind

Wash and trim the broccoli and separate the florets from the stalks. Divide the stalks into quarters and cook gently in a small amount of boiling salted water for 4–5 minutes. Add the florets and cook for an additional 5–6 minutes until just tender. Drain and place in a shallow bowl. Mix together oil, lemon juice, parsley, chives, and tarragon. Pour this dressing over the broccoli while still warm, cover, and let marinate for at least 4 hours, turning frequently. Chill, and sprinkle with the lemon rind just before serving.

## BROCCOLI WITH MAYONNAISE DRESSING

*Serves 4–6*

2 pounds fresh broccoli
Freshly ground pepper
Lemon juice
3 shallots, finely chopped
¼ cup white wine

1 tablespoon finely chopped fresh
  chives
½ cup mayonnaise
1 hard-boiled egg, sieved

Wash the broccoli in cold water and trim the stems to a maximum length of 3 inches. Boil in a little lightly salted water for 8–10 minutes, or until just tender. Drain and place in a shallow serving dish. Grind fresh pepper over the broccoli and sprinkle with a few drops of lemon juice.

Put the shallots and wine into a saucepan and cook until the liquid has completely evaporated. Add the shallots and the chopped chives to the mayonnaise and pour over the broccoli.

Chill for 2–3 hours before serving, garnished with sieved hard-boiled egg.

## BRUSSELS SPROUTS

THE BRUSSELS SPROUT is a member of the cabbage family, producing numerous small heads, instead of one. Although these sprouts seem to have been grown as early as the thirteenth century around Brussels, it was a seventeenth-century Belgian botanist who first catalogued them as a plant "bearing fifty heads the size of an egg."

Thomas Jefferson introduced the Brussels sprout to the United States in 1812, when he planted a crop in his garden at Monticello. Today, Brussels sprouts are cultivated mainly in California, New York, and Oregon, during the late autumn and winter months.

Though sprouts are not generally considered in the preparation of salads, a little experimentation will bring pleasing rewards: young Brussels sprouts are delicious dressed with an herbal vinaigrette, and they add unusual variety to a mixed winter salad bowl. When buying Brussels sprouts, look for those with firm, compact heads and a bright green color. Avoid wilted or yellow leaves and heads that have grown puffy.

## BRUSSELS SPROUT SALAD

*Serves 4–6*

2 pounds young Brussels sprouts
½ cup olive oil
2–3 tablespoons wine vinegar
Pinch of sugar
¼ teaspoon dry mustard

Salt and freshly ground pepper
4 tablespoons finely chopped fresh
  parsley
2 tablespoons finely chopped onion

Wash the sprouts thoroughly in cold water, remove any yellow or overblown leaves, and trim the butt ends. Cut an x into each stem to ensure quick and even cooking. Place the sprouts in a saucepan of lightly salted, boiling water—just enough to cover the vegetables. Simmer for 5–7 minutes, or until just tender.

While the sprouts are cooking, combine the oil, vinegar, sugar, and mustard. Beat with a fork, and add salt and pepper to taste. Set aside. Drain the sprouts, making sure to remove all excess moisture. While still warm, place in a glass bowl and add the dressing, the chopped parsley, and chopped onion. Stir well to blend all ingredients. Allow to marinate for at least 2 hours before serving.

## MIXED SPROUT SALAD

*Serves 4–5*

This is a colorful and crunchy mixture for the winter dinner table.

1 pound small Brussels sprouts
1 large leek
4 stalks celery, chopped
1 small red pepper, seeded and
  chopped
5–6 water chestnuts, cut into slivers
  (optional)

2 tablespoons chopped fresh parsley
5–6 tablespoons olive oil
2 tablespoons lemon juice
1 tablespoon grated lemon rind
Salt and freshly ground pepper

Wash and trim the sprouts as described in the preceding recipe. Cut the base off the leek and remove any bruised leaves and about 2 inches of the dark green leaves. Slice into ¼-inch rounds and wash thoroughly in a sieve. Drain both vegetables and place in a saucepan of gently boiling salted water for about 5 minutes. Plunge into cold water and drain again.

Place these vegetables in a large wooden salad bowl with the chopped celery, red pepper, and water chestnuts, if desired. Prepare the dressing from the remaining ingredients, mix well, and pour over the vegetables. Toss gently and chill before serving.

# CABBAGE

CABBAGE IS ONE of the most versatile and widely available of all vegetables. It is also one of the oldest. Both the Celts and the Romans introduced varieties of the plant to the areas they conquered. The first-century Roman cookbook of Apicius gives seven recipes for cabbage, including one with caraway seeds—a combination still popular today.

Cabbage was probably introduced to the New World by the French explorer Jacques Cartier who, in 1541, brought it to Canada, where it was cultivated by colonists and Indians alike.

The name *cabbage* covers a large family of plants, including cauliflower, broccoli, and Brussels sprouts, each treated separately in this chapter. The most popular varieties for salad are the white, red, and Chinese cabbages. In salads white, or Dutch, cabbage is generally shredded and eaten raw, as is red cabbage, though the red is sometimes parboiled to make it more digestible. Chinese cabbage can be shredded raw or cut into larger pieces, as a substitute for romaine lettuce.

## AMERICAN COLE SLAW

### Serves 6–8

There are many recipes for this classic American dish. *Cole* is Old English for cabbage (like German *kohl*) and *slaw* means a simple combination of salad. Every family and every region has its favorite version.

This recipe comes from the apple-growing Northwest, where the state of Washington alone supplies some twenty-five percent of the nation's crop.

1 medium-size firm white cabbage, coarsely shredded
2 large unpeeled Red Delicious apples, cored and diced
1 small green pepper, seeded and diced

⅓ cup mayonnaise
½ cup sour cream
1 teaspoon superfine sugar
2 tablespoons vinegar
⅓ cup light cream
Salt and freshly ground pepper

Place the shredded cabbage, diced apples, and green pepper in a salad bowl. In a separate mixing bowl, whisk together the mayonnaise, sour cream, sugar, vinegar, and light cream. Season to taste with salt and plenty of freshly ground pepper. Pour over the cabbage mixture, toss well, and refrigerate for several hours. Toss again just before serving and adjust seasoning if necessary.

## FESTIVAL CABBAGE SALAD

*Serves 6–8*

This is a seventeenth-century Scottish recipe.

2 pounds white cabbage, coarsely grated
1 medium-size onion, finely chopped
1 tablespoon finely chopped fresh chives
1 sprig thyme, finely chopped, or ½ teaspoon dried

1–2 tablespoons finely chopped fresh parsley
⅔ cup mayonnaise flavored with 1 teaspoon prepared mustard
1 small can anchovy fillets, drained and chopped
3 hard-boiled eggs, sliced

Mix together the cabbage, onion, chives, thyme, and half the parsley. Add the mustard mayonnaise and blend gently until all ingredients are covered. Put a generous portion of salad onto individual salad plates and garnish with anchovy fillets, sliced eggs, and a sprinkling of the remaining parsley.

55

# GAGHAMP AGHSTAN

### ARMENIAN CABBAGE SALAD

*Serves 4*

¼ white cabbage (approximately 1 pound), shredded

½ small green pepper, seeded and thinly sliced

1 small onion, thinly sliced

1 small tomato, seeded and finely chopped

5 tablespoons finely chopped fresh mint

4 tablespoons olive oil

2 tablespoons freshly squeezed and strained lemon juice

Salt and freshly ground pepper

Combine the cabbage, green pepper, onion, tomato, and mint in a salad bowl. Whisk the olive oil and lemon juice until well blended, and season with salt and pepper to taste. Pour the dressing over the vegetables and toss gently but thoroughly. Chill, toss again, and serve.

# SAUERKRAUT

Sauerkraut is finely shredded white cabbage that has been pickled in brine. Its origins date back to the days of the building of the Great Wall of China, when workers were sustained on a diet of rice and cabbage in summer and cabbage preserved in red wine in winter. When transported by the Tartars from China to Europe, the fermentation process for souring the cabbage was improved by substituting salt for wine, and this same method is still employed today. In the countries of Eastern Europe where sauerkraut is part of the regular diet, many families prepare their own versions in large barrels to last the winter months.

There are quite a few decent prepared sauerkrauts available in jars or cans. However, if you have never experienced the taste of freshly made sauerkraut, half an hour's work plus three weeks idle waiting will yield unexpected pleasures.

Choose firm, mature heads of white cabbage. Remove the outer leaves and discard the cores. Wash thoroughly with cold water. Shred the cabbage into pieces about the thickness of a dime.

Weigh the cabbage. To every 5 pounds cabbage, allow 3 tablespoons kosher or pickling salt. Wash a 2- to 3-gallon crock, scald it with boiling water, then place the cabbage in it, alternating cabbage with sprinklings of salt. Pack and press with each addition. The cabbage will begin to draw juice, which should, in the end, cover the cabbage. If not enough liquid has formed, prepare an additional brine by combining 1½ tablespoons salt to 1 quart boiling water. Cool the brine to room temperature and add to the crock.

The cabbage should now be weighted and covered to keep it submerged in brine. This can be done by placing a large plate that has been carefully washed in hot water on top of the shredded cabbage. On top of that a clean cheesecloth should be placed to keep out dust or other foreign particles. Skim the brine daily and place a clean plate on top. Always keep the cloth on top.

Fermentation begins within a day. Depending on the temperature of the room, sauerkraut will take from 3 to 6 weeks (75°F is the ideal temperature at which fementation should occur). The sauerkraut is ready to eat once the fermentation is complete, but it gains in flavor if stored, tightly sealed, for another month.

Once the sauerkraut has fermented sufficiently, it can be flavored with caraway, apples, cumin, or coriander. Often served hot with pork and sausages, sauerkraut also makes a delicious cold salad all year round.

## SAUERKRAUT AND CRANBERRY SALAD

*Serves 4–5*

This is a delicious accompaniment to cold duck or cold roast pork.

1 pound sauerkraut
1 tablespoon olive oil
2 teaspoons sugar
2 stalks celery, diced

1 eating apple, peeled and chopped
4 ounces cranberries, softened in
   boiling water

Pour cold water over the sauerkraut, drain, and squeeze out excess liquid. Place in a large glass bowl and mix with the oil and sugar. Add the celery, apple, and cranberries. Toss all ingredients until well mixed, and serve.

## RED CABBAGE SALAD

*Serves 6–8*

6 tablespoons vegetable oil
½ pound onions, sliced
1 medium-size (approximately 2
   pounds) red cabbage, coarsely
   shredded

4 ounces raisins
2 small cooking apples, chopped
Sea salt and freshly ground pepper
2–4 tablespoons cider or wine vinegar

Heat the vegetable oil in a large frying pan and cook the onions until just tender and translucent in appearance. Add the shredded cabbage and cover the pan. Cook over low heat for approximately 10 minutes, then add a little water, the raisins, apples, sea salt, and pepper. Cook for another 10–15 minutes, then drain off excess liquid. Add the vinegar, and additional salt and pepper if necessary, mix well, and allow to cool before serving.

## ROT KOH ISALAT

*Serves 8*

### BAVARIAN CABBAGE SALAD

2 pounds red cabbage, shredded
Salt
1–2 teaspoons caraway seeds
2–4 teaspoons sugar

3 tablespoons vinegar
3 tablespoons oil
3 slices bacon, cooked and chopped
Sour cream (optional)

In a large bowl, sprinkle the shredded cabbage with salt and allow to stand for at least 1 hour. Squeeze to remove excess water. Sprinkle caraway seeds and sugar to taste over the cabbage, then add the vinegar, oil, and chopped bacon. Toss well and leave standing for an hour or so before serving. If you like, add a few tablespoons of sour cream to the salad.

## TRICOLOR SLAW

*Serves 8–10*

½ pound red cabbage, finely shredded
1 pound white cabbage, finely
  shredded
2–3 large carrots, peeled and finely
  grated
½ large white onion, thinly sliced

3 tablespoons olive oil
2 tablespoons vinegar
2 teaspoons sugar
Salt and freshly ground pepper
½–⅔ cup plain yogurt
2 tablespoons chopped fresh chives

In a large bowl, mix together the red and white shredded cabbage, the grated carrots, and the sliced onion. Blend the oil, vinegar, and sugar in a bowl, adding salt and pepper to taste. Slowly add the yogurt, beating continuously until a smooth, creamy consistency is achieved. Pour over the vegetables, add the chives, and mix well to ensure that all ingredients are evenly moistened. Chill for several hours before serving.

## CHINESE CABBAGE SALAD

*Serves 4*

This unusual member of the cabbage (*Brassica*) family is like a pale, crisp romaine lettuce. A native of East Asia, it was introduced to Europe by eighteenth-century missionaries who brought back seeds from the Far East.

Nowadays Chinese cabbage can readily be found at many supermarkets. It makes an excellent salad on its own or in combination with other greens.

| | |
|---|---|
| 1 cucumber, peeled and diced | 1 tablespoon sesame seeds |
| 1 head Chinese cabbage, thinly sliced or shredded | 8 tablespoons olive oil |
| | 2 tablespoons wine vinegar |
| 1 large green pepper, diced | 1 tablespoon soy sauce |
| 2 tablespoons finely chopped onion | Salt and freshly ground pepper |

Drain excess water from the diced cucumber by placing it lightly salted in a sieve for 30–45 minutes. In a large bowl, combine the cabbage, cucumber, green pepper, and onion.

Toast the sesame seeds in a roasting pan under the broiler or in a deep-frying pan over low heat. Shake occasionally and remove from heat when seeds begin to pop. Add most of the toasted sesame seeds, the oil, vinegar, soy sauce, pepper, and a dash of salt to the cabbage mixture. Mix well and chill. Before serving, garnish with a sprinkling of the remaining toasted sesame seeds.

# CARROTS

THE ORANGE CARROT that we eat today is a relative newcomer to the vegetable scene. If you look at Dutch paintings of the sixteenth century you will see mainly purple and white carrots. The Dutch also developed the orange variety, which was later introduced in England and France. In these countries the carrot was not at first appreciated for its tasty root; rather, the feathery, fern-like leaves were considered a chic and stylish adornment for ladies' coiffures and brooches.

Even earlier, carrots were prized for their medicinal properties. Galen, the second-century Roman physician, remarked on their effectiveness in breaking wind and scouring the digestive tract. In the nineteenth-century Near East they were sometimes stewed with sugar to make an aphrodisiac for men. Modern doctors recommend carrots in the diet to alleviate night blindness and other symptoms of vitamin A deficiency. Carrots also are a good source for vitamins B and C and calcium.

Grated carrots make wonderfully decorative and nourishing salads in combination with raisins, nuts, or cheese. Carrots, peeled and cut into small sticks, make an ideal crudité to serve with dips.

# CARPETAS ELIXATAS

## ROMAN CARROT SALAD

*Serves 6*

2 pounds carrots
5 tablespoons dry white wine
3 tablespoons olive oil
½ teaspoon ground cumin

½ teaspoon ground coriander
½ teaspoon salt
¼ teaspoon freshly ground pepper
1 large Spanish onion, finely chopped

Wash, peel, and dice the carrots. Cook in just enough boiling salted water to cover until tender (10–12 minutes). Drain and set aside.

In a small saucepan, gently boil the wine until it is reduced by half. Cool and blend with the remaining ingredients. Pour this dressing over the carrots and chill until ready to serve.

# MINTED CARROT SALAD

*Serves 4*

1 pound baby carrots
2 tablespoons vegetable oil
2 tablespoons long-grain rice

Salt and freshly ground pepper
3–5 tablespoons chopped fresh mint
1 tablespoon lemon juice

Wash and lightly scrape the carrots, and trim the ends. Slice in half lengthwise. Heat the oil in an enamel frying pan, add the carrots, and cook gently over low heat for 3 minutes. Stir in the rice and add sufficient water to cover the ingredients. Season with a dash of salt and a few grindings of pepper.

Cook, covered, over low heat for about 20 minutes, or until the liquid has evaporated and the carrots are tender.

Remove from the heat and place in a serving dish. Add the mint and lemon juice. Stir and chill before serving.

## MOROCCAN CARROT SALAD

*Serves 4*

1 pound carrots
1 large navel orange
2–3 tablespoons lemon juice
1 teaspoon orange-flower water
1 teaspoon ground cinnamon

2 teaspoons sugar
Pinch of salt
Scant ½ cup raisins, soaked for an
   hour to soften (optional)

Wash, peel, and finely grate the carrots. Peel the orange and carefully remove all the white pith. Divide the orange into segments, removing the flesh from the membranes. Add the segments to the carrots. Squeeze the juice from the remainder of the orange into a separate bowl. Add the other ingredients and stir thoroughly. Pour over the orange-and-carrot mixture and chill for an hour before serving. Plumped-up raisins can be added just before the salad is brought to the table.

## CAULIFLOWER

CAULIFLOWER IS ANOTHER MEMBER of the cabbage family, or, as Mark Twain called it, "a cabbage with a college education." First developed by the Arabs in the Middle Ages, cauliflower has been cultivated in Europe since the sixteenth century. Besides the white variety, lovely purple and green cauliflowers are commonly grown around the Mediterranean and are occasionally available in this country.

Cauliflower is available most of the year, although the autumn-winter produce is generally cheaper and tastier.

For salads, cauliflower can be used raw or just slightly cooked. The raw florets, high in iron and vitamin C, make a nutritious addition to any selection of crudités.

When choosing cauliflower in the shops, look for compact white heads with fresh green leaves. Heads that are loose and spread out are overmature.

## GOBI KI SABZI

### INDIAN SPICY CAULIFLOWER

*Serves 4*

5 tablespoons vegetable oil
1 teaspoon mustard seeds
1-inch piece of fresh ginger, peeled
   and finely chopped
1 green chili pepper, finely chopped
   (see page 95)
1 medium-size onion, thinly sliced
½ teaspoon ground coriander

1 teaspoon turmeric
1 large cauliflower, separated into
   florets
Freshly squeezed juice of ½ lemon
Salt
1 tablespoon chopped fresh coriander
   leaves or Italian parsley

Heat the oil in a large frying pan, add the mustard seeds, and cook, covered, for 2 minutes (the seeds will pop in response to the heat). Add the ginger, chili pepper, onion, ground coriander, and turmeric, and cook for another 3 minutes. Add the cauliflower, stir all ingredients for about a minute, then sprinkle the lemon juice on top. Cover the pan, simmer gently for 15 minutes, and add salt to taste.

Turn into a serving dish and cool. Just before serving, garnish with chopped coriander or parsley.

## SALADE DE CHOUFLEURS AU ROQUEFORT ET ANCHOIS

### CAULIFLOWER WITH ROQUEFORT DRESSING

*Serves 4*

1 whole large cauliflower
Roquefort Dressing, page 29
Large lettuce leaves

2 hard-boiled eggs, quartered
4 anchovy fillets

Trim the cauliflower by removing all the leaves and the tough base. Cook or steam it whole until the stems are tender when pressed with a finger. Drain, cool thoroughly, and place in a deep bowl.

Prepare the Roquefort Dressing and pour it over the cauliflower. Let it stand for 30 minutes, basting frequently.

To serve, place the cauliflower on a serving dish lined with lettuce leaves. Pour the dressing over the cauliflower and surround with hard-boiled eggs and anchovy fillets.

## INSALATA DI CAVOLFIORE

ITALIAN CAULIFLOWER SALAD

*Serves 3–4*

1 large cauliflower, washed and trimmed
5 anchovy fillets, chopped
6 black olives, pitted and chopped
2 red pimientos, chopped
6 tablespoons light olive oil

2 tablespoons freshly squeezed and strained lemon juice
Salt and freshly ground pepper
2 tablespoons finely chopped fresh parsley
2 tablespoons capers

Cook the cauliflower in boiling salted water until just tender, about 5–8 minutes. Drain and leave until it is cool enough to handle. Separate the florets and arrange in a shallow salad bowl. Add the chopped anchovies, olives, and pimientos. Make the dressing from the oil, lemon juice, salt, and pepper. Pour over the cauliflower while still warm and toss gently but thoroughly to moisten all ingredients. Allow to stand for an hour, toss again, and garnish with chopped parsley and capers.

# CELERY

THE ORIGINAL STRONG, bitter flavor of the wild plant harvested by the Romans mainly for medicinal cures has been tempered through centuries of cultivation, and the many different-colored varieties described by the Greek naturalist Theophrastus have virtually disappeared. When occasionally crunching on a tasteless, stringy supermarket stalk, one might wistfully wonder what the seventeenth-century Englishman John Evelyn was eating when he wrote: "This herb celery is for its high and grateful taste ever placed in the middle of the grand sallet at our great men's tables, and at our proctor's feasts, as the grace of the whole board."

Celery is wonderfully versatile. It can be washed and served whole on its own, or with a bowl of salt. It can be cut into small stalks for a platter of crudités, or it can be stuffed with a variety of savory spreads and fillings. Chop it into all sorts of vegetable and fruit salads, or stew it *à la Grecque.*

Celery is generally available throughout the year. Examine the stalks closely before purchase; if they are woody or the leaves are wilted or yellow, the celery is probably tough and overripe. Keep it stored in the crisper bin of the refrigerator.

# SEDANO ALLA GRECA

### CELERY À LA GRECQUE

*Serves 4–6*

2 heads celery
1 cup dry white wine
1 onion stuck with a clove
1 carrot
Bouquet garni
6 peppercorns
Salt

Freshly squeezed and strained juice
   of 1 lemon
4 tablespoons olive oil
3 bay leaves
1 tablespoon coriander seeds
Salt and freshly ground pepper

Remove any bruised outer stalks from the celery and trim the leaves and base. Cut into 2-inch lengths and wash well in cold water. Parboil in 1 cup salted water for 3 minutes. In the meantime, place all other ingredients in a deep sauté pan and bring to a gentle boil. Add the celery and cook over low heat until tender, about 10–15 minutes. Remove the celery and place in a shallow dish. Continue cooking the stock until it has reduced by one-third. When cool, strain and pour over the celery.

# CELERY SALAD WITH COCONUT DRESSING

*Serves 4*

Coconut cream is commonly used to dress salads in many Southeast Asian countries. This salad, from Sri Lanka, is served as an accompaniment to meat dishes.

1 large head celery
1 small green pepper, seeded and
   finely chopped
1 tablespoon freshly squeezed lemon
   juice
½ teaspoon salt
½ teaspoon paprika

1 tablespoon onion juice
1 tablespoon finely chopped green
   ginger
Coconut cream from 1 coconut (see
   note) or 1 cup canned coconut
   cream

Trim leaves and base from celery and wash thoroughly. Drain, dry, and chop into small dice. Place in a bowl and add the green pepper. In a separate small dish, blend together the lemon juice, salt, paprika, onion juice, and ginger. Pour over the celery and let stand for 1 hour, tossing occasionally to remoisten all ingredients. Just before serving, pour on the coconut cream and toss again.

*Note:* Coconut cream is made by soaking the freshly grated flesh in water and squeezing out the liquid. Grate the white flesh trimmed of its brown outer skin into a bowl. Pour ½ cup hot water over the flesh and allow to stand for half an hour. Then squeeze through cheesecloth. You should have about 1 cup of cream.

## SALADE DE CÉLERI À L'ANCIENNE

*Serves 4–6*

2 heads celery
3 hard-boiled eggs
⅓ cup mayonnaise flavored with 1–2
   teaspoons Dijon mustard

¼ cup shelled walnuts
3 small tomatoes, quartered
6 each of green and black pitted olives

Trim leaves and base from celery and wash thoroughly. Drain, dry, and cut into strips approximately 1 inch long.

Mash the hard-boiled egg yolks with a fork and slowly add the mustard mayonnaise to achieve a smooth paste. Cut the whites into strips the same size as the celery. In a large bowl, blend together the celery, egg whites, and mayonnaise. Let stand in the refrigerator for several hours. Before serving, stir in the walnuts and turn the mixture out onto a shallow platter. Decorate with tomato wedges and olives.

## CELERY LEAF SALAD

The young green leaves from the heads of celery can be used to make delicious salads. They are especially tasty in combination with sliced fennel and watercress. Dress with Basic Vinaigrette, page 18.

## CELERY ROOT OR CELERIAC

THIS ANCIENT VEGETABLE is actually the enlarged root of the celery plant. Long popular on the European continent, it is now gaining wider favor in the United States. It makes a wonderfully refreshing salad in winter when peak supplies are available and is also a good source of iron. When choosing celeriac at the market, look for vegetables with a fairly smooth skin. Once cut, the pieces should be immersed in water to which a teaspoon of vinegar or lemon juice has been added to prevent discoloration.

Céleri rémoulade is the famous French hors d'oeuvre made from raw shredded celeriac mixed with a well-seasoned Sauce Rémoulade, page 25. The following recipes will add to your repertoire for preparing this undervalued vegetable.

## SELLERISALAT

### DANISH CELERIAC SALAD

*Serves 8–10*

3 medium-size celeriac
Juice of ½ freshly squeezed lemon
8–10 tablespoons heavy cream,
  whipped

8–10 tablespoons mayonnaise
1 teaspoon prepared mustard
Salt and freshly ground pepper
Chopped fresh parsley

Peel the celeriac to remove the knobbly outer skin. Cut into thin slices or shred finely with a food processor. Discard the woody core. Immerse the pieces immediately in water with the lemon juice added, to prevent discoloration. Combine the whipped cream, mayonnaise, and mustard, and season to taste with salt and freshly ground pepper. Drain the celeriac and fold into this dressing. Chill for at least 2 hours. Before serving, garnish with freshly chopped parsley.

## CELERIAC SALAD WITH CUBED HAM

*Serves 6*

2 pounds celeriac, peeled
Lemon juice
Salt
1 tablespoon Dijon mustard
1 teaspoon finely grated horseradish
2 small dill pickles, finely chopped
1 tablespoon white wine vinegar

⅔ cup mayonnaise
¼ teaspoon ground white pepper
2 tablespoons finely chopped fresh
  parsley
1 tablespoon finely chopped fresh
  chives
¼ pound ham, diced

To prevent discoloration, immerse the peeled celeriac in water to which lemon juice has been added. In a large pan, bring to a rapid boil enough salted water to cover the vegetables by at least 2 inches. Add the celeriac and cook until tender when pierced with a fork, approximately 20–30 minutes. Drain, and when cool enough to handle, cut into small cubes, place in a serving bowl, and sprinkle with lemon juice.

Combine the mustard, horseradish, pickles, and vinegar and blend with the mayonnaise. Add to the celeriac. Season with salt and pepper, then add the parsley, chives, and cubed ham.

Toss gently and chill for at least 2 hours before serving.

## SALATA DE TELINA

### RUMANIAN CELERIAC SALAD

*Serves 4–6*

| | |
|---|---|
| 1 large celeriac | 2 tablespoons finely chopped fresh |
| 5 tablespoons olive oil | parsley |
| 1 tablespoon wine vinegar | 4 small sour pickles |
| Salt and freshly ground pepper | A few black olives |

Wash and peel the celeriac. Cook as in preceding recipe. Remove from the water, drain, and cool. Cut crosswise into round slices about ⅛ inch thick. Mix the oil and vinegar with salt and freshly ground pepper to taste. Pour over the celeriac, add the chopped parsley, and toss. Allow to stand for at least an hour, tossing again from time to time.

To serve, arrange on a shallow platter and garnish with pickles and olives.

# CORN

EVERY AMERICAN SCHOOLCHILD knows the story of the friendly Indian named Squanto who showed the Pilgrim settlers how to plant corn with a fish head under each mound for fertilizer. Corn was certainly a very important crop to the early colonists, but its historical importance dates even further back to the pre-Columbian civilizations of South and Central America. There exists a plethora of legends from these early cultures telling how gods, goddesses, and sacred animals brought the gift of corn to man.

Corn can be bought throughout the year, though the stalks of spring and summer are generally the most succulent and flavorful and corn is at its best when fresh picked.

To prepare corn off the cob for salads, hold the cob downward and run a sharp knife along the length of the ear as close to the cob as possible. The kernels will need only a brief cooking period in a little lightly salted boiling water.

# SUCCOTASH

## CORN WITH LIMA BEANS

*Serves 4*

This classic North American dish was introduced to colonial cooks by the Indians and possibly was served at the first Thanksgiving dinner in 1621. Regional taste preferences dictate the right bean to mix with the corn: in the South, cooks use lima and butter beans; in the North, the cranberry bean is often favored.

1 pound lima beans
5–6 ears of corn
4 tablespoons vegetable oil
1 tablespoon cider or wine vinegar

Salt and freshly ground pepper
2 tablespoons chopped chives
  (optional)

Shell the beans and cook in boiling salted water for about 5 minutes. Drain and set aside. Prepare the corn as described above and cook in a little lightly salted boiling water for a few minutes. Drain and place in a salad bowl with the beans. Mix the oil, vinegar, salt, and pepper with the chives, if desired, and blend well. Pour over the vegetables and toss. Serve at room temperature.

# CRUNCHY CORN SALAD

*Serves 6–8*

This is a colorful and filling dish to accompany cold meats and poultry. A richer variation can be made by substituting a dressing of 2 parts mayonnaise to 1 part sour cream for the vinaigrette.

8 ears of corn
½ pound fresh bean sprouts
3 stalks celery, finely chopped
1 large red pepper, seeded and diced
4 large scallions, sliced

6 tablespoons olive oil
2 tablespoons white wine vinegar
Salt and freshly ground pepper
1 clove garlic, crushed (optional)
½ cup shelled, roasted peanuts

Prepare and cook corn as described on page 68. Drain and cool. In a large bowl, mix the corn, bean sprouts, celery, red pepper, and scallions. Mix together the oil, vinegar, salt, ground pepper, and garlic, if desired, and pour over the vegetables. Toss and chill for at least an hour. Just before serving add the roasted peanuts and toss again.

# CUCUMBER

THE CUCUMBER IS GROWN throughout the world and plays a versatile role in almost every national cuisine. It is said to have originated in the valleys of India between the Bay of Bengal and the Himalayan mountains—and some of the most interesting recipes I have included here come from Asia and the Far East. In fact, the cucumber was cultivated by most of the ancient civilizations. A Roman naturalist described a highly sophisticated method for growing it out of season for the Emperor Tiberius, who demanded that cucumber be available every day of the year. The Emperor Charlemagne included it in his imperial vegetable garden, and Columbus brought cucumber seeds to Haiti in 1494.

Two varieties of cucumber are generally cultivated today in the United States—the slightly irregular-shaped and thick-skinned ridge cucumber, easily grown at home, and the long, smooth-skinned variety, greenhouse-grown and the type most commonly found in stores. A third variety of hydroponically grown cucumber with very thin skin is widely available. Cucumbers are rich in vitamins B and C and, because of their high water content and lack of carbohydrates and fats, make an excellent low-calorie addition to diets.

Cucumbers can be bitter at the stem end. To avoid spreading the bitter taste, cut a cucumber in half first and peel it from the cut edge to within ½ inch of the ends. To remove some of the water from cucumbers—especially useful when mixing with mayonnaise, yogurt, or other creamy dressings—put the peeled, sliced cucumbers in a sieve or colander, sprinkle with salt, and let drain for at least half an hour, shaking occasionally. Rinse to remove salt, but make sure the cucumbers are quite dry before dressing.

# AGURKESALAT

### DANISH PICKLED CUCUMBERS

*Serves 6–8*

2–3 cucumbers
1 teaspoon salt
⅔ cup cider or wine vinegar
2–4 teaspoons sugar
¼ teaspoon ground white pepper

2 teaspoons finely chopped fresh dill
   or 2 teaspoons dried
2 teaspoons chopped fresh parsley
   (optional)

Wash and peel the cucumbers. Slice into paper-thin rounds (a food processor is best for this, if you have one). Place the slices in a deep bowl, sprinkle with the salt, and cover with a plate directly on top of the cucumbers. Weight this down with something heavy and let stand at room temperature for approximately 2 hours. Place the cucumbers in a sieve or colander and drain thoroughly, squeezing out any remaining juice.

   Combine the vinegar, sugar to taste, and pepper and pour over the cucumbers. Add the chopped dill, correct the seasoning, and chill for several hours before serving. If desired, sprinkle chopped parsley over the cucumber just before bringing to the table.

# KYURIMOMI

### JAPANESE CUCUMBER SALAD

*Serves 4*

The Western distinction between cooked vegetables and fresh salads is largely ignored by the Japanese. When cooked at all, vegetables are cooked only briefly, and, even then, often served cold.

   Many vegetables are marinated in vinegar and dressed with soy sauce. This recipe is topped with toasted sesame seeds and makes an excellent accompaniment to grilled fish or as a side dish with *sashimi,* sliced raw fish.

1 large cucumber
1 teaspoon salt
⅔ cup vinegar

2 tablespoons sugar
2 tablespoons light soy sauce
1 tablespoon white sesame seeds

Wash the cucumber and slice, unpeeled, into paper-thin rounds. Sprinkle with salt and place in a colander or sieve to drain for 30 minutes. If a plate is placed on top of the cucumber slices and occasionally pressed down hard, even more liquid can be removed. Place the cucumber slices in a clean dish

towel and pat dry. Transfer to a bowl or dish. Mix together the vinegar, sugar, and soy sauce. Pour over the cucumber slices and toss gently.

Toast the sesame seeds in a dry frying pan, shaking constantly until they begin to jump (they can also be toasted under the grill). Remove from the heat and crush with a mortar and pestle. Sprinkle over the cucumber slices and serve.

## KHIRA KA RAITA

### INDIAN CUCUMBER AND YOGURT

*Serves 6–8*

This condiment goes well with curries and tandoori dishes.

2 cups yogurt
2 very large cucumbers
Salt
½ teaspoon chili powder
1 teaspoon roasted and crushed cumin
  seeds

3 green chili peppers, seeded and
  finely chopped (see page 95)
1 teaspoon finely chopped fresh
  coriander leaves or Italian parsley

Strain the yogurt through a sieve lined with cheesecloth. Allow to stand for about an hour. Squeeze the cloth from time to time to extract liquid.

Peel and grate the cucumbers, salt lightly, and let drain in a sieve or colander for at least half an hour. Meanwhile, mix together the chili powder and cumin seeds. Add the chopped green chilies and coriander or parsley, and blend all the seasonings with the strained yogurt. When the cucumber is ready, rinse off the salt, pat dry in a dish towel, and add to the other ingredients.

## MICHOTETA

### MIDDLE EASTERN CUCUMBER AND CREAM CHEESE

*Serves 4–6*

Feta can be used on its own for this salad, or in combination with a small quantity of yogurt or cottage cheese for those who find the taste of feta too strong.

½ pound feta or feta/cottage cheese
    or feta/yogurt mixture
Juice of 1 lemon
2 tablespoons olive oil

1 small onion, finely chopped
½ large cucumber, peeled and diced
Freshly ground black pepper

71

Crumble the feta with 1 tablespoon water and, using a fork, blend in the lemon juice, olive oil, and yogurt or cottage cheese, if desired. Add the chopped onion and cucumber, and season to taste with freshly ground pepper.

## SPICY TROPICAL CUCUMBERS

*Serves 4–5*

2 medium-size cucumbers
1 teaspoon salt
1 large clove garlic, crushed
3–4 tablespoons freshly squeezed
    lime juice

1 tablespoon finely chopped green
    chili peppers (see page 95)
Zest of lime
Parsley sprigs

Peel the cucumbers, remove the seeds, and chop coarsely. Place in a sieve or colander, sprinkle with salt, and let drain for 20 minutes. To make the dressing, mix together the crushed garlic, lime juice, and chopped chilies. Toss the cucumbers in a bowl with the dressing. Chill and serve garnished with lime zest and parsley.

# EGGPLANT

WHOLE COOKBOOKS have been written about the eggplant. This versatile vegetable exists in many forms all over the globe and can be imaginatively prepared in many different ways.

The eggplant was originally cultivated in India and China, and its name derives from the small early varieties that resembled white and brown eggs (even today, a small, white, delicate eggplant is grown in China and Madagascar). Eggplants were brought to the West by Arab traders and made their first appearance in Italian ports in the thirteenth century.

The early reputation of this vegetable was not entirely favorable; although some championed its aphrodisiac properties, it was more widely regarded as "malaisana"—the mad apple. Nevertheless, its popularity spread, and by the 1500s it had made its way to England. It reached America somewhat later via the Spanish and Portuguese colonists.

The ubiquitous purple variety is generally available throughout the year, but at least ten different varieties are now commercially grown in the United

States, and some of the less familiar types should be sampled when they are available. Eggplants come in all sizes and shapes, with weights ranging from half a pound to as much as two pounds. Purchase vegetables that feel firm and have an unblemished, unwrinkled skin and shiny, sleek purple color.

Eggplants contain a bitter juice that should be partially removed. Eggplant can be sliced, salted, and left standing to drain while still raw or, if it is to be made into a pâté, the cooked pulp can be squeezed or the juice drained through a sieve. Either way, finish with a quick rinse under a cold tap.

## CAPONATA ALLA SICILIANA

### ITALIAN EGGPLANT SALAD

*Serves 4–6*

Caponata is a popular Mediterranean vegetable stew for which there are many recipes. This version, sharpened by the addition of olives, capers, and vinegar, also includes the unexpected taste of chocolate. Caponata will keep well in the refrigerator for several days.

| | |
|---|---|
| 3 medium eggplants (approximately 2 pounds) | 12 green olives, pitted and chopped |
| Salt | 3 tablespoons grated unsweetened chocolate |
| Vegetable oil | ⅓ cup white wine vinegar |
| 1 small head celery, diced | 2 tablespoons sugar |
| 1 tablespoon capers | Freshly ground pepper |

Peel the eggplant and cut into 1-inch cubes. Sprinkle with salt and leave in a sieve to drain for about an hour. Toss occasionally. Drain and pat dry.

Using enough oil to cover the bottom of a large frying pan, fry the eggplant, stirring constantly, until golden brown and soft. Add extra oil during cooking, if required. Remove the eggplant pieces to a large bowl and fry the celery in the same oil until translucent. Add this to the eggplant and stir in the remaining ingredients, seasoning with salt and pepper to taste.

Serve at room temperature.

# LEBANESE EGGPLANT

*Serves 4*

2 large eggplants (approximately
   2 pounds)
Salt
Vegetable oil
1¼ cups yogurt

2 cloves garlic, crushed
2 tablespoons chopped fresh mint
   or 1 tablespoon dried
Paprika

Peel the eggplant and slice into ½-inch-thick pieces. Sprinkle with salt and leave in a sieve to drain for an hour, tossing occasionally. Rinse and pat dry. Heat the oil in a large saucepan and fry the eggplant until lightly cooked. Remove from the pan and drain on paper towels.

Combine the yogurt, garlic, and salt to taste.

When the eggplant is completely cool, place it in a shallow serving dish, pour on the yogurt, and garnish with mint and a sprinkling of paprika.

# SALADE D'AUBERGINES ET CORNICHONS

### FRENCH EGGPLANT SALAD

*Serves 2–3*

*Aubergine* is the French name for eggplant, and cornichons are tiny sour French pickles, which can be purchased at specialty food stores.

1 large eggplant (1–1½ pounds)
Cornichons
3 tablespoons olive oil
1 tablespoon white wine vinegar
1 teaspoon chopped fresh chervil
   or ½ teaspoon dried

1 teaspoon chopped fresh tarragon
   or ½ teaspoon dried
Salt and freshly ground pepper
Lettuce leaves

Cut the eggplant in half, peel, and slice into pieces approximately ½ inch thick. Cook in a small amount of boiling water over low heat for 5–8 minutes, or until the vegetable is tender but firm. Drain and refresh under gently running cold water. Drain again and place in a glass bowl.

Mince 2 cornichons and whisk them with the oil, vinegar, and herbs. Correct seasoning with salt and pepper, pour the mixture over the eggplant, and gently toss. Chill for several hours. When ready to serve, line a platter with lettuce leaves and turn the eggplant mixture onto the dish. Garnish with extra cornichons.

# EGGPLANT À LA PROVENÇALE

*Serves 4–5*

This salad makes a delicious appetizer or accompaniment to cold chicken, veal, and omelets.

3 large eggplants (approximately 3 pounds)
Coarse salt
Olive oil
2 pounds ripe tomatoes
3 cloves garlic, finely chopped
2 tablespoons finely chopped fresh parsley
1 tablespoon lemon juice
⅛ teaspoon sugar
Salt and freshly ground pepper
Parsley sprig

Cut the unpeeled eggplants into long slices about ½ inch thick. Place on a cutting board, sprinkle lightly with coarse salt, and put a plate on top to help press out excess liquid. Allow to drain for about half an hour, then wipe with a damp paper towel.

Heat enough olive oil to cover the bottom of a large enamel frying pan. Add the eggplant and fry gently over medium heat, turning often, until it is tender. Remove from the pan and drain.

Plunge the tomatoes into boiling water for a few seconds, peel, and deseed them. Sauté the remaining pulp in a little olive oil until just soft. Add the garlic and the chopped parsley. Cover and reduce over medium heat for approximately 30–40 minutes. Remove from the heat, cool, and add the lemon juice, sugar, and salt and pepper to taste.

Place the eggplant in a shallow serving dish or glass bowl, pour the tomato mixture on top, and chill until ready to serve. Garnish with a sprig of fresh parsley.

# CHINESE SPICED EGGPLANT

*Serves 4*

1¾ pounds fresh young eggplant
3 tablespoons light soy sauce
2 tablespoons red wine vinegar
2 tablespoons sugar
¼ teaspoon salt
1½ teaspoon dry sherry
1 tablespoon sesame oil
1 teaspoon peanut, corn, or vegetable oil
1 tablespoon chopped fresh ginger
1 tablespoon chopped fresh garlic
1 tablespoon white sesame seeds

Place the eggplant in the top of a steamer, cover, and cook over boiling water for 30–45 minutes, until it is very soft. Cool.

75

While the eggplant is steaming, mix together the soy sauce, vinegar, sugar, salt, sherry, and sesame oil. Set aside. In a small saucepan, heat the peanut oil over a high flame, add the ginger and garlic, and cook for no more then 30 seconds. Stir in the vinegar-and-soy-sauce mixture, bring to the boil, then immediately remove from the heat. Set aside to cool.

Toast the sesame seeds in a dry frying pan over medium-low heat, or under the broiler, shaking the pan constantly to avoid burning. When the seeds are golden brown, remove from the heat, shake the pan for a few more seconds, and then set aside to cool.

Break the eggplant into pieces, discarding seeds and skin that fall away. Place in a serving dish, pour the cooked sauce on top, and garnish with the toasted sesame seeds.

If this is to be prepared in advance, keep chilled and add the seeds just before serving.

## BAINGAN BHURTA

### INDIAN EGGPLANT SALAD

#### Serves 4

Garam masala is the unusual spice that gives this typical Indian salad its distinctive flavor. It is a condiment made with cardamom, cumin, and cloves, all dry-roasted and ground (in an electric blender or food processor) or pounded (with mortar and pestle) to a fine powder. It can be purchased at specialty grocers or at Indian food stores, but for the ambitious cook who wishes to prepare garam masala at home, the proportions are: 1 ounce dark cardamom seeds, 2 ounces cumin seeds, 1 ounce cloves, and some Indian cooks also add cinnamon. When ground, store in a tightly sealed container until ready to use.

Baingan Bhurta, a puréed salad, closely resembles the "poorman's caviar" of the Balkans (see page 157).

1 large eggplant (approximately 1 pound)
2 tablespoons ghee (clarified butter)
⅔ teaspoon black cumin seeds
1 teaspoon white cumin seeds

⅔ teaspoon chili powder
1 tablespoon coriander seeds
Salt to taste
⅓ teaspoon garam masala

Pierce the eggplant skin with a fork and place under a hot broiler until the skin chars and the vegetable starts to shrivel (about 30 minutes). Turn occasionally to cook all sides. Allow to stand for 5–10 minutes, then squeeze gently to remove the bitter juices. Peel, and mash the pulp (or purée in an electric blender at low speed or in a food processor). Heat the ghee and fry the black and white cumin seeds until they turn brown; add the eggplant pulp, chili powder, coriander seeds, salt, and *garam masala.* Cook until the pulp has absorbed all the flavors and turns nicely brown. Serve at room temperature.

## SIMPOOG AGHTSAN

### ARMENIAN EGGPLANT

*Serves 3–4*

2 large eggplants (approximately 2 pounds)
2 large tomatoes, deseeded and cut into small wedges
2–3 scallions, finely chopped
¼ cup seeded and diced green pepper

½ cup peeled and diced cucumber
¼ cup chopped fresh parsley
1 clove garlic
½ cup olive oil
3 tablespoons wine vinegar
Salt and freshly ground pepper

Remove the stems from the eggplants and bake in a preheated 350°F oven for 45–60 minutes, or until they are quite soft. When cool enough to handle, peel off the skin, halve, and remove the seeds. Cut the remaining pulp into small pieces, place in a sieve to drain for 10–15 minutes, and place in a large salad bowl. Add the tomato wedges, scallions, green pepper, cucumber, and most of the parsley.

In a separate small bowl, crush the garlic with the oil, whisk several times, and then discard any remaining garlic pieces. Add the vinegar and whisk until well blended. Season with salt and pepper and pour over the salad. Toss well and chill for at least 1 hour. Toss again gently before serving and garnish with the remaining chopped parsley.

# FENNEL

NOT TO BE CONFUSED with bitter fennel—a tall, wild herb—Florence fennel, or *finocchio,* the type available in supermarkets, has large, white bulbous roots and short, round stalks topped with soft, feathery leaves. It has the same crunchy texture as celery, but its own distinctly sweet aniseed flavor.

Choose bulbs that are solid, crisp, and pale green; avoid those which have turned dark green.

Fennel makes an unusual addition to winter salads. It tastes delicious with fruits as well as vegetables. Use the leaves to season dressings.

## FENNEL WITH ORANGE SALAD

*Serves 4–6*

An excellent salad to serve with duck or game.

2 large fennel bulbs
3 large oranges
4 tablespoons sunflower or corn oil
2 tablespoons lemon juice

1 tablespoon white wine vinegar
1 large pinch sugar
1 tablespoon chopped fresh parsley
Freshly ground pepper to taste

Cut the fennel into ¼-inch slices and set aside. Remove the peel and pith from 2 of the oranges and divide into segments; grate approximately 2 teaspoons of rind from the third and squeeze out the juice. Put the fennel and orange segments into a salad bowl, arranging them decoratively in layers.

In a separate bowl mix the orange juice and rind with the remaining ingredients. Blend with a whisk and pour over the salad.

## FENNEL WITH ANCHOVIES

*Serves 4–6*

2 large fennel bulbs
1 small bunch watercress
4 anchovy fillets, cut into small pieces
1 hard-boiled egg, quartered
1 tomato, cut into small wedges

6 tablespoons olive oil
2 tablespoons lemon juice
Salt and freshly ground pepper to taste

Cut the fennel into ¼-inch slices and place in a large salad bowl. Wash, drain, and remove the damaged stalks from the watercress. Mix with the fennel. Add the anchovies and garnish with the egg and tomato wedges. Mix the oil, lemon juice, salt, and pepper and pour over the salad just before serving.

## FENNEL À LA GRECQUE

The recipe for Sedano alla Greca (Celery à la Grecque, page 64) may be adapted for fennel. Trim the feathery leaves from the bulbs before preparing them for cooking, and use as a garnish when serving.

# JERUSALEM ARTICHOKES

JERUSALEM ARTICHOKE is actually a misnomer for a kind of sunflower; it is certainly no real relation of the French globe artichoke. How this native American root vegetable acquired its strange name (in early colonial records it is sometimes referred to as "the Canadian Potato") is still somewhat of a mystery, though there seems to be some agreement on the theory that Jerusalem was a corruption of the Spanish word for sunflower, *girasol,* and artichoke was appended for the slight resemblance in flavor.

A nourishing winter vegetable, the Jerusalem artichoke is sometimes forsaken by the less adventurous because its knobby surface makes it awkward to clean. Persevere; the taste is worth the extra preparation time.

## JERUSALEM ARTICHOKE SALAD

*Serves 2–3*

1 pound Jerusalem artichokes
Juice of 1 small lemon
4 tablespoons olive oil
Salt and freshly ground pepper

2 tablespoons chopped fresh parsley
2 slices well-fried bacon, finely
   chopped (optional)

Scrub the artichokes and peel as you would a potato. Immerse in acidulated water (water to which a few drops of lemon juice or vinegar has been added) to prevent discoloration. Once peeled, cut each artichoke into walnut-size pieces and place in gently boiling, lightly salted water, along with half the lemon juice. Simmer for 7–8 minutes, or until just tender but not soft. Drain.

While the vegetable cools, blend the remaining lemon juice with the oil; add salt and pepper to taste. Place the artichokes in a glass bowl, pour on dressing, and add the chopped parsley and bacon bits, if desired.

*Note:* For a delicious variation, add one firm avocado, which has been peeled and cubed, along with 2 tablespoons chopped scallions.

# JICAMA

THE JICAMA IS A BROWN, bulbous root vegetable, popular in Mexican and Oriental cooking, with its devotees in this country, too. It looks like a very large potato with a thin skin that is easy to peel; inside, the flesh is white and crunchy—a cross between radish and potato in consistency, and apple and water chestnut in taste.

A favorite Mexican snack is jicama peeled, thinly sliced, and seasoned with salt, chili powder, and lime juice. It combines well with many fruits and vegetables and makes an excellent crudité.

## MEXICAN JICAMA SALAD

*Serves 4–6*

1 large jicama (approximately 1½ pounds)
1 tablespoon finely chopped fresh coriander
1 teaspoon salt
2 teaspoons finely grated grapefruit rind

2 tablespoons lemon juice
5 tablespoons orange juice
5 tablespoons grapefruit juice
1 large navel orange

Peel the jicama with a potato peeler and cut into dice (approximately ½ inch square). In a large bowl, mix the jicama with the coriander, salt, grapefruit rind, and fruit juices. Set aside to macerate for at least 1 hour. Peel and slice the orange into thin rounds. Line a large platter with the orange slices and spoon the jicama mixture over the top, along with some of the juice. Chill and serve.

# KOHLRABI

ALTHOUGH SIMILAR IN APPEARANCE and flavor to the turnip, kohlrabi is not a root. It is a swollen stem. Native to northern Europe, it has been known since the sixteenth century, yet it remains something of a novelty to most American cooks. Best supplies come to the market in the summer months. Choose only very young vegetables, approximately 2 inches in diameter, with thin skins.

Kohlrabi, like turnip, can be grated raw for salads or sliced and marinated in vinaigrette. Julienne-cut and lightly steamed, it is delicious with Bagna Cauda dressing (page 34).

## ORIENTAL KOHLRABI SALAD

*Serves 4*

½ pound kohlrabi, peeled
Salt
2 tablespoons light soy sauce
½ teaspoon superfine sugar
1 teaspoon Tabasco sauce

3 tablespoons Oriental sesame oil
3 stalks celery, cut into ½-inch pieces
3–4 scallions, chopped, including
  3 inches of green stem

Coarsely grate the kohlrabi and place in a deep glass bowl. Sprinkle lightly with salt and allow to stand for half an hour. Rinse several times in cold water and turn into a sieve or colander to drain.

In a separate small bowl, blend the soy sauce, sugar, and Tabasco. Gradually add the sesame oil while whisking constantly with a fork.

Dry the glass bowl and return the kohlrabi. Add the celery, scallions, and the dressing. Toss well to thoroughly coat all ingredients. Chill for about an hour, toss again, and serve.

## LEEKS

LEEKS ARE THE MILDEST and most delicately flavored members of the onion family. Their ancestry dates back to ancient times, when they were cultivated by most of the early Mediterranean civilizations. The Romans were especially fond of leeks, and the vain Emperor Nero is said to have eaten them to improve his singing voice.

The leek figures most importantly in Welsh history. In A.D. 640 the Welsh defeated the Saxons, a victory partly attributed to the leeks pinned to their hats, preventing them from attacking one another by mistake. Ever since, the leek has been the Welsh national emblem.

In spite of this distinguished pedigree, the leek has been largely ignored in the United States. Food of the European peasantry for hundreds of years, the leek is today still an expensive delicacy here.

When choosing leeks, look for smallish tender ones with several inches of

81

blanched or white skin at the root end, and fresh, green tops. Leeks must be washed thoroughly under cold running water to remove all the grit. If a recipe calls for whole leeks, it is a good idea to first stand them, green ends down, in cold water for half an hour. Then rinse under a running tap.

## PRASSA ME DOMATA

### GREEK-STYLE LEEKS

*Serves 4–5*

2 pounds leeks
1 cup canned tomatoes
1 cup chicken stock or broth
1 medium-size onion, coarsely
   chopped
1 stalk celery, chopped

2 tablespoons chopped fresh parsley
1 teaspoon dried oregano
3 tablespoons vegetable oil
Salt and freshly ground pepper
2 tablespoons lemon juice

Trim the stem ends of the leeks and remove the tough green tops. Wash thoroughly and cut into 1-inch slices. Soak in hot water for 5–10 minutes, then drain. In a large enamel saucepan combine the tomatoes, stock, onion, celery, parsley, oregano, and oil. Add the leeks, season with salt and pepper, and cook over a low heat for 12–15 minutes, or until the leeks are tender, adding the lemon juice during the last 5 minutes of cooking.

Remove the vegetables from the pan and bring the liquid to a rapid boil, cooking until the quantity has been reduced by one-third. Pour the reduced liquid over the leeks and chill for several hours before serving.

## PORROS IN BACA

### LEEKS AND OLIVES

*Serves 4–5*

This is a recipe said to have graced the banquet tables of Imperial Rome.

8 young crisp leeks
¾ cup white wine
3 tablespoons olive oil
¼–½ teaspoon cumin
¼–½ teaspoon ground coriander

¼ teaspoon caraway seeds
⅛ teaspoon freshly ground black
   pepper
16 pimiento-stuffed green olives

Rinse the leeks and trim about 3 inches from the root end. Trim the darker green tops to remove any bruised leaves. Cut the leeks into ¼-inch slices and wash well. Drain.

Put the wine, oil, cumin, coriander, caraway seeds, and pepper in a saucepan and bring to a gentle boil. Add the leeks and simmer until tender (10–12 minutes). In the meantime, chop the olives coarsely. Add these to the leeks as soon as they are removed from the heat. Refrigerate in a covered container until serving time.

## LEEKS VINAIGRETTE

*Serves 4*

| | |
|---|---|
| 8 young thin leeks | Salt and freshly ground pepper to |
| 4 tablespoons olive oil | taste |
| 1 tablespoon lemon juice | Crumbled hard-boiled egg yolk |
| Pinch of sugar | |

Trim the roots and coarse green top leaves from the leeks, and remove any damaged outer leaves. Clean by running the leeks under a cold tap and then immersing them in cold water.

Cook the leeks whole in just enough boiling salted water to cover, for 10 minutes, or until just tender. Drain and place on a serving dish to cool.

Mix the oil, lemon juice, sugar, salt, and pepper, and pour over the leeks just before serving. Garnish with a sprinkling of crumbled hard-boiled egg yolk.

## LOTUS ROOT

THIS VEGETABLE is the underwater root of the water-lily plant and features regularly in the cooking of the Far East. It is an unusually attractive plant, once described by food writer Robin Howe as looking like "a transverse section of a bullet-chamber of a six-shooter."

In the United States, lotus root can be bought fresh or precooked in cans from most Chinese groceries. When using the fresh vegetable, prepare as follows: Clean and peel the lotus root. Cut into ¼-inch slices and place immediately in a saucepan filled with acidulated water to prevent discoloration. Bring to a boil and simmer gently for 2–3 minutes, until the slices are tender but still crisp. Remove from the heat, drain, and place in a serving bowl.

## LOTUS ROOT SALAD

*Serves 4–6*

½ cup sake
2–3 tablespoons superfine sugar
1 tablespoon white wine vinegar
½ teaspoon salt
1 cooked lotus root, or one 19-ounce
 can, drained, sliced into ¼-inch
 pieces

2 small red peppers, seeded and
 thinly sliced into rings

In a small saucepan, combine the sake, sugar (to taste), vinegar, 4 tablespoons water, and salt. Stir, and bring gently to the boil. When the sugar has completely dissolved, remove from the heat and pour over the lotus root slices. Add the red pepper rings, toss to ensure that all ingredients are well covered with dressing, and chill for at least an hour. Toss again before serving.

# MUSHROOMS

FEW VEGETABLES arrive at the table heralded by as much history, myth, and legend as the mushroom. "Food of the gods" to more than one ancient civilization, the mushroom has garnered both fear and delight in equal measure, and not without cause. Of the thirty-eight thousand known varieties, there are sufficient fatally poisonous and hallucinogenic types to arouse suspicion and awe. Some famous victims of mushroom poisoning include the Roman emperors Tiberius and Claudius, Russia's Alexander I, Pope Clement VIII, and France's Charles V.

In her excellent book *The Mushroom Feast,* Jane Grigson describes the origins of the mushroom. The word comes to us from the French *mousseron* by way of the late Latin *mussiriones,* and the plant was noted in the sixth century by Anthrimus, doctor to the Ostrogoth King Theodoric. However, the actual cultivation of mushrooms as a proper crop did not begin until the seventeenth century, when the French botanist Marchant was able to demonstrate a suitable method.

*Agaricus bisporus* and *Agaricus campestris* are two of the basic varieties grown for market consumption. Unfortunately, the tastier wild mushrooms perish too easily to be a successful commercial crop. Cultivated mushrooms are sometimes sold in three grades: "button" mushrooms are the smallest—

crisp, white, and fresh-tasting; "cup" are medium-size but still retain the half-spherical shape of their smaller cousins; and "flat" or "open" mushrooms are the large, mature variety, generally strongest in flavor.

Fresh mushrooms should be cleaned with as little water as possible—a quick rinse under the tap will generally remove the loosely clinging dirt; or they can be gently wiped clean with a moistened paper towel. They do not need peeling, although the woody bottom of the stem should be removed.

A number of dried mushrooms feature prominently in Oriental cooking. Their color varies from black to speckled brown or gray, and they must be soaked in hot water for at least half an hour before using. The stems are always discarded, but the soaking water can be added to stock for cooking. *Mo-er* or cloud-ear mushrooms are a Szechuan specialty. They are thin and brittle dry chips which, after soaking, expand into clusters of dark brown petals.

There are also continental dried mushrooms, mainly French and Italian, with which to experiment when seeking a flavorful salad garnish. An Oriental white mushroom called Enok, with a long, thin stem and a tiny cap, has recently appeared in supermarkets. It is somewhat chewy but clean-tasting, and its distributors recommend it for salads as well as cooked dishes.

## RAW MUSHROOM AND ORANGE SALAD

*Serves 4–5*

A traditional English salad and a splendid accompaniment to poultry and game.

| | |
|---|---|
| 1 pound large flat-capped mushrooms | 6–8 tablespoons olive oil |
| 4 medium-size oranges | 2 tablespoons white wine vinegar |
| Salt and freshly ground pepper | 1 clove garlic, finely chopped |
| 1 small head Boston lettuce, washed and dried | ¼ cup coarsely chopped walnuts |

Trim the woody bottoms from the mushroom stems, then wash and dry gently with a dish towel. Slice thinly and place in a bowl. Squeeze the juice from 1 orange over the mushrooms, sprinkle with salt and pepper, and set aside.

Peel the 3 remaining oranges, removing all the white membrane and pith. With a very sharp knife, slice each one into thin circles. Line the bottom of a shallow dish or platter with crisp lettuce leaves and sprinkle with a few drops of oil. Follow with a layer of orange slices and then one of mushrooms. Repeat the orange and mushroom layers, and dress with a mixture of oil, vinegar, garlic, salt, and pepper. Chill for at least an hour. Just before serving, garnish with chopped walnuts.

# MUSHROOM AND PEPPER SALAD

*Serves 6*

2 green peppers
2 red peppers
1 pound button mushrooms
6–8 tablespoons olive oil
1 tablespoon lemon juice

2 tablespoons white wine vinegar
1 clove garlic, finely chopped
Salt and freshly ground pepper
3 tablespoons chopped fresh parsley

Peel the peppers by placing them under the broiler until they begin to turn black and blister. Keep turning to ensure that all sides are done. When cool enough to handle, peel off the skins under a cold running tap. Cut the peppers in half and remove the seeds and ribs. Slice thinly and place in a glass salad bowl.

Wipe the mushrooms with a damp dish towel or wet paper towel. Trim the woody bottoms from the stems, then slice thinly and add to the peppers.

In a separate bowl, mix the oil, lemon juice, vinegar, and garlic. Season with salt and pepper and add half the chopped parsley. Pour this dressing over the salad, toss well, and garnish with the remaining chopped parsley.

# SALADE DE CHAMPIGNONS QUERCYNOISE

### FRENCH MUSHROOM SALAD

*Serves 4*

Choose very fresh, large flat mushrooms or, if you live in the country, pick field mushrooms.

12 mushrooms
1 cup olive oil
12 small pearl onions
2 small heads Boston lettuce
2 large tomatoes
2 stalks celery, diced
Juice of 1 small lemon

2 teaspoons tomato paste
1 sprig fresh thyme, chopped, or
    ½ teaspoon dried
1 bay leaf
1 teaspoon coriander seeds
4 ounces dry white wine
Salt and freshly ground pepper

Clean the mushrooms by gently wiping with a damp dish towel or paper towel. Leave the caps whole, but chop the stems coarsely. Fry both caps and stems in half the oil until soft. Remove the mushrooms and set aside to drain. Discard the used oil.

Peel the onions, cut the lettuce into quarters, and slice the tomatoes. Put the onions, lettuce, and tomatoes into a pan with the celery, lemon juice, tomato paste, thyme, bay leaf, coriander seeds, wine, and the remaining ½ cup oil. Season with salt and pepper and simmer for 20–25 minutes, or until the onions are tender.

Remove the mushrooms to a shallow serving dish and bring the remaining ingredients to a rapid boil for 4–5 minutes. Pour over the mushrooms and chill until ready to serve.

## MUSHROOMS À LA GRECQUE I

*Serves 3*

⅓ cup water
¼ cup olive oil
¼ cup lemon juice
½ teaspoon coarse sea salt
2 tablespoons chopped scallions or
    shallots
1 stalk celery, with leaves
1 sprig fresh fennel or ⅛ teaspoon
    fennel seeds

1 sprig fresh thyme or ½ teaspoon
    dried
5–6 sprigs parsley
10–12 whole black peppercorns
8 coriander seeds
1 pound button mushrooms
3 tablespoons chopped fresh parsley

Place all the ingredients except mushrooms and chopped parsley in a covered saucepan and simmer gently for 10 minutes.

Meanwhile, wash the mushrooms under a cold running tap and trim the woody bottoms from the stems. Any large mushrooms should be halved or quartered.

Add the mushrooms to the simmering liquid, stir to cover completely with liquid, replace the lid, and continue to simmer for another 10 minutes.

Remove the mushrooms with a slotted spoon and set aside in a serving dish. Boil the liquid rapidly until it has reduced to about ⅓ cup. Add more salt and freshly ground pepper if desired, and strain the liquid over the mushrooms. Cover the dish and chill until ready to serve. Garnish with the chopped parsley just before serving.

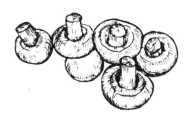

# MUSHROOMS À LA GRECQUE II

*Serves 3–4*

| | |
|---|---|
| 1 cup dry red wine | 12 whole black peppercorns |
| ¼ cup raisins | 12 coriander seeds |
| 1 small onion, thinly sliced | ¼ teaspoon dried thyme |
| 3 tablespoons tomato paste | 1 pound button mushrooms |
| 5 tablespoons olive oil | Salt and freshly ground pepper |
| ½ tablespoon sugar | Fresh chopped parsley |

Put the wine, 2½ cups water, raisins, onion, tomato paste, oil, sugar, peppercorns, coriander seeds, and thyme into a large saucepan. Bring to the boil and simmer gently for 5 minutes. Add the mushrooms, stir to cover completely with liquid, and simmer for another 10–15 minutes. Remove the mushrooms with a slotted spoon and set aside in a serving dish. Continue to boil the liquid until it is reduced by one-third. Adjust the seasoning with salt and pepper, and pour over the mushrooms. Toss and chill until ready to serve, garnished with chopped parsley.

# OKRA

KNOWN AS *gombo* in South America, "lady's fingers" in England, and *bamia* in the Middle East, okra probably had its origins in Africa, crossing the Atlantic with the slave trade. Together with tomato, okra forms the basis for the popular Southern gumbo stew (the stew shares its name with the vegetable because its defining characteristic is a sauce thickened by the juice of the okra).

Okra can be purchased throughout most of the year, but best supplies are available between July and October. The pods look somewhat like pale green ridged chilies, and they are best eaten when slightly underripe and about 2½ inches long. The gluey substance in the pods can be removed by soaking the okra in vinegar (approximately ½ cup per pound) before using. Discard the gluey liquid, rinse, and drain.

## MIDDLE EASTERN BAMIA WITH TOMATO AND ONIONS

*Serves 4–6*

The addition of *taklia*—garlic crushed with ground coriander—a favorite Arab combination, gives this dish its distinctive Middle Eastern flavor. A few chopped coriander leaves make an excellent garnish.

1 pound ripe tomatoes
2 pounds fresh young okra or two
   10-ounce packages frozen
¾ pound small pearl onions
5 tablespoons olive oil

2 cloves garlic, crushed with 1
   teaspoon ground coriander
Salt and freshly ground pepper
Juice of 1 small lemon

Immerse the tomatoes in rapidly boiling water for several seconds. Remove and, when cool enough to handle, peel off the skins. Slice the tomatoes. Wash, scrub, and drain the okra. Remove the hard stems. Peel the onions, but leave them whole.

Heat the oil in a large frying pan. Add the onions and crushed garlic with coriander and fry over medium heat until the onions become soft and translucent. Add the okra and continue frying for another 5 minutes; then add the tomatoes and cook for a few more minutes, stirring constantly. Season with salt and pepper, then add just enough water to cover. Simmer gently for 30–45 minutes, or until the okra is very tender. Add the lemon juice, stir, and cook for another 5 minutes. Allow to cool, then chill for at least 2 hours before serving.

# ONION

THROUGHOUT HISTORY, onions have been celebrated and maligned, prescribed and prohibited, perhaps more than any other vegetable. First domesticated somewhere in the Fertile Crescent area, and used for both culinary and medicinal purposes, the onion was also regarded as a symbol of the universe and eternity because of its spherical shape. John Evelyn writes in *Acetaria:* "How this noble *Bulb* was deified in Egypt we are told, and that whilst they were building the *Pyramids,* there was spent in this Root *Ninety Tun of Gold* among the workmen."

The Greeks and Romans had many imaginative uses for the onion. The Roman poet Martial commended its aphrodisiac and rejuvenating powers and advised, "If your wife is old and your member is exhausted, eat onions in plenty."

The onion in its many forms—garlic, leeks, and chives are also members of the onion family—is a mainstay of any cook's kitchen. The most popular varieties are listed below.

*Pearl onions* measure about 1 inch in diameter (about 18–24 onions per pound) and are generally available during the summer months and early autumn. The smallest are used for pickling and as cocktail onions.

*Shallots* are an essential ingredient in French cooking. This delicately flavored cousin of the onion was probably introduced to Europe during the Crusades and to the New World in 1543, by the explorer Hernando de Soto. Generally copper-colored and walnut-size, the shallot dries up quickly and should be purchased in small quantities, as needed. Best supplies available between July and October.

*Bermuda onions* are the most common member of the onion family and are available all year round. The skin may be white, tan, or even red. An average-size onion weighs 5–8 ounces. Sweet and mild in flavor, this is a good all-purpose onion.

*Spanish onions* are larger, milder, and sweeter than ordinary onions and at their best during the summer months.

*Yellow onions* are the strongest of the dry onions and used mainly in cooking.

*Italian onions,* reddish purple in color, with a sharp, sweet flavor, are the perfect salad onion and an excellent complement for slices of beefsteak tomato dressed with oil, vinegar, and lots of freshly ground pepper.

*Scallions* are almost always used raw. The bulb can be substituted for shallots, and the green stems make a respectable substitute for chives. Scallions keep best when stored in the refrigerator.

## SWEET-AND-SOUR ONIONS

*Serves 6–8*

2 pounds pearl onions
2 cups dry white wine
3 tablespoons sugar
⅓ cup plumped-up (presoaked) raisins
4 tablespoons tomato purée
1–2 teaspoons chopped fresh dill
5 tablespoons olive oil

2–4 tablespoons wine vinegar or the juice of 1 small lemon
Salt and freshly ground pepper
Dash of cayenne pepper
1 bay leaf
2 tablespoons coarsely chopped fresh parsley

Place the onions in a bowl, cover with boiling water, and leave for 5 minutes. Drain and peel. In a saucepan, combine 1½ cups water, wine, sugar, raisins, tomato purée, dill, and olive oil. Add the vinegar or lemon juice, salt, freshly ground pepper, cayenne, and bay leaf. Add the onions and simmer for 30 minutes, or until they are tender but still firm. With a slotted spoon, remove the onions to a glass salad bowl or serving dish. Bring the liquid to a rapid boil and reduce the quantity by half. Pour over the onions and chill for several hours. Just before serving, garnish with chopped parsley.

*Note:* Instead of raisins, use 8 crushed juniper berries and season with 1 tablespoon chopped fresh basil instead of dill.

# CACHOOMBAR

### INDIAN SPICED ONION SALAD

*Serves 4–6*

1 small cucumber
1 teaspoon salt
3 large firm tomatoes
2–3 large Spanish or Bermuda onions
½ cup white wine vinegar

4 tablespoons chopped coriander
   leaves or Italian parsley
4 green chili peppers, chopped and
   seeded (see page 95)

Peel and chop the cucumber into small dice. Sprinkle with salt and allow to drain in a sieve or colander for 20–30 minutes. Peel the tomatoes after immersing briefly in boiling water, then coarsely chop. Peel and chop the onions.

    Mix these ingredients with the vinegar, coriander, and chilies in a shallow dish. Tossing occasionally, allow to stand for 30 minutes before serving.

# SLAPHAKSKEENTJIES

### CAPE TOWN COOKED ONION SALAD

*Serves 2–3*

1 pound pearl onions
2 eggs

2 tablespoons sugar
2 tablespoons vinegar or lemon juice

Cook the onions in simmering salted water until tender but not soft, approximately 20 minutes. Remove the onions and allow to cool. To make the dressing, whisk the eggs with the sugar. Add the vinegar or lemon juice and 2 tablespoons water and put the mixture into the top of a double boiler over simmering water. Stir occasionally until it thickens. Pour this over the onions, cool, and serve at room temperature.

## PERSIAN ONION SALAD

*Serves 4–6*

A good accompaniment with lamb or mutton dishes.

2–3 large Spanish onions
Salt
4 tablespoons chopped fresh mint or
   2 tablespoons dried

4–5 tablespoons white wine vinegar

Slice the onions into thick half-circles. Place in a bowl and sprinkle with salt; add the mint and vinegar. Toss and allow to stand for at least 1 hour, tossing again from time to time before serving.

## ENSALADA DE CEBOLLITAS

### MEXICAN SCALLION SALAD

*Serves 6–8*

Although truly a mixed salad, the onion flavor strongly dominates this dish. Like many Mexican salads, it is cooked.

16 scallions with well-formed bulbs
½ pound zucchini
2 large green peppers
3 small, firm but ripe avocados

6 tablespoons olive oil
2 tablespoons white wine vinegar
Salt and freshly ground pepper

Chop the scallion bulbs coarsely. Reserve about 8 unbruised stalks for garnish. Wash and cut the zucchini into slices approximately 2 inches thick. Cook the scallions and zucchini separately, each in a very small quantity of lightly salted boiling water, until just tender. Drain and place both in a large salad bowl.

Wash, seed, and cut the green peppers into very thin, shredlike strips. Peel and cut the avocados into small chunks. Add to the salad bowl with the peppers.

Whisk the oil and vinegar with salt and pepper to taste and pour over the vegetables. Toss gently, chill, and toss again just before serving. Garnish with the scallion tops, snipped into small circles.

# PEAS

PEAS HAVE BEEN AROUND for a long time. Excavations of Bronze Age sites in Switzerland, for instance, produced evidence that peas were eaten by our early ancestors, though only as a dried vegetable. The Chinese were probably the first to eat them green, and they were introduced to England by the Dutch in the sixteenth century. Initially received as exotic, expensive "fit dainties for ladies," they were nevertheless being widely cultivated during the seventeenth century.

Thomas Jefferson, ever the keen gardener, helped to popularize the cultivation of peas in the United States. The annual competition in the neighborhood of Monticello to produce the first peas was a great event, culminated by a dinner at the home of Mr. George Divers, the usual winner.

Peas grow best in a somewhat cool climate. For best flavor, they should be eaten during the early summer months. Pick young ones and eat them at once.

Nowadays, the quality of frozen peas is of a very high standard, and these can be substituted when fresh peas are out of season; but avoid canned peas to which artificial coloring and preservatives have been added.

Snow peas (known in Europe as *mange-touts* because they are eaten whole) are a variety of pea popular in Chinese cooking. Like the ordinary green pea, these need only the slightest cooking (3–4 minutes).

The newly introduced snap peas, like snow peas, are eaten pod and all. They are best raw and make a delicious addition to assorted crudités.

## ARAKA ME ANGINARES

### GREEK GREEN PEAS WITH ARTICHOKES

*Serves 6–8*

This method of stewing vegetables to be eaten as a cold dish is popular all over Greece.

3 cups shelled fresh green peas or
  2 packages frozen
6–8 fresh young artichokes
Juice of 1 lemon
⅓ cup olive oil
1 small bunch scallions, chopped,
  including 3 inches green stem

½ cup canned tomato sauce
2 cloves garlic, cut into slivers
1 teaspoon dried marjoram
Salt and freshly ground pepper
½ teaspoon sugar
4 tablespoons chopped fresh parsley

Wash and drain the peas. If using frozen peas defrost and drain them. Remove the outer leaves of the artichokes and cut off the stems. Remove the remaining leaves above the base of the heart. With a teaspoon, remove the choke, then immerse in water with lemon juice added, to avoid discoloration while the sauce is being prepared.

Heat the oil in a large, heavy frying pan. Sauté the scallions until translucent. Stir in the tomato sauce and ½–⅔ cup water (dilute to taste), and season with garlic, marjoram, salt, pepper, and sugar.

Drain the artichokes and place in the pan. Add the peas and stir gently to ensure that the vegetables are moistened with sauce. Cover and simmer on low heat for half an hour. The sauce should thicken. Adjust the seasoning and allow to cool to room temperature. Serve garnished with a sprinkling of chopped parsley.

*Note:* If artichokes are not in season, try substituting cauliflower or broad beans, but add these vegetables slightly later to the stewing peas than you would the fresh artichokes.

# PEPPERS

THERE ARE TWO BASIC TYPES of peppers: sweet peppers, generally known as bell peppers, and chili peppers. Both probably had their origin in South America. Various artifacts of Peruvian civilizations dated back two thousand years attest to their early existence. Europeans first encountered the pepper when Columbus's Spanish fleet landed at Hispaniola. The green and scarlet pods that he observed the natives eating were of such fiery hotness that he mistook them for relatives of *Piper nigrum,* the Spanish plant from which we get our black pepper seasoning.

While the chili pepper found instant favor when introduced by the Spaniards to the colonies of the American South, only the milder green pepper was fully accepted in the North. Our Puritan forefathers feared that chili peppers might encourage passionate excitement.

Bell peppers begin green, turn to yellow-orange, and finally become red as they reach maturity. There is little difference between green and red peppers; the red ones may be a little bit softer and somewhat sweeter. Peppers are generally chopped or sliced for salads. They can also be left whole and stuffed (after cleaning and deseeding) with an infinite variety of fillings, such as ratatouille, chicken salad, crab salad, spiced and herbed cottage cheese, and so on.

The chili pepper, though used more judiciously in cooking, was at one time highly valued as a cure for flu, sore throat, and yellow fever. Chilies are cultivated, among other places, in California, Texas, Arizona, and New Mexico. Of the many different varieties (with names varying from place to place) some common types of mild peppers are *poblano* and *ancho,* and of hotter ones, *seranno, jalapeño,* and *pequin.* The sizes and colors are also diverse, ranging from 1 to 6 inches, in all shades of green, red, and even black. We also use chili in its dried forms—cayenne, paprika, and chili powder—or as the basis for Tabasco and other chili sauces.

Chilies should be handled with care. The capsaicin secreted from their flesh can make the eyes smart and the skin burn.

If possible, wear rubber gloves and try not to touch your face. Clean the chilies by rinsing under cold running water. If they are to be left whole, break off the stems but do not cut. If the recipe calls for deseeding, pull out the stem and any seeds attached to it, then cut open the pod and brush out any remaining seeds with your fingers. After handling chilies, always wash your hands thoroughly with soap and warm water.

## MIXED PEPPER SALAD

*Serves 4*

This is a delicious salad to serve with cold meats, especially salami and ham, and crusty French bread.

2 large red peppers
2 large green peppers
2–3 tablespoons olive oil
1 tablespoon lemon juice or white
  wine vinegar

Salt and freshly ground pepper to
  taste
2 tablespoons chopped fresh parsley

Place the peppers under a hot broiler and turn until all sides are well charred (10–15 minutes). Remove from the heat and, when cool enough to handle, cut away the stalk, remove the inner pith and seeds, and carefully peel away

95

the skin. Rinse and allow the excess juices to drain through a sieve for several minutes. Cut into thin strips and place in a large glass bowl.

Combine the oil, lemon juice or vinegar, salt and pepper, whisk and pour over the salad. Chill for about an hour, toss, and garnish with the chopped parsley just before serving.

## SCHLADA L'FILFIL

### MOROCCAN GREEN PEPPER SALAD

*Serves 8*

A delicious accompaniment for couscous.

6 large green peppers
6 large firm tomatoes
1 large clove garlic, finely minced
1 teaspoon ground cumin
2 red chili peppers, seeded and
  finely chopped (see page 95)

1 teaspoon salt
3 tablespoons olive oil
2–3 tablespoons freshly squeezed
  lemon juice

Place the green peppers under a hot broiler and turn until all sides are well charred, about 10–15 minutes. When cool enough to handle, remove the stems, pith, and seeds; peel off the skin and rinse the green peppers under a cold tap. Allow to drain, then slice into thickish, lengthwise strips. Place in a salad bowl.

Peel the tomatoes after immersing briefly in boiling water. Cut into ½-inch dice. Add to the green peppers. In a small bowl, whisk the remaining ingredients to form a dressing. Pour this over the vegetables and marinate for at least 2 hours, tossing occasionally, before serving.

# POTATOES

THE POTATO may first have been domesticated by the primitive civilizations of Latin America, but its more notorious history begins in sixteenth-century Europe. So overwhelmingly dismissed were the early attempts to encourage widespread cultivation of the potato that it is difficult to imagine how it came to play such a crucial role in the later economic history of the European continent.

Sir Walter Raleigh, on his return from Virginia, planted a potato crop on his estate at Youghal in Ireland, but he neither cared for nor understood this plant, and ordered the vegetables to be rooted out. In Scotland, the Presbyterian clergy declared potatoes unfit to eat because the Bible made no mention of them. When first introduced to French society in the sixteenth century, the potato was admired solely for its blossoms; and a Dutch chemist, writing at the time, expressed his countrymen's skepticism in stating that "potatoes cannot become a staple diet without the eaters not only dwindling in physical condition, but growing more dull and torpid in intellect."

Possibly the first Europeans to wholly appreciate the potato were the Germans. The 1581 publication of *Ein Neu Kochbuch* included several recipes for potato dishes. Later, Frederick the Great actually sponsored the cultivation of potatoes by distributing free seed potatoes with growing instructions to the Prussian peasantry. In France, the potato gained favor through the efforts of Antoine Auguste Parmentier. While a prisoner in Germany during the Seven Years' War, he survived on a diet of potatoes. Returning to his native land, he established a soup kitchen using potatoes and earned the praise of his king, Louis XVI: "France will thank you for having found bread for the poor." Less appreciative were members of the British aristocracy, horrified to see the growing popularity of the potato. Stephen Switzer, the eighteenth-century garden designer, typified upper-class conservatism when he commented, "That which was heretofore reckon'd a food fit only for Irishmen and clowns is now become the diet of the most luxuriously polite."

Nevertheless, the potato's adaptability to all kinds of soil and climate and its high yield made it the staple diet of the masses. Hence, the failure of the potato crops throughout Europe in the 1840s played an important role in creating the economic and political unrest that shaped the world we know today. The potato is still a major source of food internationally and has a featured role in many international cuisines.

For salads, new or early potatoes, in plentiful supply between May and September, are generally best; California Long Whites or White Roses are good choices. Although the sweet potato is rarely used in salads, a recipe for a delicious sweet potato salad is included here.

Scrub potatoes and boil without peeling to preserve the vitamins stored just below the surface. Peel, if instructed, when cool enough to handle. Be careful not to overcook: potatoes for salad should retain their firmness or they will turn to mush when the dressing is added. It is important to remember that small, young, new potatoes need only a very few minutes of cooking.

# BASIC POTATO SALAD

2 pounds new potatoes, scrubbed but not peeled
4 large scallions (tops included), finely chopped
1–2 cloves garlic, finely chopped (optional)

2 tablespoons chopped fresh parsley
4–6 tablespoons light olive oil
1–2 tablespoons lemon juice
Salt and freshly ground pepper to taste

Cook the potatoes for 8–10 minutes in enough gently boiling salted water to cover. Drain and peel while still warm. Cut into dice or slice and mix with the scallions, garlic (if desired), and parsley.

In a separate bowl, blend the oil and lemon juice, adjusting quantities to taste. Add salt and freshly ground pepper and pour over the potatoes while still warm. Toss gently and let stand at room temperature for at least an hour before serving, so that the dressing flavors can be absorbed.

*Note:* For variety, try adding 1 tablespoon of capers or finely chopped anchovies.

# BASIC POTATO SALAD WITH GREEN MAYONNAISE

### Serves 4–6

Some people prefer a creamy dressing for potato salad. Mayonnaise is the most common, but dressings made with cream, yogurt, or sour cream are also popular.

To transform a vinaigrette-dressed potato salad to a creamy salad, simply add 4–5 tablespoons cream just before serving and toss well. For something a little different and especially lovely with cold poached fish, try this green mayonnaise dressing.

2 pounds small young potatoes, scrubbed but not peeled
4 tablespoons mayonnaise
4 tablespoons heavy cream
2 tablespoons wine vinegar
4 tablespoons olive oil
¼ pound fresh spinach leaves, coarsely chopped

1 small bunch scallions, tops removed, coarsely chopped
2–3 cloves garlic
Salt and freshly ground pepper
Parsley sprigs

Cook the potatoes as for Basic Potato Salad (preceding recipe).

For best results, use an electric blender or food processor to prepare the dressing.

Stir the mayonnaise and cream together in a bowl. Put the vinegar, oil, chopped spinach leaves, scallions, garlic, salt, and lots of black pepper into the blender or processor and blend thoroughly. Add slowly to the mayonnaise mixture. If it is too thick, add a little cream; if too thin, add a little more mayonnaise. Use just enough of this mixture to bind the potatoes; the remainder can be stored in the refrigerator in a tightly sealed jar. Garnish the salad with a few sprigs of fresh parsley.

# FRENCH POTATO SALAD

*Serves 4–6*

"A dish as simple as potato salad," wrote Alice B. Toklas, "must be served surrounded by chicory. To serve it with any other green is inconceivable."

There are rules and there are rules. Chicory makes an excellent base for French potato salad, but any sturdy green may be substituted. Watercress, romaine, and spinach leaves are all excellent.

2 pounds new potatoes, scrubbed but not peeled
2 tablespoons dry white vermouth
2 tablespoons chicken stock or bouillon
1 teaspoon prepared mustard
2 tablespoons wine vinegar

Salt and freshly ground pepper to taste
2 tablespoons chopped scallions or shallots
5–6 tablespoons light olive oil
2 tablespoons chopped fresh parsley

Cook the potatoes as for Basic Potato Salad, page 98. Drain and peel when cool enough to handle. Cut into rough dice, place in a large bowl, and pour on the vermouth and stock or bouillon. Toss and let stand for several minutes.

In a separate bowl, combine the mustard, vinegar, salt, pepper, and chopped scallions or shallots. Add the oil slowly, drop by drop, beating continuously with a wire whisk. Pour this dressing over the potatoes, add the chopped parsley, and toss gently. Serve at room temperature.

# AMERICAN-STYLE POTATO SALAD

*Serves 5–6*

Each region of the country has its distinctive way of preparing this popular dish. In the South and Midwest, a variety of boiled dressings are made with whipped cream or mayonnaise, and some typical garnishes are pimientos and olives. In the East, chopped cucumber, chopped eggs, minced onion, and celery seed may be mixed with sour cream or mayonnaise to form a dressing.

Here is an old New England recipe from the days when salt pork was more commonly used in cooking.

2 pounds small potatoes, scrubbed but not peeled
¼ pound salt pork, cut into ¼-inch dice

Oil
1 large onion, finely chopped
1 teaspoon salt
2 tablespoons vinegar

Boil the potatoes in lightly salted water over medium heat for 10–12 minutes, or until tender. Drain and set aside. Meanwhile, fry the salt pork in a little oil. When golden brown, remove from heat and set aside.

Place the chopped onion in a large bowl. Add the salt and crush into the onion. Next add the vinegar, stir, and let stand for 5 minutes. When the potatoes are cool enough to handle, peel and cut into small pieces. Add to the onion mixture, toss, and add the salt pork. Blend well and serve at room temperature. If the salad is stored in the refrigerator, be sure to remove it an hour or so before serving to let stand at room temperature.

# ALU RAITA

### PAKISTANI POTATO SALAD

*Serves 4*

Raita, a popular Indian and Pakistani relish or accompaniment, is made from a base of thick yogurt.

1½–2 cups yogurt
3–4 medium-size potatoes
2–3 medium-size firm tomatoes
½ teaspoon cumin seeds, roasted
Salt and freshly ground pepper

1 teaspoon chopped green chili pepper (see page 95)
2 tablespoons chopped coriander leaves or Italian parsley

It is important to partially strain the yogurt so that the raita does not turn out watery. This is done by placing a piece of cheesecloth or muslin in a sieve, pouring the yogurt into the sieve, and allowing the liquid to drain through. Leave for 15 minutes, then place the yogurt from the sieve in a mixing bowl.

Meanwhile, cook the potatoes in their skins in gently boiling salted water, for 15 minutes or until tender when pierced with a fork. Peel, slice thinly, and set aside.

Peel the tomatoes after immersing in boiling water for a few seconds. Cool and slice, discarding seeds and core. Add to the potatoes.

Mix the strained yogurt with the cumin seeds and salt and pepper to taste, and pour over the tomatoes. Add the chopped chilies and toss lightly to blend all ingredients. Chill before serving, garnished with chopped coriander or parsley.

# BATATA BHAJI

### INDIAN POTATO SALAD

*Serves 3–4*

1 pound medium-size potatoes
⅓ cup ghee (clarified butter)
1 small onion, finely chopped
1–2 teaspoons chili powder
1 teaspoon turmeric
Salt

2 teaspoons ground coriander
1 teaspoon cumin seeds
1 teaspoon grated coconut
3 tablespoons finely chopped
   coriander leaves

Peel the potatoes and cut each into 8 pieces. Heat the ghee in a frying pan and sauté the onion until translucent. Add the chili powder, turmeric, salt to taste, ground coriander, and cumin seeds, and fry for 2 minutes, stirring constantly. Add the potatoes and fry gently for 10–15 minutes, until lightly browned. Next add ½ cup water to the pan and simmer gently until the liquid is nearly absorbed and the potatoes are soft.

Cool, turn into a serving dish, and garnish with grated coconut and chopped coriander.

# KEDNAKHINTZER AGHTSAN

## ARMENIAN POTATO SALAD

*Serves 6*

5 medium-size potatoes
6 tablespoons olive oil
2 tablespoons freshly squeezed
and strained lemon juice
Salt and freshly ground pepper to
taste
3 tablespoons chopped fresh dill or
1 tablespoon dried

4 scallions (including tops), finely
chopped
1 small cucumber, peeled and thinly
sliced
1 large tomato, cut into 8 wedges
8 black olives
3 sprigs fresh parsley
Paprika

Scrub the potatoes and cook, unpeeled, in lightly salted boiling water for about 15 minutes, or until just tender. Drain and peel. Cut into cubes and place in a bowl.

Mix together the oil, lemon juice, salt, pepper, and dill. Pour this over the potatoes while still warm and add the chopped scallions. Toss and let stand for 15 minutes.

Turn the mixture onto a large serving dish and surround with the cucumber slices and tomato wedges. Garnish with olives, parsley sprigs, and a sprinkling of paprika.

# LOUISIANA SWEET POTATO SALAD

*Serves 4*

The sweet potato was native to Central America. Columbus brought it back to Spain in 1493. It was introduced to England by Sir John Hawkins in 1553, where it enjoyed brief popularity as a conserve, sometimes sold in crystallized slices as an aphrodisiac. It has never been as popular in Europe as it is in Africa and South and Central America. It is also a great favorite in the cooking of the Southern states and a feature nationwide of many Thanksgiving feasts.

1 cup peeled and grated sweet
potato
2 cups peeled and diced apples,
sprinkled with lemon juice
½ cup coarsely chopped pecans

¾ cup raisins
½ cup finely chopped celery
3 tablespoons mayonnaise
A few lettuce leaves

In a large glass bowl, mix the grated sweet potatoes with the apples, pecans, raisins, and celery. Stir in a spoonful of mayonnaise at a time and blend all ingredients with a wooden spoon. Chill and serve on a platter lined with lettuce leaves.

# RADISHES

IN ANCIENT EGYPT, the radish was prized by the pyramid builders as a source of energy and physical strength. To the Greeks, it was worthy of offering to the gods (there is a saying that Athenian artists made replicas of turnips in lead, beets in silver, but radishes were fashioned from gold).

The radish was probably introduced to England in the fifteenth century and was such common fare by the time the British colonized the New World that most of the early English settlers boasted a radish patch in their kitchen gardens.

The red varieties are the most commonly cultivated here, but in the Far East, the *daikon* or *mooli*—a long, white vegetable—is ubiquitous. White radishes are also cultivated in the United States, and the Mediterranean black radish is sometimes available.

Radishes make excellent garnishes and crudités. They are delicious simply dipped in coarse salt. Rich in vitamin C and very low in calories, their peppery taste makes a flavorful addition to the salad bowl all year round.

## MINTED RADISH SALAD

*Serves 4*

¾ pound white radishes
1 large firm tomato
1 small onion, finely chopped
2 tablespoons finely chopped fresh
  mint

2 tablespoons olive oil
1 tablespoon lemon juice
Salt and freshly ground pepper

Wash and peel the radishes and slice into thin rounds. Immerse the tomato in boiling water for several seconds to loosen the skin. Drain and when cool enough to handle, peel and chop, discarding the seeds and core.

Place the radishes, tomato, onion, and mint in a bowl. In a separate bowl, mix the oil, lemon juice, and salt and pepper to taste. When thoroughly blended, pour over the vegetables, and toss gently. Chill for several hours before serving.

# DAIKON NAMASU

### JAPANESE RADISH AND CARROT SALAD

*Serves 3–4*

¼ pound carrots
¾ pound *daikon* (white radishes)
½ teaspoon salt

⅔ cup white wine vinegar
1 tablespoon light soy sauce
2 tablespoons light-brown sugar

Wash and peel the carrots and radishes. Cut both into julienne strips about 1 inch long. Place in a sieve and sprinkle with salt. Allow to drain for half an hour, then press out excess water with the hands. In a glass bowl, mix together the vinegar, soy sauce, and brown sugar. Add the vegetables, toss to cover thoroughly with dressing, and chill for at least an hour before serving.

*Note:* As a variation, try adding 2 ounces plumped-up raisins or 1 tablespoon toasted sesame seeds (see Oriental Salad Dressing, page 31).

# RUSSIAN RADISH SALAD

*Serves 4*

2 bunches radishes
1 hard-boiled egg
1½ cups sour cream

3 scallions (tops included), chopped
½ teaspoon salt
Freshly ground pepper

Wash the radishes, trim the tops, and slice thinly. Cut the egg in half, sieve the white, and mash the yolk with a fork. In a bowl, blend the yolk with the sour cream and add the radishes, scallions, salt, and pepper to taste. Mix well, garnish with the egg white, and chill.

# SALSIFY

THIS UNUSUAL and much-forgotten vegetable is often referred to as the "oyster plant" or "vegetable oyster" because of its slightly sealike flavor. In appearance, the salsify resembles an underdeveloped, white-fleshed parsnip or a white, elongated carrot. Two kinds of salsify are sold in the United States: the common, white-skinned variety and the more delicate black salsify. Both require careful scrubbing before cooking and should be soaked in acidulated water after peeling, to prevent discoloration.

Salsify can be served as a salad simply boiled *al dente* and dressed with a vinaigrette or mayonnaise. It also mixes nicely with other winter vegetables and herbs.

## SALSIFIS À LA MAYONNAISE

*Serves 4–6*

2 pounds salsify  
Juice of 1 small lemon  
⅔ cup mayonnaise

10 anchovy fillets, chopped  
6 black olives

Wash, scrub, and peel the salsify. Cook in boiling salted water to which a little of the lemon juice has been added, for 10–15 minutes, until tender but crisp. Drain, cut into 1-inch dice, place in a salad bowl, and chill.

Prepare the mayonnaise and season with lemon juice, according to taste. Blend with the salsify and add the chopped anchovies. Stir well and garnish with the olives.

# SPINACH

SPINACH WAS INTRODUCED into Europe by the Moors in Spain, and for many years after, as its popularity spread, it was known as the "Spanish vegetable."

Spinach can usually be purchased all year round, but the delicately flavored spring and summer varieties are more tender, and therefore better for salad making. When buying loose, bulk spinach, look for crisp, dark-green, moist leaves. Bulk spinach needs careful cleaning to remove all the dirt that clings

105

to its leaves; it needs equally careful handling, since the leaves bruise easily. Bagged spinach is prewashed, so a quick rinse and removal of the coarse stems will suffice.

# SPINACH, BACON, AND MUSHROOM SALAD

*Serves 4–6*

1 pound fresh young spinach leaves
¼ pound button mushrooms
8 sprigs watercress
4 slices bacon, fried and broken
   into small pieces
6 tablespoons olive oil

2 tablespoons lemon juice or white
   wine vinegar
¼ teaspoon dry mustard
Salt and freshly ground pepper
1 hard-boiled egg, thinly sliced
   (optional)

Clean the spinach carefully, drain, and dry thoroughly. If the leaves are large, break them into smaller pieces. Wipe the mushrooms clean with a damp paper towel, trim the bottoms, and slice.

Place the spinach, mushrooms, and watercress in a large wooden salad bowl and add half the crumbled bacon.

In a separate small dish, mix the oil, lemon juice or vinegar, mustard, and salt and pepper to taste. Blend thoroughly and pour over the salad. Toss gently but well, so that the mushrooms do not collect at the bottom of the bowl. Sprinkle the remaining bacon on top and garnish, if desired, with the hard-boiled egg.

*Note:* A delicious variation is Joe Allen's Deluxe Spinach Salad, made at the well-known New York restaurant. For each person, add 2 large shrimp (boiled and peeled), a few tomato wedges, and one artichoke heart to your salad bowl. Arrange decoratively around the top.

# SPANAKI SALATA

### GREEK SPINACH SALAD

*Serves 4*

2 pounds fresh young spinach leaves
4 tablespoons olive oil
Juice of 1 lemon

Salt and freshly ground pepper
2 sprigs fresh mint
A few chives, finely chopped

Wash the spinach thoroughly and remove the stalks and damaged leaves. Drain and cook in a large covered saucepan, without any additional water, for about 8 minutes, until the spinach is quite tender. Place in a sieve and drain off as much liquid as possible (pressing with the back of a spoon helps force out the liquid). Arrange in a shallow serving dish, and gradually add the oil, lemon juice, and salt and pepper to taste. Toss thoroughly to ensure that each leaf is well coated with dressing. Garnish with mint and chives.

## JAPANESE-STYLE SPINACH SALAD

*Serves 2*

1 pound fresh young spinach leaves
3 tablespoons light soy sauce

3 tablespoons white sesame seeds
1 tablespoon sugar

Wash the spinach carefully and cook, covered, in a little lightly salted boiling water for a maximum of 4 minutes. Rinse in cold water and drain well. Chop coarsely and place in a bowl with 1½ teaspoons soy sauce.

Toast the sesame seeds in a dry frying pan or under the broiler until they begin to jump. Shake constantly so that they do not burn. Remove from the heat and crush in a mortar or Japanese *suribachi*.

Mix the seeds with the remaining 1½ teaspoons soy sauce and the sugar. Pour over the spinach, toss to blend all ingredients, and chill for about an hour before serving.

## SALADE D'ESPINARDS AUX MOULES

### SPINACH AND MUSSEL SALAD

*Serves 4–6*

2½ pounds fresh spinach
1 pound fresh mussels, cooked and
    removed from their shells
6 tablespoons light olive oil

2 tablespoons white wine vinegar
1 teaspoon prepared mustard
1 hard-boiled egg
Salt and freshly ground pepper

Wash the spinach thoroughly and remove the stems. Cook covered in a small quantity of lightly salted boiling water for approximately 6 minutes, or until tender. Place in a sieve, rinse with cold water, and drain, pressing out the excess liquid with the back of a spoon.

Drain the mussels and place in a large salad bowl. Add the spinach.

Place the oil, vinegar, mustard, hard-boiled egg, and salt and pepper to taste in an electric blender. Blend for a few seconds at medium speed until creamy in texture. Pour over the salad, toss carefully, and chill for at least an hour before serving.

## SPANAKH VER MADZOON AGHTSAN

### ARMENIAN SPINACH WITH YOGURT

*Serves 3*

1 pound fresh spinach
1 clove garlic, crushed
1 tablespoon freshly squeezed
  and strained lemon juice
2 tablespoons finely chopped fresh
  mint or 2 teaspoons dried

Salt and freshly ground pepper
1 cup yogurt
2 tablespoons chopped walnuts
  (optional)

Wash the spinach thoroughly, remove the stalks, and drain. Place in a large saucepan with a little lightly salted boiling water. Cover and cook over a low heat for about 6 minutes, or until tender. Place in a sieve, rinse with cold water, and drain, pressing out excess water with the back of a large spoon.

Chop the spinach and place in a shallow serving bowl. Add the garlic, lemon juice, mint, and salt and pepper to taste. Stir, then gradually add the yogurt, mixing constantly. Correct the seasoning and chill in a covered dish for several hours. If desired, garnish with chopped walnuts just before serving.

## SQUASH

THE LARGE VARIETY of vegetables called squash—from the American-Indian word *askutasquash*, meaning "green thing eaten green"—can be confusing. Basically, there are two types, winter squash and summer squash. The former category, including pumpkin, acorn, and butternut squash, is generally eaten baked, mashed, or puréed and is not suitable for salads. Of the summer varieties, zucchini (treated separately on pages 114–16) is an ideal salad vegetable. Yellow crookneck squash and chayotes are also suitable for salads.

Choose young crooknecks for salads. When well washed, they can be eaten raw, skins and all. The chayote, or vegetable pear, is much used in African and Central and South American cooking. It resembles a ridged and faded green pear and is best parboiled in its skin for use in salads.

In addition to the following recipes for summer squash, these vegetables can be substituted in many of the recipes for zucchini.

# MACEDOINE OF SQUASH

*Serves 4–6*

1 chayote
1 large zucchini
1 crookneck squash
12 cherry tomatoes
5 scallions, including 3 inches of
  green stem, chopped
12 large black olives
1 tablespoon white wine
2 tablespoons white wine vinegar

¼ teaspoon dry mustard
1 tablespoon chopped fresh dill or
  1 teaspoon dried
2 tablespoons chopped fresh parsley
6 tablespoons sunflower oil
Salt and freshly ground pepper
Romaine lettuce leaves
½ cup grated Monterey Jack cheese

Parboil the chayote until tender (about 10–20 minutes), peel, and cut into bite-size pieces. Cut the zucchini and crookneck squash into ¼-inch pieces. Place these vegetables in a large salad bowl with the cherry tomatoes, chopped scallions, and olives. In a small separate bowl, blend the wine, vinegar, mustard, dill, and parsley. Gradually whisk in the oil, and season to taste with salt and plenty of pepper. Pour the dressing over the vegetables and toss thoroughly to coat. Line a large platter with romaine leaves and cover with the vegetable mixture. Garnish with grated cheese and chill until ready to serve.

# ISRAELI SQUASH SALAD

*Serves 4–6*

6 small crookneck squash, unpeeled
  and sliced into ¼-inch rounds
1 cup yogurt
1 clove garlic, crushed

2 tablespoons finely chopped fresh
  mint
Salt and freshly ground pepper

109

Steam the squash for 2–3 minutes. Drain well and chill. In the meantime, blend the yogurt with the garlic and most of the mint. Season to taste with salt and pepper. Just before serving, place the squash in a glass salad bowl, pour on the dressing, and gently toss. Garnish with a few grindings of pepper and a sprinkling of the remaining chopped mint.

# TOMATOES

SIXTEENTH-CENTURY SPANISH EXPLORERS found the natives of the New World growing a strange plant which bore small yellow fruits called *tomate.* When brought back to Europe, this intriguing fruit became known to the Italians as *pomo d'oro* for its golden color, and to the French as *pomme d'amour,* for what were thought to be its aphrodisiac powers.

In England, where the tomato was introduced in 1596, it was shunned as food but used for ornamentation. The early American settlers were also cautious in introducing tomatoes into their diet. There is no record of tomatoes being grown in the colonies until Thomas Jefferson planted a crop in 1781. Much influenced by French tastes from his years as United States envoy to France, Jefferson happily consumed these little fruits at his White House dinner table, while most Americans still regarded them as poison apples.

Today tomatoes are available all year round in many shapes and sizes. Standard red globe tomatoes (about 3–4 per pound) are good, everyday tomatoes; cherry tomatoes are juicy, bite-size fruits usually sold in 1-pint containers; plum, bell, or Italian tomatoes are sometimes red, sometimes golden, and plum-shaped (about 5–6 per pound); and beefsteak tomatoes are the very large, firm variety popular for slicing in salads and for sandwiches.

Tomatoes are a wonderfully versatile salad ingredient—sliced, in simple combinations with other vegetables and dressed with vinaigrette; stuffed, with almost anything; or chopped and mixed in the salad bowl with all sorts of exotic vegetables and spices. Alas, it is increasingly difficult to find anything but tasteless imitations of this fruit in modern supermarkets. The odds are better in summer, but best of all is the freshly picked home-grown tomato— easy to cultivate and unbeatable in flavor.

## SLICED TOMATO WITH CHOPPED BASIL

*Serves 4*

1½ pounds firm ripe tomatoes
6 tablespoons light olive oil
2 tablespoons white wine vinegar
1 clove garlic, finely chopped
1 teaspoon prepared Dijon mustard

Salt
Freshly ground pepper
2 tablespoons coarsely chopped
   fresh basil

Slice the tomatoes into ¼-inch rounds. Prepare the dressing from the oil, vinegar, garlic, and mustard. Blend well and add salt.

Dress the tomatoes just before serving, and garnish with generous turns of the pepper mill and chopped basil.

## AMERICAN STEAKHOUSE SALAD

*Serves 4–5*

This simple first course is standard steakhouse fare all across the U.S.A. Choose large, firm beefsteak tomatoes, if available.

3 very large tomatoes
1 large red onion
A few sprigs parsley

Oil
Vinegar
Salt and pepper

Simply slice the tomatoes and onion into evenly sized rounds and arrange on a serving dish in an attractive pattern. Garnish with the parsley sprigs.

The salad should be dressed individually with the remaining ingredients by each partaker, according to his or her own palate.

## TOMATO AND MOZZARELLA CHEESE

*Serves 4*

1 pound firm ripe tomatoes
8 ounces mozzarella cheese
6 tablespoons olive oil
1 tablespoon lemon juice
1 teaspoon dried oregano

1 tablespoon finely chopped fresh
   parsley
1 tablespoon finely chopped fresh
   basil
Salt and freshly ground pepper

111

Slice the tomato thickly. Cut the mozzarella into slices approximately ⅛ inch thick. Arrange the tomatoes and cheese alternately on a large shallow serving dish. Mix the oil and lemon juice and pour over the salad. Sprinkle on the oregano and fresh herbs and season with salt and generous turns of the pepper mill.

## SALADE DE TOMATES CUITES

### COOKED TOMATO SALAD

*Serves 5–6*

This is an ideal salad to serve with cold sliced beef.

1 medium-size cucumber
Salt
1 large stalk celery
2 pounds tomatoes

½ cup olive oil
Freshly ground pepper
Pinch of powdered ginger or sage
Juice of 1 small lemon

Peel the cucumber and cut into large dice. Place in a sieve and sprinkle with salt; leave for 20 minutes to allow excess liquid to drain off. Cut the celery into small dice.

Peel the tomatoes after immersing in boiling water for several seconds. Cut into quarters and deseed.

Heat the oil in a large frying pan and add the vegetables. Sprinkle with salt and pepper and add the ginger or sage. Cook over medium heat until most of the liquid has evaporated. Take off the heat and leave to cool. Just before serving, correct the seasoning and add the lemon juice.

## ENSALADA DE JITOMATES

### MEXICAN TOMATO SALAD

*Serves 4*

1 large ripe avocado
Salt and freshly ground pepper
1–2 teaspoons olive oil
¼–½ teaspoon wine vinegar
2 slices cooked ham (approximately 2 ounces)

4 medium-size firm tomatoes
4–5 large lettuce leaves
A few sprigs of fresh parsley

Halve the avocado, remove the stone, and scoop the flesh into a small bowl. Season with salt and pepper, oil, and vinegar to taste. Mash with a fork until well blended.

Chop the ham into small pieces and blend with the avocado. Cut the tomatoes into fairly thin slices.

Line a serving dish with the lettuce leaves and arrange the tomatoes on top. Cover the slices with the avocado mixture and garnish with parsley.

## STUFFED TOMATOES

A large, firm tomato, hollowed and filled with any of an infinite variety of mixtures, makes a most attractive appetizer or a pleasant light lunch or supper.

There are three important basic instructions to remember when preparing tomatoes for stuffing: (1) Always choose large, firm tomatoes. Overripe fruit will be too soft to hold the filling. (2) Slice only a small cap from the top with a sharp knife, allowing the maximum base for the stuffing. (3) Once the pulp has been scooped out and reserved (if required for filling), lightly sprinkle the tomato shell with salt and pepper and turn upside down to drain for 15 minutes.

Suggested stuffings are: Michoteta, page 71; Crunchy Corn Salad, page 68; Napoleon's Bean Salad, page 137; Salade de Riz Colorée, page 150; and Tuna Fish Salad, page 182. See also recipes for Hawaiian Chicken Salad in Tomato Petals, page 164, and Dannevang Salad, page 170.

## TURNIPS

BECAUSE IT IS SO RARELY EATEN in its uncooked state, it may come as a surprise to learn that the turnip is quite tasty raw. The most popular variety of this edible root has a white flesh with a purple top. Turnips can generally be found all year round, but the young fresh vegetables available from April to July are best for eating raw. Buy smooth, firm, fairly round vegetables of small or medium size.

Rutabaga is a variety of turnip with a very large, elongated, yellowish top. Its flesh is also more yellow than turnip flesh. Rutabaga is in plentiful supply during the winter months.

Both turnip and rutabaga, peeled and cut into julienne strips, make excellent crudités. They are also delicious peeled and grated, then simply dressed with a vinaigrette or a sauce rémoulade.

113

## TURNIP SALAD

*Serves 4–6*

1 pound young turnips, peeled
Salt
1 small onion, thinly sliced

¼ teaspoon sugar
Soy sauce
4 tablespoons Oriental sesame oil

Slice the turnips thinly. Place in a sieve, sprinkle with salt, and rinse well with cold water. Drain and pat dry in a clean kitchen towel.

In a glass bowl, mix the turnip slices with the onion rings, sprinkle with sugar, and toss. Add soy sauce to taste—usually several teaspoons—and, just before serving, heat the sesame oil and pour over the vegetables. Toss well.

## MAINE RUTABAGA SALAD

*Serves 4–6*

1 cup peeled and grated rutabaga
3 stalks celery, thinly sliced
4 scallions, chopped, including 2
  inches of green stem
4 large radishes, washed and thinly
  sliced
1 small head romaine lettuce, washed,
  drained, and shredded
¼ teaspoon dry mustard

¼ teaspoon superfine sugar
1 teaspoon finely chopped fresh
  basil
1 tablespoon wine vinegar
4 tablespoons olive oil
Salt and freshly ground pepper
2 slices bacon, crisply fried and
  crumbled

In a large salad bowl combine the rutabaga, celery, scallions, radishes, and shredded romaine. In a small separate bowl, blend the mustard, sugar, and chopped basil with the vinegar. Gradually whisk in the oil, and season to taste with salt and plenty of freshly ground pepper. Pour the dressing onto the vegetables and toss well. Just before serving, sprinkle the top with the crumbled bacon.

## ZUCCHINI

ZUCCHINI IS A MEMBER of the squash family. Like yellow squash, it is best eaten when young and should not be kept for too long after purchase. It can be used in salads, either cooked—*al dente*—or raw.

114

## ZUCCHINI À LA GRECQUE

*Serves 4–6*

2 pounds small zucchini
6 tablespoons olive oil
1 large onion, finely chopped
1 large clove garlic, finely chopped
⅔ cup dry white wine
Bouquet garni
12 coriander seeds

12 black peppercorns
Freshly squeezed and strained juice
    of 1 lemon
Salt
3 tablespoons finely chopped fresh
    parsley

Wipe the zucchini with a damp cloth. Trim the ends and slice thickly cross-wise. Set aside.

In a large pan or casserole, heat 3 tablespoons of the olive oil and add the onion and garlic. Sauté until transparent. Add the wine, ⅔ cup water, bouquet garni, coriander seeds, peppercorns, most of the lemon juice, and salt to taste. Bring to the boil and simmer gently for 5 minutes. Add the zucchini to this stock and continue cooking over low heat for another 6–8 minutes, or until just tender.

With a large, slotted spoon, remove the zucchini and place in a deep serving dish. Discard the bouquet garni and continue boiling until the liquid is reduced by half. Pour over the vegetables and chill for at least an hour. Just before serving, add the remaining olive oil. Check the seasoning, adding more salt if required, and garnish with chopped parsley and a sprinkling of lemon juice.

## KOLOKYTHIA YIACHNI

### GREEK STEWED ZUCCHINI

*Serves 6*

A delicious hors d'oeuvre for summer, when fresh mint and dill are available.

2 pounds small zucchini
⅔ cup olive oil
2 large onions, coarsely chopped
1 pound ripe tomatoes
1 teaspoon sugar

1 tablespoon finely chopped fresh
    dill
2 teaspoons finely chopped fresh mint
Salt and freshly ground pepper

Trim the ends of the zucchini, but leave them whole if they are small; other-wise, cut them in half. Heat the oil in a large pan or casserole and gently fry the onions for 5 minutes, until translucent. Peel the tomatoes after immersing in boiling water for several seconds, and either sieve them or put them in a blender to make a smooth purée. Add the purée to the onions, along with the sugar, and cook for 10 minutes. Stir in $\frac{2}{3}$ cup water, bring to a gentle boil, and add the zucchini, dill, mint, and salt and pepper to taste. Cover and simmer gently for about 20 minutes, until the zucchini are quite tender.

Cool, adjust the seasoning, and chill until ready to serve.

# ENSALADA DE CALABACITA

### MEXICAN ZUCCHINI SALAD

*Serves 4–6*

In Mexico, this recipe is often prepared using chayote, a vegetable pear, instead of zucchini. The *cebollas encurtidas,* a kind of Mexican relish, is well worth the extra effort to make this salad an authentically spicy Mexican dish. You must, however, make this condiment at least two days before you plan to serve it.

| | |
|---|---|
| $1\frac{1}{2}$ pounds zucchini | 1 teaspoon dried oregano |
| 1 firm avocado, cut into strips | *Cebollas encurtidas* (see note) |
| 6 tablespoons olive oil | 8 green olives |
| 2 tablespoons wine vinegar | One $3\frac{1}{2}$-ounce package cream cheese, |
| Salt and freshly ground pepper | cut into strips |

Trim the ends of the zucchini and slice thickly crosswise. Cook in lightly salted boiling water for 5–8 minutes, or until just tender. Drain, cool, and place in a large bowl. Add the strips of avocado. Blend together the oil, vinegar, salt and pepper to taste, and the oregano. Pour over the vegetables and toss gently. Garnish with *cebollas,* olives, and strips of cream cheese.

*Note:* To prepare *cebollas encurtidas,* place 1 large thinly sliced onion, 10 peppercorns, $\frac{1}{2}$ teaspoon dried oregano, 2 cloves garlic (peeled and sliced), and $\frac{1}{2}$ teaspoon salt in a 16-ounce glass jar. Pour over this mixture approximately $\frac{1}{3}$ cup wine vinegar mixed with $\frac{2}{3}$ cup water. Cover tightly and store in a cool place for at least 48 hours.

If kept in a tightly sealed jar, *cebollas encurtidas* will last indefinitely.

# A SELECTION OF MIXED-VEGETABLE SALADS

MIXED-VEGETABLE SALADS are a popular hors d'oeuvre in many countries. A Russian formal dinner might well commence with a colorful spread of cold *zakushki*, including a variety of mixed-vegetable salads known as *vinigrets*. In France, the mixed-vegetable salad often starts the day's main meal. The popular *mezze* of the Middle East feature salads of finely chopped raw vegetables dressed with oil and lemon juice. And the vegetable salads of Italian *antipasti* need almost no introduction.

Here are recipes for some familiar and less familiar vegetable salads.

## MEXICAN SALAD

*Serves 6–8*

"Food goes through the eyes before it passes the mouth" is a Mexican saying well illustrated by this decorative salad. The selection of ingredients from the serving dish is for each individual to choose.

1 pound new potatoes, scrubbed
4 large carrots, peeled and diced
2 turnips, peeled and diced
1 small cauliflower
Basic Vinaigrette, page 18

6–8 small gherkins
2 tablespoons capers
12 black olives
2 teaspoons Dijon mustard
½ cup mayonnaise

Cook the potatoes in their skins until tender when pierced with a fork. Set aside.

Cook the carrots and turnips separately in lightly salted boiling water for 8–10 minutes, until tender but still crisp. Drain and set aside.

Divide the cauliflower into florets and cook in lightly salted boiling water just until tender, about 5 minutes. Drain and set aside.

While still warm, dress each of the cooked vegetables with a little vinaigrette. Arrange on a large serving dish as follows: pile the gherkins in the center and surround with capers and olives; follow with a ring of cauliflower, and finally a ring of alternating groupings of carrots, potatoes, and turnips.

Blend the mustard and mayonnaise and spread between the rings of cauliflower and mixed vegetables. Serve at room temperature.

## SALADE DE PEPINO

### PORTUGUESE MIXED SALAD

*Serves 6*

The Portuguese serve a salad with most meals. Tomatoes, peppers, and onions are regular features and form the base for this rather festive salad.

1 large red onion
2 tart green apples, such as Granny
　Smiths
1 medium-size cucumber
2 large green peppers
2 large firm tomatoes
1 clove garlic, halved

6–8 tablespoons olive oil
2 tablespoons freshly squeezed
　and strained lime juice
Salt and freshly ground pepper
6 whole chestnuts
2 hard-boiled eggs
6 strips pimiento

Peel the onion and slice into thin rounds. Peel and core the apples and slice into thin wedges. Without peeling, slice the cucumber into thin rounds. Remove the stem and deseed the peppers; slice into thin strips. Cut each of the tomatoes into 8 wedges of equal size.

Rub the inside of a large wooden bowl with half the cut garlic and fill it with the apples, cucumber, peppers, onion, and tomatoes.

In a separate small bowl, combine the oil and lime juice. Season with salt and pepper to taste, and, if desired, crush the remaining garlic half into the dressing. Whisk to blend. Pour over the salad, toss well, and allow to stand for at least an hour, tossing again once or twice. In the meantime, boil the chestnuts for about 15 minutes; peel and grate while still warm. Set aside.

Separate the hard-boiled egg whites from the yolks and sieve each. Set them aside.

Just before serving, garnish the salad as follows: sprinkle the sieved egg yolks in the center and surround with a ring of grated chestnut, followed by a ring of egg white. Decorate with pimiento strips, pinwheel fashion, around the outside of the bowl.

## HORIATIKI SALATA

### GREEK VILLAGE SALAD

*Serves 4–6*

This most traditional of Greek salads is served throughout the year, varying only with seasonal vegetables. The ubiquitous taverna favorite is a combination of cucumbers, tomatoes, onions, green peppers, olives, and feta cheese.

4–5 medium-size firm tomatoes
2 medium-size green peppers
1 medium-size Spanish onion or
    4 large scallions
1 clove garlic, halved
1 large cucumber, peeled and thickly
    sliced
6 ounces feta cheese, broken into
    bite-size pieces

16 Greek olives
Salt and freshly ground pepper
1 tablespoon chopped fresh parsley
1 heaping teaspoon dried oregano
Capers (optional)
Wine vinegar or lemon juice
    (optional)
Olive oil

Cut the tomatoes into quarters. Remove the tops from the peppers, deseed, and slice into thin rounds. Peel and slice the onion into thin rounds or thinly slice the scallions, including at least 2 inches of green stem.

Rub a large wooden bowl with the cut garlic and add the cucumber, tomatoes, onion or scallions, green peppers, half the feta, and 8 olives. Sprinkle with salt and plenty of freshly ground pepper. Toss. Crumble the remaining feta across the top and sprinkle on the parsley and oregano. Decorate with the remaining olives and some capers, if desired. Then gradually pour on olive oil to taste, beginning at the outer edges and steadily moving, in circular motion, toward the center.

The Greeks tend to dress their salads with olive oil alone—usually a flavorful local variety—but add a sprinkling of vinegar or lemon juice, if you prefer.

## FATTOUSH

*Serves 6*

Fattoush is a Syrian peasant salad made with leftover bread and fresh vegetables.

1 large cucumber, chopped into
  1-inch pieces
Salt
3 pieces of pita or 6 slices of white
  bread
4 firm tomatoes, chopped into
  1-inch pieces
1 medium-size Spanish onion or 6
  scallions, chopped, including 2
  inches of stem
1 medium-size green pepper, seeded
  and chopped
3 tablespoons finely chopped fresh
  parsley

2 tablespoons finely chopped fresh
  coriander or 1 tablespoon extra
  of parsley if coriander is
  unavailable
2 tablespoons finely chopped fresh
  mint or 1 tablespoon dried
Freshly ground pepper
6–8 tablespoons olive oil
Juice of 1 lemon, freshly squeezed
  and strained
2 cloves garlic, crushed

Sprinkle the chopped cucumber with salt and allow to drain in a colander or sieve for about half an hour.

Place the pieces of bread in a large bowl and moisten with water. Drain off any excess liquid that has not been absorbed by the bread. Add the chopped vegetables and herbs, and season generously with salt and freshly ground pepper. Prepare a dressing with oil, lemon juice, and crushed garlic. Pour over the salad just before serving and toss well.

# CRUNCHY BELGIAN SALAD

*Serves 4–6*

A cooked salad to be served slightly warm with main-course dishes.

¼ pound bacon
1 pound green beans
¾ pound new potatoes
1 medium-size Bermuda onion,
  finely chopped

1 tablespoon butter
3–4 tablespoons wine vinegar
Salt and freshly ground pepper
2 tablespoons chopped fresh parsley

Cut the bacon crosswise into small strips.

Trim and wash the beans. Wash the potatoes, but do not peel. In separate saucepans, cook the beans and potatoes in lightly salted boiling water just until tender.

Meanwhile, fry the bacon over low heat. When it turns translucent, add the chopped onion and butter. Stirring constantly, fry the onion until it is soft, but do not allow to brown. The bacon should become crisp. When cooking is nearly completed, add the vinegar and reduce to very low heat.

Drain the boiled vegetables. Slice the potatoes into pieces ¼ inch thick and place, with the beans, in a serving bowl. Season to taste with salt and plenty of freshly ground pepper.

Pour the bacon-and-onion mixture over the warm vegetables and toss gently but thoroughly. Sprinkle with chopped parsley and serve.

# TOMATE, ESCAROLA Y ALCACHOFAS

SPANISH TOMATO, CHICORY, AND ARTICHOKE SALAD

*Serves 6*

1 small head chicory
4 medium-size firm tomatoes
5 canned artichoke hearts, drained
  and quartered
3 hard-boiled eggs
6 tablespoons mayonnaise

1 clove garlic, crushed
6 tablespoons heavy cream, whipped
1 egg white, whipped to form peaks
Salt and freshly ground pepper
A few sprigs of parsley

Wash the chicory, drain thoroughly, and break into pieces. Place in the center of a large serving dish. Immerse the tomatoes in boiling water for several seconds. When cool enough to handle, remove the skin, deseed, and chop

121

coarsely. Mix the artichokes with the tomatoes and arrange on the dish. Surround with quartered hard-boiled egg whites (sieve the yolks and set aside for garnish).

To the mayonnaise add the garlic, whipped cream, and a few tablespoons of beaten egg white. (Vary the amounts according to taste and desired consistency.) Season well with salt and freshly ground pepper. Chill for an hour, then pour over the salad.

Just before serving, decorate with the sieved egg yolks and a few sprigs of parsley.

## CRUNCHY HEALTH SALAD

*Serves 4–6*

4 large carrots, peeled and coarsely
   grated
6 stalks celery, cut into ½-inch pieces
¼ small white cabbage, shredded
½ pound cooked beets, peeled and
   diced
1 green pepper, seeded and diced
3 tablespoons finely chopped
   Bermuda onion

1 large crisp apple, cored and diced
½ cup coarsely chopped almonds,
   walnuts, or hazelnuts
5 tablespoons sunflower oil
2 tablespoons cider vinegar
½ teaspoon brown sugar
Salt and freshly ground pepper

Place carrots, celery, cabbage, beets, green pepper, onion, apple, and nuts in a large bowl. Whisk together the oil, vinegar, and brown sugar, season to taste with salt and plenty of freshly ground pepper, and gently mix into the salad ingredients. Chill before serving.

## CHINESE-STYLE MIXED SALAD

*Serves 6*

1 pound fresh snow peas or three
   6-ounce packages frozen
1 small head cauliflower
5-ounce can water chestnuts, drained
   and thinly sliced
3 tablespoons chopped pimiento
5 tablespoons vegetable oil (see note)
1 tablespoon lemon juice

1 tablespoon wine vinegar
1 teaspoon sugar
1 small clove garlic, crushed
½ teaspoon salt
2 tablespoons toasted sesame seeds
   (see Oriental Salad Dressing,
   page 31)

If fresh snow peas are used, snap off the tops and remove the strings. Parboil in lightly salted water for 1 minute. Drain and set aside. If using frozen snow peas, prepare according to directions on the package. Wash the cauliflower and break into small florets. Cook in lightly salted water for 3 minutes, or just until tender. Drain.

In a large bowl, combine the snow peas, cauliflower, water chestnuts, and chopped pimiento. Cover and chill.

To prepare the dressing, place the oil, lemon juice, vinegar, sugar, garlic, and ½ teaspoon salt in a small jar. Cover and shake well. Pour the dressing over the salad, toss to blend thoroughly, and, just before serving, sprinkle on the toasted sesame seeds and toss again.

*Note:* A mixture of 3 parts corn or sunflower oil to 1 part Oriental sesame oil makes a delicious combination.

## ORIENTAL SALAD BOWL

*Serves 4–5*

½ cucumber
Salt
1 small head iceberg lettuce
10 litchi nuts, peeled and pitted
½ pound bean sprouts, steamed for
   1 minute
¼ pound melon, diced
2 stalks celery, diced

5 tablespoons vegetable oil
1 tablespoon wine vinegar
1 teaspoon soy sauce (or more, if
   desired)
1 teaspoon sugar
¼ teaspoon prepared mustard
1 clove garlic, crushed

Peel the cucumber and chop. Place in a sieve or colander, salt lightly, and let drain for half an hour.

Wash the lettuce, drain, and dry thoroughly. Break into bite-size pieces, or shred coarsely. Cut the litchi nuts into quarters.

Combine the lettuce, bean sprouts, cucumber, melon, celery, and litchi nuts in a large bowl.

In a small jar, mix the oil, vinegar, soy sauce, sugar, mustard, and garlic. Shake well and add more soy sauce if desired. Pour over the salad, toss thoroughly, and chill. Just before serving, toss again.

123

# SALADE AU PAPRIKA

### PAPRIKA SALAD

*Serves 6*

1 medium-size celeriac
3 heads Belgian endive
3 large mushrooms
1 tart green apple, such as Granny
 Smith
½ cup almonds, chopped

Salt and freshly ground pepper to
 taste
¾ cup mayonnaise
Paprika
1 pimiento, cut into strips

Peel the celeriac and cut into matchstick pieces about 3 inches long. Parboil in acidulated water for about 5 minutes. Drain and cool.

Wash the endive, drain, and chop coarsely. Trim the stalks from the mushrooms, wipe clean with a damp paper towel, and slice. Wash and core the apple, but do not peel. Dice the apple.

Place all these ingredients in a large bowl and add the chopped almonds, reserving 1 tablespoon for garnish. Season with salt and pepper and blend in the mayonnaise. Chill for about an hour. Just before serving sprinkle generously with paprika and decorate with the pimiento and reserved almonds.

# MARTINIQUE SALAD BOWL

*Serves 6*

This salad should not be prepared too far in advance, since the bananas may discolor.

4 green (unripe) bananas
1 large tomato
1 medium-size cucumber, peeled
 and coarsely chopped
Salt
6 tablespoons olive oil
2 tablespoons wine vinegar

1 teaspoon Dijon mustard
1 clove garlic, crushed
Freshly ground pepper
1 small head iceberg lettuce
6 stalks celery, diced
2 large carrots, peeled and shredded

Peel the green bananas carefully, so that they remain whole. Place in a saucepan with enough lightly salted cold water to cover. Bring to the boil, cover, and simmer until tender, approximately 10 minutes. Drain, cool, and cut crosswise into ½-inch slices.

Meanwhile, immerse the tomato in boiling water for several seconds. Remove the skin, seeds, and chop coarsely. Set aside.

Place the chopped cucumber in a sieve or colander, salt lightly, and let drain for half an hour.

Prepare the dressing by blending the oil, vinegar, mustard, and garlic. Season with salt and pepper to taste.

Line a large bowl with the lettuce leaves. In a separate bowl, mix the bananas, cucumber, tomato, celery, and shredded carrots. Pour on the dressing and toss thoroughly. Spoon the mixture onto the lettuce leaves; chill for an hour and serve.

# RUSSIAN VEGETABLE SALAD WITH SATSIVI

*Serves 4*

*Satsivi* is a Russian walnut sauce.

| | |
|---|---|
| 1 medium-size cucumber, peeled and chopped | 1 tablespoon wine vinegar |
| Salt | 2 tablespoons finely chopped fresh parsley |
| 1 large tomato, seeded and diced | 2 tablespoons chopped fresh |
| 4 stalks celery, chopped | coriander leaves or ½ teaspoon |
| ½ cup shelled walnuts | dried and ground coriander seeds |
| 1 small clove garlic | 2 tablespoons finely chopped onion |
| Pinch of cayenne pepper | 10–12 large romaine lettuce leaves |

Place the chopped cucumber in a sieve or colander and salt lightly. Allow to drain for half an hour. In a large bowl, combine the cucumber, tomato, and celery. Sprinkle with salt.

Pound the walnuts to a paste with the garlic and cayenne. Gradually stir in the vinegar and 3 tablespoons cold water until well blended. Add to the cucumber, tomato, and celery, toss, add the parsley, coriander, and onion, and toss again. Chill for at least an hour.

Line a large bowl with the lettuce leaves. Fill with the vegetable mixture and serve.

125

# RATATOUILLE PROVENÇALE

*Serves 4–6*

This delicious mixture of Mediterranean vegetables is served as an hors d'oeuvre or as a side-dish salad—either way, there should be plenty of crusty bread on hand to soak up the tasty juice.

| | |
|---|---|
| 2 medium-size Bermuda onions | Bouquet garni |
| 2 large eggplants | 2 cloves garlic, peeled |
| Coarse sea salt | 6–8 black peppercorns, crushed |
| 4 medium-size zucchini | 12 coriander seeds |
| 2 large green peppers | 1 tablespoon chopped fresh basil |
| 1 pound tomatoes | 2 tablespoons chopped fresh parsley |
| Light olive oil | |

Peel the onions and chop or slice into very thin rounds. Cut the eggplant into ½-inch-square dice (do not peel), and place in a colander. Salt lightly and allow to drain for 20–30 minutes. Slice the zucchini into ½-inch-thick rounds. Halve the peppers, remove the seeds and ribs, and slice into strips about ½ inch wide. Chop the tomatoes coarsely.

Cover the bottom of a large frying pan with a thin layer of olive oil and sauté the onions over low heat until they become translucent, about 8 minutes. Add the eggplant, peppers, bouquet garni, and zucchini. Stir for 2 minutes, then cover and simmer for another 10 minutes. Uncover, stir again, and add the garlic, chopped tomatoes, crushed black pepper, and coriander seeds; season to taste with salt. Continue cooking and stirring until the tomatoes have started to soften. (If necessary, add another 1–2 tablespoons oil, but be careful not to make the mixture too liquid, since the vegetables will themselves give off a lot of juice.) Cover and simmer an additional 10–15 minutes.

Remove from the heat, take out the bouquet garni, and allow to cool. Just before serving, garnish with chopped basil and parsley.

# RATATOUILLE CREOLE

*Serves 6–8*

A dish from the French Caribbean islands, its special feature is the *gros concombre,* a huge light-green cucumber weighing about a pound. Ordinary cucumbers will do just as well.

½ pound green peppers
1 pound zucchini
1 pound cucumbers
Salt
1 pound eggplant
1 pound tomatoes
6 tablespoons olive oil

1 teaspoon sugar
Freshly ground pepper
12 coriander seeds
2 tablespoons chopped fresh parsley
1 tablespoon chopped fresh tarragon
    or 1 teaspoon dried

Halve the peppers, seed, and cut into ½-inch slices. Trim the zucchini and cut into ½-inch slices. Peel the cucumbers and cut into ½-inch crosswise slices; salt lightly and place in a sieve or colander to drain for 20 minutes. Peel the eggplant and cut into crosswise slices 1 inch thick. Place in a colander, sprinkle with salt, and let drain at the same time as the cucumbers. Immerse the tomatoes for a few seconds in boiling water, slip off the skins, deseed, and chop coarsely.

Heat the oil in a large earthenware or enamel casserole. Place the eggplant on the bottom, then add the cucumbers, zucchini, tomatoes, and peppers. Season with sugar and plenty of freshly ground pepper, the coriander seeds, and half each of the parsley and tarragon. Cover and cook gently for 15 minutes.

Uncover and check the seasoning, adding salt and more pepper if desired. Stir well and continue to cook, uncovered, for another 15 minutes, or until most of the liquid has evaporated. If there is too much liquid when the cooking time is completed, remove the vegetables with a slotted spoon to the serving dish, increase the heat under the casserole, and reduce the liquid to the desired quantity. Pour over the vegetables and chill until ready to serve. Garnish with the rest of the chopped herbs.

# PESADUMBRE

### MEXICAN CHILLED VEGETABLE SALAD

*Serves 6*

*Pesadumbre,* which literally means "sadness," is a traditional Lenten dish—spicy and vinegary—served as an accompaniment to meat and beans. According to the prescriptions of the *curandero* (herb doctor), the use of cumin strengthens the heart; laurel or bay leaf stimulates the affections; thyme reinforces the veins and firms the breasts; and the small vegetables fortify and relax the stomach.

This salad must be made three days ahead of time.

2 pounds zucchini
1 clove garlic, peeled
2 tablespoons chili powder
½ teaspoon cumin
1 tablespoon chopped fresh thyme
    or 1 teaspoon dried
1 pound fresh peas, cooked *al dente*
    (see note)

2 stalks celery, chopped
⅔ cup red wine vinegar
1 bay leaf
Salt
¼–⅓ cup olive oil
Freshly ground black pepper
    (optional)

Trim the ends off the zucchini and cut into ½-inch rounds. Mash the garlic with chili powder, cumin, and thyme. Place in a bowl with the zucchini, peas, and celery. Boil ½ cup water and the vinegar and pour over the vegetables. Add the bay leaf and season with salt. Cover the bowl with a plate and let the *pesadumbre* stand at room temperature for 48 hours.

Before serving, chill for at least 2 hours, then gradually stir in the olive oil, to taste. Remove the bay leaf and season with additional salt and a few grinds of black pepper if desired.

*Note:* You may substitute either frozen or canned peas for fresh. When using frozen peas, cook in boiling water for 2–3 minutes. If you use canned peas, buy only the best *petit pois* variety and drain off all the liquid.

## MOROCCAN RELISH SALAD

*Serves 5–6*

A finely chopped Middle Eastern salad, perfect with couscous or other hearty casserole dishes.

2 cucumbers
1 large tomato
1 large Bermuda onion, peeled
2–3 red chili peppers, seeded (see
    page 95)

3 tablespoons olive oil
1 tablespoon wine vinegar
Salt

Chop each of the vegetables into very small dice. If desired, peel the cucumbers and tomato first. Place the vegetables in a large glass bowl, adding oil, vinegar, and salt to taste. Chill for 1–2 hours before serving. This allows the hotness of the chili peppers to permeate the other vegetables.

# THE DETOXICATING SALAD

Grayshott Hall Health Centre near Hindhead, Surrey, England, has developed a marvelous one-day salad diet, the perfect antidote to overindulgence and prolonged holiday excesses. Although the detoxicating effect depends on following the strict regime, the salad itself is delicious—a blend of sweet and sour flavors, crunchy and moist textures—as a pleasant and healthful light meal anytime.

3 medium-size carrots, scrubbed
3 apples, scrubbed
3 stalks celery
A handful of raisins
½ cucumber, washed but not peeled

1 small green pepper
2 pears
1 orange (if subject to liver troubles or migraine take ½ grapefruit instead of orange)

Commence the day with a glass of hot water with a little lemon juice added. For the rest of the day drinks may be lemon juice in hot water or not more than three cups of tea with lemon—no sugar or sweetening of any kind—and no milk. The drinks should be taken between meals.

The meals consist of three equal parts of the special salad mixture given above. All the ingredients should be chopped up in the morning and well shaken together in a container. The total is then divided into three portions—one for each meal. With the mixed salad a cup of yogurt flavored with a little lemon juice may also be taken—no sweetening.

If this regime is carried out for one day per week, or following any day on which a little "dissipation" has been unavoidable, the weight will be kept down and toxic accumulation from ordinary meals will be considerably reduced.

# EGG AND CHEESE SALADS

## EGGS

THE POPULARITY of egg salad of the sandwich-filler variety should not deter the creative cook from trying some of the more exotic ways that hard-boiled eggs can be turned into salads.

## PHOOL KA ACHAR

### NEPALESE EGG SALAD

*Serves 6–8*

Served as a chutney in Nepal, often with finely chopped tomatoes, this dish makes an excellent accompaniment to curries and other spicy meals. The yogurt, which is usually prepared from buffalo milk in the East, can sometimes be bought ready-made from Indian grocers. Thick, unsweetened yogurt makes a reasonable substitute.

1 tablespoon butter
3 teaspoons fresh chopped chili
   pepper (see page 95)
1 teaspoon cumin seeds, pounded
   and crushed
¼ teaspoon cardamom seeds,
   pounded and crushed

1½–2 cups yogurt
10 tablespoons coarsely chopped
   fresh coriander or parsley
1 small lime *with* peel, finely chopped
10–12 hard-boiled eggs, halved

Heat the butter and gently fry the chili pepper, cumin, and cardamom to rid them of their "raw" odor. Remove from the pan and drain on a paper towel. In a large glass bowl, beat the yogurt with the coriander or parsley and chopped lime. Add the drained spices and mix until well blended. Drop in the egg halves gently so they do not break. Chill.

# EGG SALAD AND "CAVIAR"

### *Serves 10–12*

This recipe is my mother's creation, and it makes a beautiful dish for a party buffet. Lumpfish roe is hardly caviar, but it's tasty enough and provides a striking contrast to the egg salad.

24 hard-boiled eggs
2 tablespoons finely chopped fresh
   chives
Salt and freshly ground pepper
1 jar pimientos (approximately
   8 ounces)
1 cup mayonnaise

1 teaspoon butter or margarine
Lettuce leaves
One 4-ounce jar black lumpfish roe
12 tomato wedges or 12 cherry
   tomatoes
A few sprigs of parsley

In a large wooden bowl, chop the hard-boiled eggs, add the chives, and season with salt and pepper. Drain the pimientos, set one aside for garnish, and cut the rest into small dice. Add to the eggs with the mayonnaise and stir gently until well blended.

   Grease an 8-inch ring mold with the butter or margarine and spoon the egg salad mixture into the mold, making sure it is firmly packed, with no holes. Cover with a plate or piece of kitchen foil and chill overnight.

When ready to serve, turn onto a large platter lined with lettuce leaves. Fill the center with lumpfish roe and garnish the top with strips of pimiento. Decorate the platter with the tomatoes and parsley.

## HUEVOS, JUDIAS VERDES Y GUISTANTES

### HARD-BOILED EGGS, SPANISH STYLE

*Serves 5–6*

A pleasant antipasto, excellent with the Spanish sausage chorizo.

¾ pound fresh green beans
½ pound shelled peas
3 tablespoons olive oil
1 tablespoon wine vinegar
1 teaspoon prepared mustard

½ teaspoon salt
6 hard-boiled eggs, halved
Freshly ground black pepper
1 cup mayonnaise

Trim the green beans, wash, and cook in gently boiling salted water for 8 minutes, or until just tender. Drain. Boil the peas in the same manner, drain, and add to the beans. Make a dressing by whisking together the oil, vinegar, mustard, and salt, and add to the vegetables while still warm. Place this mixture on a large serving dish and surround with the hard-boiled eggs. Garnish generously with black pepper and serve with a bowl of mayonnaise.

## HAVGIT AGHTSAN

### ARMENIAN EGG SALAD

*Serves 3–4*

4 hard-boiled eggs, sliced
½ small onion, thinly sliced
1 medium-size tomato, sliced
1 small green pepper, deseeded and
  sliced
8 black olives
3 tablespoons olive oil

2 tablespoons freshly squeezed and
  strained lemon juice
1 tablespoon finely chopped fresh
  mint
1 tablespoon finely chopped fresh
  parsley
Salt and freshly ground pepper

On a large platter, arrange the eggs, onion, tomato, and green pepper in an attractive pattern. Garnish with black olives.

Blend together the oil, lemon juice, and fresh herbs. Season to taste with salt and pepper, and pour over the eggs and vegetables.

## HERBED EGG AND PEPPER SALAD

*Serves 4*

1 large green pepper
1 large red pepper
4 tablespoons olive oil
1 tablespoon white wine vinegar
1 tablespoon *each* of finely chopped fresh parsley, tarragon, chervil, and chives (if fresh herbs are unavailable, reduce quantity to 1 teaspoon each dried)

1 clove garlic, finely chopped
Salt and freshly ground pepper
2 ripe but firm tomatoes
2 hard-boiled eggs
8 green or black olives
4 anchovy fillets

Clean the peppers, removing the core and seeds. Slice crosswise into circles and set aside.

Prepare the dressing by combining the oil, vinegar, herbs, garlic, and salt and pepper to taste. Whisk well and set aside.

Slice the tomatoes thinly and place them, overlapped, in the bottom of a glass salad bowl. Sprinkle with some of the dressing.

Next, add a layer of green pepper slices and sprinkle again with a little dressing. Follow with a layer of red pepper slices and more dressing. Finally, slice the eggs and place in a circle around the rim of the bowl. Pour on the remaining dressing and decorate with the olives and anchovy fillets. Chill for an hour before serving.

## CHEESE

GRATED CHEESE and cheese-flavored dressings are popular salad adornments, but cheese can also be the main ingredient in a salad. Cottage cheese is especially good: a large scoop garnished with chopped vegetables (raw or cooked) or seasonal fruits is not only wholesome and filling but also low in calories.

# INSALATA DI FONTINA

## ITALIAN CHEESE SALAD

*Serves 4–6*

Fontina is a lovely Italian cheese, smooth in texture and mild-tasting, produced in the Aosta Valley of northern Italy.

3 large yellow or red peppers
½ pound fontina cheese, diced
6 large green olives, pitted and
   chopped
2–3 tablespoons olive oil

2–3 tablespoons heavy cream
1 teaspoon Dijon mustard
Salt and freshly ground pepper
2–3 sprigs parsley

Wash the peppers and cut them in half. Remove the cores, ribs, and seeds and broil for 10–15 minutes, or until the skins blister. Remove from the heat and when cool enough to handle, peel away the thin outer skin. Cut the remaining flesh into strips about ½ inch wide. In a shallow bowl, mix the peppers, cheese, and olives. Mix the oil, cream, and mustard with salt and plenty of freshly ground pepper. Pour over the salad, stir gently, and allow to chill for at least 2 hours. Stir again just before serving, and garnish with parsley.

# BERNARD SHAW'S CHEESE SALAD

*Serves 3*

The playwright George Bernard Shaw was a committed vegetarian from the age of twenty-five. This is a favorite salad that his housekeeper, Mrs. Alice Laden, used to prepare for him.

1 head Boston lettuce
½ cucumber, peeled
¼ pound hard Cheddar cheese
1 teaspoon caraway seeds

3 tablespoons sunflower oil
1 tablespoon cider vinegar
Salt and freshly ground pepper

Wash and dry the lettuce leaves. Arrange them on a large dish. Slice the cucumber into thin rounds and place on top of the lettuce. Grate the cheese and put in the center of the dish. Sprinkle with caraway seeds. Mix the oil and vinegar and season to taste with salt and pepper. Pour over the salad and serve immediately.

# BEANS AND SPROUTS

## BEANS

FOR ECONOMICAL NOURISHMENT, you can't beat dried beans, or pulses, as they are known to nutritionists: there is a wonderful variety from which to choose; they provide a cholesterol-free source of protein; dry, they store well and go a long way—½ pound of dried beans should easily serve a family of four; they mix well with all sorts of herbs, spices, and seasonings; they combine well with cold meats and fish to make delicious buffet salads; and cooked, they will keep for days in the refrigerator, making an excellent party dish that can be prepared in advance.

While dried beans and grains have been a staple in the diets of most Third World nations and handsomely treated as gourmet fare by Europeans, Americans have made only limited use of this wonderfully versatile food.

Dried beans should usually be soaked and always cooked. The larger beans, such as red kidney beans, lima beans, and butter beans, often need several hours or overnight soaking, whereas lentils, small white beans, and flageolets need

2 hours or less in fresh cold water. After soaking, drain well and simmer in a large pot with plenty of fresh water for at least 45 minutes (some beans need much longer cooking time—the best way to test their readiness is to remove one and bite into it: it should be soft but not mushy). To enhance the flavor, add a bouquet garni, bay leaf, garlic, or a small onion stuck with a few cloves, but do not add salt until the final 15 minutes of cooking time. Drain and dress while the beans are still warm, since they readily absorb a flavorful vinaigrette just after cooking.

Cans of ready-cooked beans can be substituted for last-minute convenience, but they lack the crisp, fresh taste of home-cooked beans and will not absorb the dressing flavor as well as the warm beans you prepare yourself.

# GERMAG LUPIA AGHTSAN

### ARMENIAN BEAN SALAD

*Serves 4–5*

| | |
|---|---|
| 1 cup dried white beans, such as Great Northern | 1 clove garlic, crushed |
| Salt | Freshly ground pepper |
| 1 small green pepper | 3 tablespoons chopped fresh parsley |
| 4 tablespoons olive oil | 6 tablespoons scallions (including 2 inches of green top), chopped |
| 2 tablespoons freshly squeezed and strained lemon juice | 2 medium-size tomatoes, peeled and chopped |
| 1 tablespoon white wine vinegar | |

Soak the beans for several hours in fresh cold water. Drain and rinse. Place in a large pot, cover with more fresh water, and bring to the boil over a high flame. Reduce the heat and simmer, partially covered, until the beans are tender but not mushy. (Add extra boiling water, if necessary, during cooking to keep the beans covered.) Add salt to taste just before cooking is completed. While the beans cook, seed, core, and chop the green pepper. Prepare the dressing by blending the oil, lemon juice, vinegar, garlic salt, ground pepper, and 2 tablespoons parsley with a wire whisk or fork.

Drain the beans and place in a serving bowl. While still warm, add the dressing and toss. Allow to stand for 2 hours. Just before serving, mix in the scallions, tomatoes, and green pepper. Adjust the seasoning and garnish with remaining tablespoon chopped parsley.

# NAPOLEON'S BEAN SALAD

*Serves 4*

In her wonderful cookbook *Good Things,* Jane Grigson tells us that Napoleon in exile on St. Helena used to eat this bean salad at lunchtime every other day. For a delicious variation, add thick slices of spicy salami sausage cut into bite-size cubes.

½ pound dried small white beans
Salt
2 tablespoons tarragon vinegar
5 tablespoons light olive oil
1 teaspoon French Pommery mustard

1 tablespoon finely chopped shallots
1 heaping tablespoon each of
    coarsely chopped fresh parsley,
    tarragon, and chives
Freshly ground pepper

Soak the beans for 2–3 hours, drain, and cook over low heat in plenty of fresh water until they are soft but not disintegrating (approximately 1 hour). Add salt to taste just before cooking is completed.

    While the beans are cooking, prepare a dressing of the vinegar, oil, mustard, and chopped shallots. Drain the beans and while still warm, add the chopped herbs and dressing. Mix well, adding plenty of freshly ground pepper and more salt, if necessary, and allow to stand for several hours before serving.

# SALADE DE HARICOTS BLANCS

### FRENCH WHITE BEAN SALAD

*Serves 4–5*

1 cup dried small white beans, such
    as Great Northern
6 tablespoons light olive oil
2 tablespoons tarragon vinegar
1 clove garlic, crushed
1 teaspoon Dijon mustard

Salt and freshly ground pepper
1 ounce black olives, pitted and
    coarsely chopped
3 hard-boiled eggs, sliced
3 medium-size tomatoes, coarsely
    chopped

Prepare the beans as in Germag Lupia Aghtsan, page 136.

    While the beans cook, combine the oil, vinegar, garlic, mustard, and salt and pepper to taste, blending with a fork until smooth.

    Drain the beans, place in a serving bowl, and add the dressing. Add the olives, eggs, and tomatoes. Toss carefully and allow to stand for at least 2 hours before serving.

# CALIFORNIA GARBANZO SALAD

*Serves 4–6*

The chick-pea—or garbanzo, as it is more commonly known throughout most of the Americas—was introduced to the Indian tribes of the New World by the conquering and colonizing Spaniards. They remain today a feature of the Spanish- and Mexican-influenced cooking of the Western and Southern states, and regularly appear in salads like the following.

| | |
|---|---|
| ½ pound garbanzo beans | ½ teaspoon ground cumin |
| Salt | 2 tablespoons olive oil |
| 2 tablespoons minced scallions | 1 tablespoon red wine vinegar |
| 2 tablespoons minced green pepper | Freshly ground pepper |
| 1 teaspoon minced green chili pepper | Large romaine lettuce leaves |
|   (see page 95) | Parsley sprigs |

Soak the garbanzos overnight. Drain and place them in a large cooking pot with plenty of fresh cold water. Simmer beans, covered, for 1–1½ hours, or until tender; about 15 minutes before cooking is completed, add salt to taste.

Drain the beans and place them in a large mixing bowl. While still warm, add the scallions, green pepper, chili pepper, and cumin. Dress with oil and vinegar, toss, and season to taste with salt and freshly ground pepper. Allow to stand for a couple of hours before serving, tossing occasionally. Line a large platter with the lettuce leaves and cover with the salad. Garnish with parsley sprigs.

# CHICK-PEA SALAD

*Serves 6*

| | |
|---|---|
| ½ pound chick-peas | Juice of 1 lemon, freshly squeezed |
| Salt |   and strained |
| Freshly ground pepper | 2 tablespoons finely chopped fresh |
| 5 tablespoons olive oil |   parsley |
| 1 clove garlic, crushed | |

Soak the chick-peas overnight in plenty of fresh cold water. Drain and rinse. Place in a large pot and cover generously with cold water. Bring slowly to the boil and simmer for 1–1½ hours, or until tender but not mushy. Add extra boiling water if necessary during cooking to keep beans covered. Add salt 10–15 minutes before cooking is completed.

Drain the peas, place in a large bowl, and season with additional salt and plenty of pepper. Blend together the oil, garlic, and lemon juice. Pour over the chick-peas while they are still warm, and sprinkle with chopped parsley. Toss and allow to stand for at least 2 hours before serving.

## HOPPING JOHN SALAD

*Serves 8*

Black-eyed peas are a Southern favorite. Available fresh during the summer months in some parts of the country, they are mainly eaten dried and cooked. This traditional cooked dish is transformed into a delicious salad by the addition of a simple oil-and-vinegar dressing.

3 cups black-eyed peas
½ pound salt pork
1 large onion, finely chopped
¼ teaspoon hot red chili pepper,
   finely chopped (see page 95)
1 bay leaf

Salt
3 cups cooked white or brown rice
6 tablespoons Basic Vinaigrette,
   page 18
2 tablespoons chopped fresh parsley

Soak the peas overnight in plenty of fresh cold water. Drain. Place the salt pork in a large pot along with 4 cups of water. Bring to a boil and cook over medium heat for 30 minutes. Add the peas, onion, chili pepper, and bay leaf. Reduce heat and simmer for another half an hour. Add salt to taste and cook for another 15 minutes, until the beans are tender but not mushy. Drain thoroughly. Remove the salt pork and cut into small pieces. In a large glass salad bowl, combine the black-eyed peas, salt pork, and rice. Add the vinaigrette and chopped parsley, toss well, and serve at room temperature.

## FAGIOLI E TONNO

### ITALIAN BEAN SALAD WITH TUNA FISH

*Serves 6*

The large white Tuscan bean is the ubiquitous antipasto favorite, but any white bean can be used for this salad. For a colorful variation, substitute red kidney beans. Some people prefer to dress this salad with oil only. Crushed or finely chopped garlic can also be added to the dressing, or experiment with oregano or basil, two favorite Italian herbs.

139

½ pound dried white beans
1 carrot, peeled and sliced
1 stalk celery
1 bay leaf
1 large Spanish onion, cut in half
Salt

Freshly ground pepper
6 tablespoons olive oil
2 tablespoons white wine vinegar
One 7-ounce can white meat tuna fish
2 tablespoons chopped fresh parsley

Soak the beans for several hours in cold water. Drain and place in a large pot, covered with plenty of fresh cold water, along with the carrot, celery, bay leaf, and half the onion. Bring to the boil, reduce the heat, and simmer gently for at least an hour. The beans should be tender but not mushy. Just before the end of the cooking period season with salt.

Drain and discard the vegetables. Put the beans in a large bowl and sprinkle generously with black pepper and additional salt, if required. Blend the oil and vinegar and pour over the beans while they are still warm.

Slice the remaining half onion into thin rings and add to the beans. Pile onto a large flat dish and garnish with chunks of tuna fish, drained of its oil. Sprinkle with chopped parsley and serve.

## WYOMING BEAN SALAD

*Serves 6*

Farmers in Wyoming cultivate many varieties of bean—lima, pinto, kidney, navy, garbanzo, and so on—and their bean dishes are often a mixture of three or four kinds.

2 ounces each of kidney beans, lima
  beans, and chick-peas, individually
  soaked
Salt
6 tablespoons olive oil
2 tablespoons wine vinegar
1 teaspoon Worcestershire sauce
½ teaspoon sugar
½ teaspoon dry mustard

Pinch of cayenne pepper
Freshly ground pepper
2 tablespoons peeled and chopped
  cucumber
2 tablespoons chopped green pepper
2 tablespoons chopped onion
A few large lettuce leaves
2 hard-boiled eggs, quartered

Drain the soaked beans. It is best to cook the different beans separately, since the cooking time will vary slightly. Follow the general method described on pages 135–36, using plenty of fresh water and adding salt only at the very end of the cooking time.

While the beans cook, make the dressing with the oil, vinegar, Worcester-shire sauce, sugar, dry mustard, cayenne, and salt and ground pepper to taste. Whisk all ingredients with a fork or shake in a jar until creamy smooth.

Drain the cooked beans and place them in a large bowl. Pour on the dressing, add the chopped cucumber, green pepper, and onion, and toss until thoroughly blended.

Line a large serving dish with lettuce leaves. Place the beans on top and decorate with the quartered eggs.

## LENTIL SALAD

*Serves 4*

Brown lentils cook quickly without becoming mushy and are therefore ideal for salads.

| | |
|---|---|
| 1¼ cups brown lentils | 1–2 tablespoons wine vinegar |
| 1 bay leaf | 1 clove garlic, crushed |
| 3 slices bacon | Salt and freshly ground pepper |
| 4 tablespoons olive oil | 1 small onion, chopped |

Soak the lentils for about 2 hours in plenty of cold water. Drain and place in a large pot, covered completely with fresh water. Add the bay leaf and bring to the boil. Reduce the heat and simmer gently for about half an hour, or until the lentils are tender but still slightly crunchy. (Lentils tend to absorb water quickly, so you may have to add more boiling water during the cooking.)

While the lentils cook, fry the bacon until crisp, drain, and crumble into small pieces. Prepare a dressing from the oil, vinegar, garlic, and salt and pepper to taste.

About 10 minutes before the cooking is completed, season the lentils with salt to taste, and stir. When cooked, remove from the heat and drain, discarding the bay leaf. Place the lentils in a large bowl and add the bacon, chopped onion, and dressing. Toss gently until well blended, adjust seasoning, and let stand, stirring occasionally, for at least 2 hours before serving.

# YEMISER SELATLA

ETHIOPIAN LENTIL SALAD

*Serves 4–6*

1¼ cups brown or green lentils
1 bay leaf
2–3 fresh green chili peppers
  (approximately 3 inches long)
3 tablespoons red wine vinegar

3 tablespoons vegetable oil
Salt and freshly ground pepper
8 large shallots, peeled and halved
  lengthwise
1 tablespoon chopped fresh parsley

Prepare the lentils as in preceding recipe, cooking with bay leaf. Drain and set aside. Cut the chili peppers into strips approximately 1 inch long and ⅛ inch wide, discarding cores and seeds (see page 95).

In a large bowl, combine the vinegar, oil, salt to taste, and a few grinds of pepper, and whisk to blend thoroughly. Add the lentils, shallots, and chili peppers; toss gently to coat with dressing. Correct the seasoning and let the beans stand (stirring occasionally) for at least 2 hours before serving. Garnish with chopped parsley.

# SPROUTS

SPROUTS HAVE BEEN CULTIVATED in the Orient for more than five thousand years. In East Asia and Europe, sprouts were used first as a medicine. It was not until the nineteenth century that Westerners began to take note of sprouts (especially the soybean) as a major foodstuff, influenced largely by missionaries' accounts of the traditional Oriental dishes in which bean sprouts so frequently appear; but only recently in the West has the use of sprouts as a medicine—either a preventive one, as a supplementary source of protein, or a curative one, as in the treatment of scurvy—been surpassed by the use of sprouts as a food.

Mung bean or Chinese sprouts are those most commonly found in markets —fresh or canned; but they can be easily grown indoors at home, requiring no special equipment, no garden soil or sun. Many other varieties of bean and seed can also be sprouted, such as alfalfa, aduki, soybean, fenugreek, chick-pea, and lentil. Each of these will yield six times its original weight. The basic method requires a glass jar, a piece of cheesecloth, and a rubber band. Place about 3 tablespoons of seeds or beans in a jar, cover with the cloth, and secure tightly with the rubber band. (Chick-peas and mung beans grow better if they have first been soaked overnight.) Fill the covered jar with warm water, shake well, and turn upside down to drain. Place the jar on its side away from a radiator or any direct source of heat. Repeat the washing and draining process morning and evening until the sprouts are ready (2–9 days, depending on the variety). They should be 1½–2 inches long, and nicely plump. Wash and use as soon as possible.

# ALFALFA SALAD BOWL

*Serves 4*

¼ pound bacon
3 hard-boiled eggs
4 tablespoons vegetable oil
1 tablespoon wine vinegar
1 teaspoon Dijon mustard
1 clove garlic, crushed
Salt and freshly ground pepper

½ pound alfalfa sprouts
8 radishes, sliced
4 scallions, cut in ½-inch pieces
2 stalks celery, diced
¼ pound button mushrooms, sliced
1 tablespoon chopped fresh parsley

Fry the bacon until crisp. Drain and crumble. Cut 2 of the eggs into quarters; sieve or finely chop the remaining egg, and set aside.

Prepare a dressing with the oil, vinegar, mustard, and garlic. Season to taste with salt and pepper.

Place the alfalfa, radishes, scallions, celery, and mushrooms in a large salad bowl. Pour on the dressing and toss to cover all ingredients. Surround the vegetables with the quartered eggs and decorate the top with the crumbled bacon, the sieved or chopped egg, and the parsley. Serve immediately.

# SOOK CHOO NA MOOL

### KOREAN BEAN SPROUT SALAD

*Serves 6*

4 tablespoons vegetable oil
2 tablespoons white wine vinegar
2 tablespoons soy sauce
1 clove garlic, minced
Freshly ground pepper and salt
8–10 ounces mung bean sprouts

1 small red pepper, cored, seeded,
   and finely chopped
4 scallions, trimmed and chopped
2 tablespoons toasted sesame seeds
   (see Oriental Salad Dressing,
   page 31)

To make the dressing, mix together the oil, vinegar, soy sauce, garlic, and ground pepper. Add salt sparingly, since soy sauce is quite salty in itself. Place the bean sprouts, red pepper, and scallions in a large salad bowl. Pour the dressing over the salad and toss gently. Chill for at least an hour. Just before serving, add the toasted sesame seeds and toss again.

## HONEY-DRESSED SPROUT SALAD

*Serves 4–5*

8–10 ounces mung bean sprouts
1 large apple, coarsely chopped
3 carrots, peeled and grated
¼ cup raisins
Salt and freshly ground pepper

2 tablespoons honey
Juice of ½ lemon, freshly squeezed
 and strained
2 tablespoons sunflower oil

Steam the mung bean sprouts for 2–3 minutes, and let them cool.

Place the chopped apple, carrots, raisins, and sprouts in a large bowl. Season with salt and pepper. In a separate small bowl, blend the honey, lemon juice, and oil. Pour over the vegetables and toss gently. Chill for at least an hour before serving.

# PASTA, RICE, AND BULGUR SALADS

## PASTA

UNTIL RECENTLY, delicatessen-style macaroni salad was the only form in which pasta found its way into salads. Today all kinds of pasta are being used in salads to make inexpensive and satisfying dishes that can be served as a meal on their own or to accompanying cold meats and other salads.

In addition to traditional pasta shapes made from semolina flour and eggs, try whole-wheat pasta and green noodles (made from spinach and flour) in your salads.

## ANTIPASTO MACARONI

*Serves 8*

This is delicious served with crusty Italian bread.

1 pound elbow macaroni
6 tablespoons Basic Vinaigrette, page 18, flavored with 1 clove garlic, crushed
1 cup cubed mozzarella cheese
¼ pound peperoni, diced
1 small can anchovy fillets, drained and chopped

10–12 small black olives, pitted and chopped
2 tablespoons chopped Italian parsley
1 teaspoon dried oregano
Freshly ground pepper and salt

Cook the macaroni in several quarts of lightly salted boiling water just until tender (approximately 8–10 minutes). Drain and place in a large bowl. Dress with half the vinaigrette and toss well. Add the cheese, peperoni, anchovies, and olives. Add the remaining dressing and season with chopped parsley, oregano, plenty of freshly ground pepper, and salt to taste. Toss again and serve at room temperature.

## PASTA WITH MINCED CLAMS

*Serves 4–6*

½ pound pasta shapes: *pipette, pennergate, pagliaci,* etc.
Salt
8 tablespoons olive oil
One 10-ounce can minced clams, drained

Juice of 1 small lemon
2 large cloves garlic, peeled
1½ ounces fresh parsley
1 ounce fresh mint
¼ cup grated Parmesan cheese
Freshly ground pepper

Cook the pasta in several quarts of lightly salted boiling water for approximately 8–10 minutes, stirring occasionally, until the pasta is *al dente.* Drain in a colander. Place the pasta in a large salad bowl, sprinkling it with 1 tablespoon of the oil to prevent sticking. Add the drained clams.

In a blender, combine the remaining 7 tablespoons oil, lemon juice, garlic, parsley, mint, and grated cheese. Season with salt and plenty of freshly ground pepper. Pour over the pasta and clams, stir well, and chill for several hours before serving. Stir again before bringing to the table.

## WHOLE-WHEAT PASTA WITH PEAS AND SMOKED HAM

*Serves 6*

¾ pound whole-wheat macaroni
4–6 tablespoons olive oil
¼ pound smoked ham, cubed
½ pound cooked young peas (fresh or frozen)
2 fresh scallions, chopped (including 2 inches of green stem)

2 ounces freshly grated Parmesan cheese
Juice of ½ lemon
½ teaspoon oregano
2 tablespoons chopped Italian parsley
Salt and freshly ground pepper

Cook the macaroni in lightly salted boiling water just until tender (approximately 8–10 minutes). Drain and place in a large bowl. Add the olive oil (as much as you like) and toss well. Add the ham, peas, scallions, and grated cheese. Squeeze in the lemon juice and add the oregano and parsley. Season to taste with salt and freshly ground pepper, and toss again before serving.

## FARFALLE WITH BEANS AND TUNA

*Serves 8*

1 cup dried white beans
¾ pound farfalle (pasta bows)
5–6 tablespoons Basic Vinaigrette, page 18, seasoned with 1 clove garlic, crushed
1 red onion, thinly sliced

2 tablespoons chopped Italian parsley
One 7-ounce can tuna, drained
1 small red pepper, seeded and sliced into julienne strips
Freshly ground pepper and salt

Soak and cook the beans as described on pages 135–36. Drain and set aside. Cook the farfalle in lightly salted boiling water until just tender (approximately 6–8 minutes). Drain and place in a large bowl. Add the vinaigrette to the pasta and combine with the onion and parsley. Toss well. With a fork, flake the tuna into large pieces. Add half to the pasta along with the red pepper and beans. Toss again. Season with plenty of freshly ground pepper and salt, to taste. Toss and garnish with the remaining tuna. Serve at room temperature.

# TORTELLINI SALAD

*Serves 4–6*

½ pound meat-filled tortellini
1 tablespoon olive oil
2 tablespoons ricotta cheese
6–8 tablespoons light cream
¼ pound fresh button mushrooms,
   thinly sliced

3–4 slices prosciutto, chopped
½ pound cooked young peas, fresh
   or frozen
1 tablespoon chopped Italian parsley
1 teaspoon dried oregano
Salt and freshly ground pepper

Use fresh tortellini if possible. Cook for several minutes in lightly salted boiling water just until tender. Drain and place in a large bowl. Add the olive oil and toss well. In a separate small bowl, blend the ricotta cheese and cream with a wooden spoon until smooth. Pour the dressing over the pasta and toss again. Add the mushrooms, prosciutto, and peas. Season with parsley, oregano, salt, and plenty of freshly ground pepper. Toss thoroughly and serve.

# MIDDLE EASTERN PASTA SALAD

*Serves 4–6*

½ pound small pasta shapes
1 large clove garlic
2 teaspoons salt
2 tablespoons finely chopped fresh
   mint or 1 teaspoon dried

1–1½ cups yogurt
2 ounces pine nuts
1 tablespoon butter, melted

Prepare the pasta as in Pasta with Minced Clams, page 146.

With a mortar and pestle, crush the garlic, salt, and mint to a rough paste. Add to the yogurt and blend well. Pour this mixture over the cooked pasta.

Fry the pine nuts in hot melted butter until golden brown; drain and add to the salad. Serve at once.

# RICE

COLD WHITE RICE mixes well with raw and cooked vegetables, leftover meats, seafood, nuts, dried fruits, and fresh herbs. It takes well to both oil and cream dressings. It keeps well in the refrigerator and can be prepared in advance in large quantities.

Brown rice is the unpolished grain and is more nutritious than polished rice. It also has more flavor.

## CURRIED RICE SALAD

*Serves 8*

½ cup seedless raisins
1 pound long-grain rice
3 tablespoons curry powder
1 cup hazelnuts
1 large can *petit pois,* drained

1 cup mayonnaise, strongly flavored
  with lemon juice, or 1 cup
  Vinaigrette au Citron, page 19
Salt and freshly ground pepper

Plump up the raisins by soaking for 1 hour in warm water. Prepare the rice according to package directions, adding the curry powder to the boiling water just before the rice is sprinkled in. Drain in a colander and rinse with hot and then cold water. Drain again.

In a large serving bowl, combine the rice, hazelnuts, and peas. Drain the raisins and add to the salad. Dress with either lemon mayonnaise or lemon vinaigrette sauce. Season to taste with salt and freshly ground pepper.

## SALADE DU 15 AOÛT

*Serves 8*

This salad is served on Assumption Day (August 15) in France.

1 pound long-grain rice
½ cup yellow raisins
1 large green pepper
1 large red pepper
1 pound fresh green peas, shelled,
  or ½ pound frozen
4 medium-size firm tomatoes

2 ounces large black olives, pitted and
  chopped
1 cup heavy cream
Juice of 2 lemons, freshly squeezed
  and strained
Salt and freshly ground pepper
A few sprigs of parsley

Prepare the rice according to package directions, drain well, and chill. Soak the raisins in warm water for 1 hour. Grill the peppers under the broiler until the skins blister (turn occasionally to ensure that all sides cook), about

10–15 minutes. When cool enough to handle, remove the skins, core, and seeds. Slice into thin strips.

Cook the peas in a little boiling salted water until just tender. Drain and cool.

Cut the tomatoes into thin slices and set aside. Drain the raisins.

In a large mixing bowl, combine the rice, peppers, chopped olives, peas, and raisins. When ready to serve, make a dressing with the cream and lemon juice and pour over the rice mixture. Season with salt and pepper, and stir thoroughly to blend all ingredients.

Turn onto a large serving dish and surround with tomato slices, saving a few slices to decorate the top. Garnish with parsley sprigs.

## SALADE DE RIZ COLORÉE

### COLORED RICE SALAD

*Serves 8*

½ pound dried prunes
A pot of strong tea
1 pound long-grain rice
1 small can pimientos (approximately
    4–5 pieces)

½ cup slivered almonds
3 tablespoons chopped fresh parsley
½ cup Basic Vinaigrette, page 18

Place the prunes in a large Pyrex (or heatproof) bowl and cover with strong hot tea. Soak for 1 hour and drain.

Prepare the rice according to package directions. While it cooks, drain the pimientos and cut into small dice. Pit the prunes and cut into pieces the same size as the pimientos.

In a large salad bowl, mix the rice, pimientos, prunes, almonds, and 2 tablespoons of parsley. Add the vinaigrette and stir well to blend thoroughly. Chill and sprinkle with the remaining tablespoon of chopped parsley.

## RICE STUFFING FOR COLD VEGETABLES

*Serves 5–6*

A delicious filling for green peppers, large hollowed-out tomatoes, and artichokes; also excellent for stuffing vine leaves and cooked cabbage leaves. Vary the herbs with what is seasonally available.

⅔ cup olive oil
2 small onions, chopped
½ pound long-grain rice
1 tablespoon tomato purée
1 tablespoon currants

2 tablespoons pine nuts, chopped
1 tablespoon chopped fresh sage
1 tablespoon chopped fresh mint
Salt and freshly ground pepper
1 tablespoon sugar

In a large frying pan, heat the olive oil and lightly fry the onions until translucent but not brown. Add the rice and cook over low heat for approximately 15 minutes, stirring frequently. Add 1¼ cups boiling water, tomato purée, currants, pine nuts, sage, and mint. Season to taste with salt and pepper. Stir well, cover tightly, and cook over low heat for 15–20 minutes. Remove from the heat and stir in the sugar. All the liquid should by now be absorbed; if not, drain off any surplus. Let the rice cool before stuffing the vegetables.

## SAFFRON RICE SALAD WITH SEAFOOD

*Serves 4–6*

Any mixture of seafood can be substituted for the ingredients given below: leftover fish, canned (but well-drained) sardines or tuna fish, cooked mussels, crabmeat, or calamari.

½ teaspoon powdered saffron
6 tablespoons dry white wine
3½ cups chicken stock
¾ pound long-grain rice
6 tablespoons olive oil
2 tablespoons white wine vinegar
2 cloves garlic, crushed
4 tablespoons chopped fresh parsley

1 teaspoon Dijon mustard
Salt and freshly ground pepper
½ pound peeled shrimp
¾ pound cooked haddock, cod, or
  other white fish
2 ounces black olives
1 large tomato, thinly sliced
A few sprigs fresh parsley

Dissolve the saffron in the white wine. Place in a large saucepan with the stock. Wash the rice and add to the pan. Bring to a rapid boil, stir, reduce to a gentle simmer, and cook, covered, for approximately 15 minutes, or until the rice is tender and has absorbed all the liquid. While the rice cooks, prepare a dressing by mixing the oil, vinegar, garlic, chopped parsley, mustard, and salt and pepper to taste.

Place the rice in a colander to drain off any excess liquid, then turn into a large mixing bowl. While still warm, add the dressing and stir to blend thoroughly. Add the seafood and olives; toss gently and place on a large serving dish. Decorate with the sliced tomatoes and parsley sprigs.

# ARROZ CON ADÁN

## SPANISH RICE MOLD

*Serves 4–6*

This salad, with its multicolored layers of rice and vegetables, makes a lovely buffet centerpiece. Use a 9- to 10-inch ring mold.

| | |
|---|---|
| ½ pound long-grain rice | 1 clove garlic, crushed |
| 2–3 green peppers | Lettuce leaves |
| 5–6 medium-size tomatoes | 3 hard-boiled eggs, quartered |
| 1 bunch scallions | A few sprigs of parsley |
| Olive oil | Mayonnaise or Aïoli, page 24 |

Prepare the rice according to package directions in plenty of boiling salted water. While it cooks, grill the green peppers under the broiler until all sides blister—approximately 10–15 minutes—and when cool enough to handle, remove skins, core, and seeds. Cut into strips. Immerse tomatoes in boiling water for several seconds. Peel, deseed, chop, and set aside. Clean the scallions, removing damaged outer leaves and all but 2 inches of green stem. Chop and set aside.

When the rice is tender, drain in a colander, rinse with hot water, and drain again. Place the colander in a 275°F oven for a few minutes to dry the rice.

Heat enough oil to just cover the bottom of a frying pan and add the garlic. Add the rice and cook, stirring, for several minutes. Remove from the heat.

Grease the ring mold and pack the rice and vegetables in alternating layers, as follows: rice, tomatoes, rice, green peppers, rice, scallions, rice. Make sure the mold is packed solidly. Place a light weight on top and refrigerate for several hours. When ready to serve, line a large platter with lettuce leaves. Turn the mold onto the center of the platter and surround with the quartered hard-boiled eggs. Garnish with parsley sprigs and serve with a bowl of mayonnaise or Aïoli.

# WILD RICE

TODAY AN EXPENSIVE GOURMET DELICACY, wild rice, just a few decades ago, was considered unpalatable by all but the wild mallard duck and the American Indian.

The North American Indians first introduced this grain (wild rice is not actually rice, but an aquatic seed which grows in shallow lakes and rivers) to the white traders and trappers who moved across northern Minnesota, Wisconsin, Manitoba, and Ontario.

Although traditionally served hot as an accompaniment to game and roast meats, wild rice makes a delicious salad; and because of its high cost and the time it takes to prepare properly, it makes sense to know some tasty ways of using up the leftovers.

Instructions for boiling vary from brand to brand. Always follow the method described on the package. In general, better results are obtained when the rice has been soaked overnight and washed in several changes of water before cooking. It will triple in size when cooked.

## SPICY WILD RICE SALAD

*Serves 6–8*

This salad is a superb accompaniment to cold duck, turkey, pheasant, pork, or veal.

½ pound uncooked wild rice
5–6 tablespoons butter
1 medium-size onion, finely shredded
1 large green pepper, seeded and
    coarsely shredded
½ cup blanched almond slivers
¾ cup raisins, plumped up in cold
    water and drained

12 whole cloves
2 tablespoons vegetable oil
1 tablespoon wine vinegar
Salt and freshly ground pepper
A few sprigs of parsley

Boil the rice according to package instructions and set aside.

Melt the butter in a large frying pan and sauté the onion and green pepper for 5 minutes over low heat. Add the almonds and the raisins, and continue cooking until both the onions and the nuts have turned golden brown. Add the boiled rice and the cloves. Stir with a wooden spoon to thoroughly blend all ingredients. Remove from the heat and place the mixture in a large serving bowl. Allow to cool and dress with the oil and vinegar, seasoned to taste with salt and pepper. Garnish with parsley sprigs.

## SAVORY RICE WITH BACON AND MUSHROOMS

*Serves 6–8*

½ pound uncooked wild rice
6 slices bacon
1 medium-size onion, finely shredded
Butter (optional)
½ pound button mushrooms, sliced
1 tablespoon chopped fresh marjoram
   or ½ teaspoon dried

2 teaspoons chopped fresh thyme or
   ½ teaspoon dried
½–1 teaspoon dried oregano
Salt and freshly ground pepper
2 tablespoons olive oil
1 tablespoon wine vinegar

Boil the rice according to package directions and set aside. Fry the bacon in a large pan until very crisp. Remove and drain on a paper towel. Next, sauté the onion in the bacon fat, adding a little butter only if the pan becomes dry. After 5 minutes add the mushrooms and continue cooking over fairly low heat for 2–3 minutes more. Finally, add the rice and herbs, stir well, and season with salt and pepper.

Place the mixture in a large serving bowl and allow to cool. Just before serving, crumble the bacon into the mixture, dress with the oil and vinegar, and toss lightly.

# BULGUR

## TABBOULEH BURGHUD

CRACKED WHEAT SALAD

*Serves 8*

This Middle Eastern favorite has many variations. The indispensable ingredient, however, is the fine cracked wheat—bulgur—with its rich earthy flavor. It is first soaked, then flavored with large quantities of parsley, mint, and lemon. Sometimes chopped vegetables—tomatoes, green peppers, onions, and cucumbers—are incorporated or simply used as garnish along with extra sprigs of parsley and black olives.

Bulgur can be bought at most Hellenic or Middle Eastern food shops.

½ pound bulgur
¼ pound Italian parsley, finely chopped
4 tablespoons finely chopped fresh mint
¼ pound scallions, trimmed and finely chopped

2–3 medium-size tomatoes, chopped
4 tablespoons olive oil
4 tablespoons lemon juice
Salt and freshly ground pepper
Romaine lettuce leaves or cooked vine leaves

Soak the bulgur in plenty of cold water for about an hour. It will soften and expand. Drain and squeeze out the excess water with your hands. Spread the bulgur on a clean dish towel and let dry while you chop the parsley, mint, and scallions.

Place the bulgur in a large bowl and add the mint, parsley, scallions, and tomatoes. Mix well and gradually add the oil, followed by the lemon juice. Season to taste with salt and pepper and add additional lemon juice, if necessary, to make the flavor quite tart.

Allow to stand for at least two hours. Tabbouleh should be served on individual plates, with romaine lettuce leaves or vine leaves to use as scoops.

## BAZARGAN

*Serves 6–8*

Another Middle Eastern salad made from cracked wheat and highly seasoned with Oriental spices. This salad is a delicious accompaniment to roast lamb and pork.

½ pound bulgur
1 large onion, finely chopped
5 tablespoons sunflower oil
4 tablespoons finely chopped fresh parsley
¼ cup walnuts, coarsely chopped
½ teaspoon allspice

1 teaspoon powdered cumin
1 teaspoon powdered coriander
½ cup tomato purée
Dash of cayenne pepper
Salt and freshly ground pepper to taste

Wash the bulgur in a sieve and soak in plenty of fresh cold water for half an hour. Drain and squeeze out excess water. Spread on a clean towel to dry.

In the meantime, sauté the chopped onion in the oil until translucent but not brown.

In a large bowl, mix the bulgur and onion with the remaining ingredients. Blend thoroughly, cover, and store in the refrigerator for several hours so that all the flavors are absorbed into the bulgur.

# CREAMY SALADS

PURÉED VEGETABLES, exotically seasoned with herbs and spices, are served as salads in many countries. This chapter contains some of the most popular and some of the more unusual recipes I have discovered. You will also find here recipes for dishes like Greek Taramasalata and the Turkish Cacik, which, though eaten mainly as *meze,* or hors d'oeuvres, are considered part of the salad repertoire in their countries of origin.

A selection of these salads served with crudités, crackers, or small slices of toast (pita bread cut into triangles or strips is excellent for this purpose) makes a wonderful predinner or party spread.

Skordalia is actually a sauce, but it is eaten as an accompaniment to vegetables and therefore belongs functionally to this section rather than to the chapter on dressings.

# PATLICAN SALATZI

### TURKISH EGGPLANT SALAD

*Serves 4*

There are many variations of this eggplant pâté—often known as "poorman's caviar"—throughout the Balkan countries and the Middle East. Experiment with the proportions of garlic, oil, and lemon juice according to taste preference.

2–3 large eggplants
3–4 tablespoons olive oil
Juice of 1 lemon
1–2 cloves garlic, crushed

Salt and freshly ground pepper
Onion slices
1 tablespoon chopped fresh parsley

Lightly score the skin of the eggplants with a knife. Place them on a baking sheet and cook in a moderate oven for 45 minutes, or until they are completely soft and in a collapsed state.

When cool enough to handle, halve, and scoop the pulp out into a sieve. Allow to stand for 15–20 minutes to drain off the bitter juice. Turn the pulp into a large bowl and pound or mash until fairly smooth. Stirring continuously, trickle in the oil, then the lemon juice. Add the garlic, and season to taste with salt and pepper. Chill for at least an hour and stir again before serving. Garnish with raw onion slices and a sprinkling of chopped parsley.

*Note:* This recipe can be prepared quickly in a blender. Add the oil and lemon juice gradually, as above.

# BABA GHANOUSH

### EGGPLANT SALAD WITH TAHINI

*Serves 4–6*

A Middle Eastern favorite, combining two distinctive flavors. More or less tahini may be used, according to taste. Tahini may be purchased in health-food stores or Middle Eastern groceries.

3 large eggplants
2 cloves garlic, peeled
Salt
½ teaspoon ground cumin
½–1 cup tahini paste

Juice of 2 small lemons, strained
2 tablespoons finely chopped parsley
Black olives
Thin tomato slices

157

Lightly score the skin of the eggplants with a knife. Place them under the broiler and cook for 20–30 minutes, turning frequently, until the skins have blistered and charred and the flesh is soft. (In the Middle East, they would be cooked over an open charcoal fire, giving a distinctive smoky flavor to the dish.) When cool enough to handle, cut them in half and scoop the pulp out into a sieve. Allow to drain for 20 minutes to remove the bitter juice.

In the bottom of a large bowl, crush the garlic with salt. Add the eggplant and pound or mash until fairly smooth. Add more salt, if desired, and the cumin.

Gradually add the tahini, alternating with drops of lemon juice, and blending after each addition. The exact quantities of tahini and lemon juice are very much a matter of personal taste.

Chill for an hour before serving, sprinkle on the parsley, and garnish with black olives and tomato slices.

## HUMUS ME TAHINI

### CHICK-PEAS WITH TAHINI

*Serves 6*

½ pound dried chick-peas
2 tablespoons tahini paste
Juice of 1 lemon, strained
2–3 tablespoons olive oil

2 cloves garlic, peeled
Salt and freshly ground pepper
1 tablespoon chopped fresh parsley

Wash the chick-peas and soak overnight in cold water. Drain and rewash, then cover with fresh cold water in a deep saucepan. Bring very slowly to the boil and simmer until tender, at least 1½ hours, possibly more. Replenish the water as necessary. The peas are cooked when they can be easily crushed between the fingers.

Drain the chick-peas, reserving ½ cup of the cooking liquid. Push the peas through a medium-mesh sieve (discarding any coarse fibers that remain in the sieve) or a food mill. Set aside.

Put the tahini in a small bowl and slowly add *no more* than ½ cup of the cooking liquid to dissolve the tahini until smooth. Beating briskly with a whisk, add the tahini mixture—a teaspoonful at a time—to the chick-peas, alternating with lemon juice and olive oil. Crush the garlic over the mixture, blend, and season to taste with salt, pepper, and chopped parsley.

# GUACAMOLE

*Serves 4–6*

This Mexican avocado salad is excellent with potato, corn, or taco chips.

2 small tomatoes
2 large ripe avocados
1 tablespoon grated onion
1–2 green chili peppers, chopped
  (see page 95)

2 tablespoons lemon juice
1 tablespoon olive oil
Salt and freshly ground pepper

Immerse the tomatoes in boiling water for several seconds to loosen the skins. When cool enough to handle, peel and chop, discarding the seeds and as much juice as possible. Set aside.

Halve the avocados lengthwise, remove the stones, and scoop the flesh out into a large bowl. Mash, but make sure the consistency remains lumpy. Add the chopped tomatoes, onion, and chopped chilies. Gradually stir in the lemon juice and olive oil. Season to taste with salt and pepper. Cover and chill for about an hour. Before serving, stir again.

# CACIK

### TURKISH HERBED YOGURT AND CUCUMBER SALAD

*Serves 4–5*

Also known by its Greek name, *tzaziki,* this refreshing salad is a favorite throughout the Middle East. Most commercial yogurt is not as thick as the homemade variety and should be strained.

2 cups yogurt
1 large cucumber
Coarse salt
2 cloves garlic, peeled

Pinch of white pepper
3 tablespoons finely chopped fresh
  mint or 1 tablespoon dried
Black olives

To strain the yogurt, line a sieve with a piece of cheesecloth. Turn the yogurt into this and rest over a bowl. Let stand for 15–20 minutes, then close the top of the cloth (like a laundry bundle) and gently squeeze. The yogurt remaining will now be much thicker.

Peel the cucumber and chop into small dice. Place in a sieve, lightly salt, and allow to drain for 20 minutes.

In a large bowl, crush the garlic with a little salt. Add a few tablespoons of yogurt and blend with a pinch of white pepper. Add the remaining yogurt, most of the mint, and the cucumber. Season with salt to taste and mix well. Chill for several hours before serving so that the mint can fully permeate the salad. Garnish with a few black olives and a sprinkling of the remaining mint.

# SALATA DE CASTRARETI

### RUMANIAN CUCUMBER SALAD

*Serves 4–6*

| | |
|---|---|
| 2 medium-size cucumbers | 4–6 tablespoons olive oil |
| Salt | 1–2 tablespoons wine vinegar |
| 3 slices white bread, crusts removed | Freshly ground black pepper |
| 1 clove garlic, crushed | 1 tablespoon chopped chives |

Peel the cucumbers, cut in half, and place in a bowl of iced water for approximately 20 minutes. Remove from the water, drain, and pat dry. Cut crosswise into paper-thin slices (a food processor is a great boon in achieving uniformly thin pieces), and place these in a sieve. Salt lightly and leave for half an hour, pressing occasionally with a small plate or wooden spoon, to remove as much water as possible.

Meanwhile soak the bread in water, squeeze it to remove excess liquid, then combine it with the crushed garlic. Gradually trickle olive oil into the mixture, stirring constantly with a whisk or fork. After 4 tablespoons have been added, blend in 1 tablespoon of vinegar. This mixture should have a semiliquid consistency; add more olive oil and vinegar if the paste is either too lumpy or too thick.

Place the well-drained cucumbers in a shallow serving dish and pour on the garlic mixture. Season with plenty of freshly ground pepper and a little salt. Blend carefully with a wooden spoon and garnish with chopped chives and a trickle of olive oil.

# TARAMASALATA

### GREEK FISH ROE SALAD

*Serves 4–6*

This salad should have a uniform creamy consistency and is best prepared with an electric blender or food processor. Tarama can be purchased at Greek and gourmet food shops.

6 ounces tarama (smoked cod or
 carp roe)
2–3 slices white bread, crusts removed,
 soaked in milk, and squeezed to
 remove excess moisture
2 tablespoons lemon juice
1 clove garlic, crushed

6 tablespoons olive oil
½ teaspoon onion juice (optional)
Freshly ground pepper
Black olives
1 teaspoon finely chopped fresh
 parsley

Place the tarama, soaked bread, and lemon juice in a blender or food processor and mix at high speed for 1 minute. Add the garlic and blend for another 30 seconds. Continue blending at medium speed while gradually trickling almost all the olive oil into the mixture. Add onion juice if desired.

Place the purée in a serving dish, season with freshly ground pepper, and chill until ready to serve. Garnish with black olives, a sprinkling of chopped parsley, and an additional trickle of oil.

# SKORDALIA I

*Serves 4–6*

The use of garlic, *skordo,* in Greek cooking dates back to ancient times, when it was probably valued more for its medicinal and magical powers than as a flavoring.

I have given two typical recipes for this sauce, which is often served with cold vegetables as *mezethaki,* or with halved hard-boiled eggs. The important skill in preparing these recipes is knowing how much oil and vinegar (or lemon juice) the garlic can absorb as it is being pounded and beaten.

2 medium-size potatoes
2–3 cloves garlic, peeled
1¼ cups olive oil

4 tablespoons vinegar
Salt and freshly ground black pepper

161

Cook the potatoes in boiling salted water until tender. Drain and peel when they are cool enough to handle. Mash very finely.

Crush the garlic and mix well with the potatoes. Gradually add small, alternating amounts of oil and vinegar, beating constantly with a whisk. The right consistency has been achieved when the sauce is thick and smooth like mayonnaise. Add salt and pepper to taste.

# SKORDALIA II

4–6 cloves garlic, peeled
2 egg yolks
½–⅔ cup olive oil
2 ounces ground almonds

2 ounces fresh white bread crumbs
Lemon juice
3–5 tablespoons chopped fresh parsley

Pound the garlic in a mortar. Add the egg yolks, followed by olive oil, in the drop-by-drop method used for making mayonnaise (see page 20). When a smooth, firm consistency has been achieved, stir in the ground almonds and bread crumbs. Add lemon juice and chopped parsley to taste.

This keeps well for several days in the refrigerator.

# SALADS WITH POULTRY, MEAT, AND SEAFOOD

THERE IS A MACHO MENTALITY that applies to salads. Try offering a salad to a man who has just completed a ten-mile jog or an hour of strenuous squash and the response is likely to be, "You call that rabbit food lunch!" Yet salads can provide very satisfying, high-protein meals, especially those made with meat, poultry, or fish. This chapter should help modify the vegetarian label so often indiscriminately attached to salads.

## POULTRY SALADS

### MRS. GLASSE'S SALAMAGUNDI

*Serves 6 or more*

This eighteenth-century English favorite was intended to form a centerpiece for a supper table. It was always served on a large platter with all the ingredients—shredded and minced in different ways—arranged artistically in separate rings.

The size of your chicken will determine the number of servings.

½ pound green beans, trimmed and halved
1 small cold roast chicken
1 lemon
4 hard-boiled eggs
1 can anchovy fillets, drained and rinsed

1–2 tablespoons finely chopped fresh parsley
½–⅔ cup Basic Vinaigrette, page 18
1 crisp head iceberg lettuce
12–18 small pickled onions
¼ pound seedless grapes, peeled
A few sprigs of parsley

Cook the green beans in a little boiling salted water for 6–8 minutes, or until just tender. Drain and set aside. Remove the skin from the chicken and cut all the white meat into thin strips, about 3 inches by ¼ inch. Cut the dark meat into dice.

Peel the lemon and chop into small dice, removing all the pith and seeds. Mash the egg yolks and chop 4–6 anchovies into small pieces. Cut the remaining anchovies in half lengthwise and set aside. Finely chop the egg whites.

In a large bowl, mix the diced dark meat, chopped lemon, chopped parsley, egg yolks, and chopped anchovies. Blend with half the vinaigrette and mix well.

Shred the lettuce very finely and spread it about ½ inch thick across a large serving dish. Pile the chicken mixture in the center in a mound and decorate with a few onions and a few grapes. Surround with strips of white meat, leaving spaces between the strips and an empty ring around the circumference of the chicken mixture. In this ring scatter the chopped egg whites and the green beans. In between the strips of chicken, put the remaining chopped grapes and place the anchovy strips in between the chicken strips and the grapes. Decorate the outer edge of the platter with the remaining onions and parsley sprigs.

Chill, and just before serving, pour the remaining vinaigrette over the undressed chicken and garnishes.

## HAWAIIAN CHICKEN SALAD IN TOMATO PETALS

*Serves 6*

½ cup mayonnaise
2 teaspoons curry powder
Salt and freshly ground pepper
2 ounces slivered almonds
10–12 ounces diced cooked chicken
1 apple, peeled and diced

3 stalks celery, diced
¼ pound seedless grapes, quartered
2 teaspoons grated onion
6 very large firm tomatoes
6 sprigs of parsley

Blend the mayonnaise with the curry powder and season to taste with salt and pepper.

Toast the almonds under the broiler until golden brown, shaking the pan occasionally to prevent burning.

In a large bowl, combine the chicken, apple, celery, grapes, almonds, and grated onion. Add the curried mayonnaise and stir until well blended. Chill.

When ready to serve, cut the tomatoes into sixths *almost* but not all the way through and gently separate to form petals. Scoop out some of the flesh and seeds to create a larger cavity and fill with chicken salad. Place a sprig of parsley in the center of each and serve on individual plates.

## CHINESE LEMON CHICKEN

### *Serves 6*

This dish takes time to prepare, but it makes a delicious and most unusual salad.

| | |
|---|---|
| One 3–4-pound chicken | 4–5 fresh green chili peppers, seeded |
| 10 dried black mushrooms | and cut into julienne strips (see |
| 4 lemons | page 95) |
| 3 tablespoons vegetable or peanut oil | ⅛ cup sugar |
| 4 tablespoons finely shredded fresh | Salt |
| ginger | 1–2 teaspoons lemon extract |

The authentic way to prepare the chicken is to steam it over boiling water for at least an hour, or until tender. Alternatively, it can be boiled gently until cooked, but do not overboil—the meat will become tough and rubbery.

While the chicken cooks, prepare the other ingredients: cover the mushrooms with boiling water, allow to stand for half an hour, then drain and squeeze to extract moisture. Cut off and discard the tough stems. Set aside.

Carefully peel one of the lemons into long continuous strips, avoiding as much of the pith as possible. Cut each strip into the thinnest possible shreds and set aside. Grate another lemon to make about 1 tablespoon of grated rind. Set aside. Squeeze enough lemons to make about ½ cup of juice, making sure to remove all seeds.

Let the cooked chicken cool in the steaming liquid. Then remove; strain and reserve the broth. Gently remove the breast meat and cut into small cubes. Chop the wings, legs, and thighs into small pieces with a cleaver or remove the meat from the bones and cut into small strips.

In a Chinese wok or large enamel frying pan, heat the oil over a high flame and add the mushrooms and ginger. Cook for about 1 minute, then add the chili peppers and lemon shreds. Stir and cook for another minute, then add the sugar and stir again. Add ¾ cup of the chicken broth, bring to the boil, and add lemon juice and salt, to taste. Add the chicken pieces and cook for another minute, maximum. With a slotted spoon, transfer the pieces to a large shallow bowl, arranging them neatly and symmetrically. To the liquid in the pan, add the grated lemon and lemon extract. Reboil and continue cooking to slightly reduce the quantity. Pour over the chicken and cool to room temperature. If prepared in advance and chilled, allow to return to room temperature again before serving.

## HONESALAT

### DANISH CHICKEN SALAD

*Serves 4*

6 ounces celeriac, peeled and cut into julienne strips, or 6 stalks celery, trimmed and chopped
¾ pound diced cooked chicken or turkey
½ cup heavy cream

½–1 teaspoon mild prepared mustard
Salt and freshly ground pepper
2 tablespoons capers, drained
A few large lettuce leaves
1 tomato, thinly sliced

When using celeriac, parboil the strips for 3–4 minutes in water to which a few drops of vinegar or lemon juice have been added. Drain.

In a large bowl, combine the diced meat and celeriac or celery. Whip the cream in a separate bowl with a wire whisk until it has slightly stiffened. Fold in the mustard and salt and pepper to taste. Add to the chicken along with 1 tablespoon of the capers. Gently mix until all ingredients are well blended.

Line a large platter with lettuce leaves. Turn the chicken salad onto the platter, sprinkle with the remaining capers, and garnish with tomato slices. Chill and serve.

## SALADE AUX AVOCATS ET POULET

### AVOCADO AND CHICKEN SALAD

*Serves 6*

½ ounce slivered almonds
3 firm ripe avocados
Juice of 1 lemon, freshly squeezed and strained
2–3 ounces diced cooked chicken

2 tablespoons chopped celery
2 tablespoons chopped cucumber
½ cup heavy cream
Salt and freshly ground pepper
Paprika

166

Toast the almonds under the broiler until golden brown, shaking the pan occasionally to prevent burning.

Halve the avocados and remove the stones. Sprinkle lightly with lemon juice, which will prevent discoloration of the flesh. Gently remove some of the pulp to increase the cavity. Dice the removed pulp and combine in a large bowl with the chicken, celery, and cucumber.

Whip the cream with a wire whisk until slightly stiffened and add the remaining lemon juice and salt and pepper to taste. Add to the chicken mixture along with the toasted almonds and gently stir until all ingredients are well blended.

Fill the avocado halves with the chicken salad and sprinkle paprika on top of each one. Chill until ready to serve.

# SALADE DE POULET AUX AMANDES

## CHICKEN SALAD WITH TOASTED ALMONDS

### *Serves 6–8*

| | |
|---|---|
| ½ cup raisins | 8 tablespoons olive oil |
| 1½ ounces slivered almonds | 2 tablespoons wine vinegar |
| 3–4 pounds chicken, roasted or boiled | 1 orange |
| 1 bunch watercress | Salt and freshly ground pepper |
| 4 stalks celery | |

Soak the raisins in hot water for approximately 1 hour. Drain. Toast the almonds under the broiler until golden brown, shaking the pan occasionally to prevent burning.

Remove the skin from the chicken and carve the meat into julienne strips or dice.

Wash the watercress, dry, and discard any damaged leaves and thick stems. Clean the celery and chop into small pieces.

In a large bowl, mix the chicken, chopped celery, toasted almonds, and raisins.

Mix the oil, vinegar, and juice of half the orange. Season with salt and pepper to taste, and pour over the chicken salad. Toss to blend all ingredients and turn onto a large serving dish. Surround with watercress and decorate on top with the remaining half orange, cut into thin slices.

Chill for several hours before serving.

*Note:* If a creamy chicken salad is preferred, substitute a few tablespoons of mayonnaise for half the amount of oil and vinegar in this recipe.

167

# NÔM GA

### VIETNAMESE CHICKEN SALAD

*Serves 4*

2 large chicken breasts
1 thick slice fatback pork
½ cucumber
Salt
3 small carrots

¼ cup shelled roasted peanuts
6 large cooked shrimp, peeled
4 tablespoons wine vinegar
1 teaspoon sugar

Separately boil the chicken breasts and fatback over medium heat until each is tender and thoroughly cooked. Remove from the heat, drain, and allow to cool. Peel the cucumber and cut into small dice. Place in a sieve or colander, sprinkle with salt, and let stand 10–15 minutes. Rinse and drain thoroughly.

Peel the carrots and grate coarsely. Grind the peanuts (this can be done quickly with an electric coffee grinder or blender). Set both aside.

Shred the chicken into fairly large pieces. Cut the pork into thin strips. Slice the shrimp into ½-inch pieces.

In a large bowl, combine the chicken, pork, shrimp, grated carrots, and cucumber. Add the vinegar and sugar. Mix well and correct the seasoning with salt. Chill. Just before serving, add all but 1 tablespoon of ground peanuts to the salad. Toss and sprinkle the remaining peanuts across the top.

# DUCK AND ORANGE SALAD

*Serves 6*

1 bunch watercress
1 pound diced cooked duck meat
2 tablespoons Basic Vinaigrette,
   page 18
½ pound fresh shelled or frozen
   green peas, cooked *al dente*

3 stalks celery, diced
½–⅔ cup roasted unsalted peanuts
4 tablespoons mayonnaise
Salt and freshly ground pepper
2 oranges, peeled and sliced into rings

Wash and dry the watercress, discarding any damaged leaves and thick stems. Set aside. Season the duck with vinaigrette. Add the peas, celery, and peanuts, and blend the entire mixture with mayonnaise. Adjust seasoning with salt and plenty of freshly ground pepper.

Turn the mixture onto a large serving dish and surround with watercress and orange slices, reserving a little of each to decorate the top. Chill until ready to serve.

# MEAT SALADS

## CHEF'S SALAD

*Serves 4–5*

This is a great American classic. The original chef's salad may have been the creation of Louis Diat, the late chef of the bygone Ritz-Carlton Hotel in New York. However, his use of watercress as the *only* green has certainly been supplanted by the use of lettuce, generally iceberg, in combination with other seasonal greens according to the whim, as the name suggests, of the chef.

This is a basic recipe, but it may be garnished and varied in many ways. Chef's salad should be prepared in a large glass or wooden bowl and served with a selection of dressings, such as Russian, Roquefort, or oil and vinegar. Some suggested garnishes include: olives, parsley, croutons, crumbled bacon, capers, scallions, pickled onions, artichoke hearts, asparague tips, and watercress.

1 large head iceberg or romaine lettuce
½ pound cooked turkey or chicken, cut in julienne strips
½ pound cooked ham or tongue, cut in julienne strips
½ pound Emmental, Gruyère or Jahlsberg cheese, cubed or cut into julienne strips
2–3 hard-boiled eggs, quartered
2 firm tomatoes, quartered

Wash and dry the lettuce. Break it into bite-size pieces and line the salad bowl, forming a thick bed for the other ingredients.

Arrange the julienne strips of meats and cheese, pinwheel fashion, in rotating bunches around the center. Along the outer edge of the bowl arrange the egg and tomato wedges.

Decorate with any of the suggested garnishes and serve slightly chilled. Some chefs toss, dress, and arrange the salad on individual plates—but only after first displaying the carefully arranged creation to be admired before eaten.

169

# CHEF'S SALAD, ITALIAN STYLE

*Serves 3–4*

Be sure to serve plenty of crusty Italian bread with this hearty salad.

| | |
|---|---|
| 1 head escarole lettuce | Salt and freshly ground pepper |
| 2 small spicy Italian sausages | Pinch of dried oregano |
| 3–4 tablespoons red wine | 3 ounces fontina or mozzarella cheese, |
| 5 tablespoons olive oil | cubed or cut into julienne strips |
| 1–2 tablespoons wine vinegar | 3 ounces Italian salami, cubed or cut |
| 4 anchovy fillets, drained and chopped | into julienne strips |

Wash and dry the lettuce; break into pieces and arrange in a salad bowl.

Brown the sausages in the red wine, making sure they are well cooked before removing to drain and cool. Cut into ½-inch rounds and set aside.

Put the oil, vinegar, chopped anchovies, a dash of salt, plenty of freshly ground pepper, and the oregano in a glass jar. Cover tightly and shake to blend all ingredients. Pour about a third of the dressing onto the lettuce leaves and toss lightly.

Arrange the sausage, cheese, and salami, pinwheel fashion, in alternating mounds around the center. Chill for about an hour.

Bring to the table for display before adding the rest of the dressing. Toss and serve.

# DANNEVANG SALAD

### DANISH STUFFED TOMATOES

*Serves 6*

| | |
|---|---|
| 1 small head Boston lettuce | ½ pound Danish Samsoe cheese, |
| 6–8 tablespoons olive oil | cubed |
| 2–3 tablespoons tarragon vinegar | 6 ounces cooked ham, cubed |
| 1 tablespoon chopped fresh parsley | 6 ounces cooked chicken, cubed |
| 1 tablespoon chopped fresh chives | 6 large tomatoes |
| 1 teaspoon salt | Sprigs of parsley |
| 1 teaspoon dry mustard | Green olives |
| Freshly ground pepper | |

Wash the lettuce, removing any bruised or rough dark green outer leaves. Dry thoroughly in a lettuce basket or colander and shred.

170

In a small bowl, blend the oil, vinegar, chopped parsley and chives, salt, mustard, and plenty of freshly ground pepper.

Combine the shredded lettuce, cheese, ham, and chicken with the dressing, and toss well.

Cut a large slice off the top of the tomatoes and carefully scoop out enough flesh to form a large cavity. Fill the tomatoes with the salad mixture, then arrange them in a circle on a large serving dish, placing any leftover salad in the center. Decorate with parsley sprigs and green olives.

*Note:* You may substitute Edam, Gouda, or fontina for the Samsoe cheese.

## RUSSIAN VINIGRET

*Serves 4–5*

½ pound cold roast beef, cubed
½ pound cooked beets, peeled and
    cubed
½ pound potatoes, boiled and cubed
3 large carrots, peeled, diced, and
    boiled for 6–8 minutes, or until
    just tender

4 small gherkins, chopped
1 small can baby shrimp, drained
Mayonnaise
Salt and freshly ground pepper
A few large lettuce leaves
8–10 black olives
2 hard-boiled eggs, quartered

Place the beef, beets, potatoes, carrots, gherkins, and shrimp in a large bowl and add enough mayonnaise (up to 4 tablespoons, according to taste) to bind the mixture. Season with salt and pepper to taste, and turn onto a large serving dish that has been lined with lettuce leaves. Decorate with black olives and quartered eggs, and chill for several hours before serving.

## HUZARENSLA

### DUTCH MIXED SALAD

*Serves 4–5*

The Dutch claim this salad originated in the small garrison towns where the hussars were once stationed. Army food being nearly inedible, the young soldiers were encouraged to find kitchen maids as girl friends—preferably ones who worked for rich families. After the dinner hour, the soldier would sneak around to his sweetheart's kitchen and charm her into preparing a salad of leftovers.

2 hard-boiled eggs
8–10 ounces cooked veal or pork, cubed
2 tart green apples, such as Granny Smiths, peeled, cored, and diced
1 medium-size cooked beet, peeled and diced
4 small gherkins, chopped
2 scallions, chopped, including 2 inches of green stem

8–10 small new potatoes, boiled and quartered
5 tablespoons olive oil
1–2 tablespoons vinegar
Salt and freshly ground pepper
A few large lettuce leaves
4–5 tablespoons mayonnaise
1 medium-size firm tomato, thinly sliced

Chop one of the hard-boiled eggs and set aside the other for garnish.

In a large bowl, combine the meat, apples, beet, chopped egg, gherkins, scallions, and potatoes.

Prepare a dressing of oil and vinegar and season with salt and pepper.

Pour the dressing over the salad mixture, and toss to coat thoroughly. Turn the salad onto a large serving dish lined with lettuce leaves. Arrange in a neat mound and spread a thin layer of mayonnaise over the top.

Decorate with tomato slices and the remaining egg, quartered.

## BRAZILIAN BEEF SALAD

### Serves 4

A friend who has lived for many years in Rio de Janeiro says this is a popular and simple salad recipe for using up leftover meat.

12–14 ounces cooked beef
1 large Spanish or Bermuda onion
8 tablespoons olive oil
Juice of ½ lemon, freshly squeezed and strained

1 clove garlic, crushed
Salt and freshly ground pepper
1 tablespoon chopped green chili pepper (see page 95) (optional)

Slice the beef into thin strips. Peel and slice the onion into thin rounds. Place both in a shallow serving bowl.

Prepare a dressing from the oil, lemon juice, and garlic. Pour over the salad

and season well with salt and plenty of pepper. If desired, add the chopped chili pepper. Toss to cover all ingredients with dressing and marinate in the refrigerator for at least 2 hours, stirring occasionally, before serving.

## JAPANESE PORK WITH TOFU DRESSING

### *Serves 4–6*

Tofu, or soybean curd, is a soft, white, custardlike cake made from the cooking, pounding, and filtering of white soybeans. It is very high in protein and is therefore a staple element in many Oriental diets.

| | |
|---|---|
| 1 pound cooked lean pork | 1–2 tablespoons sugar |
| ¾ pound green beans, trimmed | 2 tablespoons light soy sauce |
| 5 tablespoons white sesame seeds | 1–2 tablespoons chicken stock |
| 1-pound piece tofu | |

Cut the pork into julienne strips, about 1½ inches by ¼ inch.

Cook the beans in lightly salted boiling water for about 8 minutes, or just until tender. Drain and mix with the pork.

Roast the sesame seeds in a dry frying pan or under the broiler, shaking the pan to prevent the seeds from burning. The seeds should then be crushed in a mortar (or Japanese *suribachi*), or put through a coffee or nut grinder. Add the crushed seeds to the tofu along with the sugar and soy sauce. Add stock gradually, while stirring, to thin out the sauce. Pour over the pork and beans, toss gently, and serve at once.

## SALVADOR DALI'S RED SALAD

### *Serves 4–5*

In *The Artist's Cookbook*, published by the Museum of Modern Art in New York, it says of Dali: "He does not have time to entertain as much as he would like, but when he does, he has dinners for 20–25 friends. His table is always exquisitely presented and always white—white porcelain, white damask, and white flowers in crystal vases." This beautiful salad makes a striking contrast to that background. Crusty French bread and a full-bodied red wine are good accompaniments.

5 tablespoons heavy cream, chilled
1 tablespoon tomato purée
1 teaspoon sugar
1 large shallot, finely chopped
Dash of cayenne pepper
2 tablespoons freshly squeezed
  and strained lemon juice
½ pound cooked beets, peeled and
  diced

¾ pound red cabbage, finely grated
½ pound smoked tongue or ham,
  diced
1 small head iceberg lettuce, broken
  into pieces
Salt and freshly ground pepper

Make the dressing by combining the cream, tomato purée, sugar, chopped shallot, and cayenne. Beat with a wire whisk until light and foamy (approximately 3 minutes). Gradually beat in the lemon juice to taste.

Put the beets, red cabbage, and tongue or ham in a large bowl. Add the dressing and toss to blend thoroughly. Cover and chill for at least 2 hours.

Just before serving, line a large serving dish with lettuce leaves. Season the salad mixture with salt and pepper, and arrange it in the center of the platter.

## SALADE BAGRATION

*Serves 6–8*

This salad takes its name from a Russian general who fought in the Napoleonic Wars. Because he employed the celebrated French chef Atonin Carême, his name graces many French dishes. Here is a variation of an Alice B. Toklas recipe.

1 small celeriac
¼ pound macaroni
5 large hard-boiled eggs
6–8 thick slices of cooked tongue or
  ham

6–8 canned artichoke hearts, drained
  and cut into thirds
Salt and freshly ground pepper
½–⅔ cup mayonnaise
3 tablespoons tomato purée

Peel and shred the celeriac, then parboil (3–4 minutes) immediately in lightly salted water to which a few drops of lemon juice or vinegar have been added. Drain and set aside.

Add the macaroni to approximately 1 quart rapidly boiling salted water. When the water comes back to the boil, reduce the heat and cook gently about 10 minutes, or until the macaroni is tender but not too soft. Drain in a colander and set aside.

Chop the egg whites and yolks in 2 separate bowls. Set aside. Cut the meat into julienne strips and set aside.

Place the macaroni in a large bowl with the artichokes and celeriac. Season with salt and pepper. Combine the mayonnaise and tomato purée and blend into the macaroni mixture.

Turn the salad onto the center of a large serving dish and surround first with a ring of egg yolk, then meat strips, and finally egg whites. Sprinkle the chopped parsley on the center mound and chill for at least 2 hours before serving.

# FISH AND SEAFOOD SALADS

## HAWAIIAN CRABMEAT AND PAPAYA SALAD

### *Serves 6*

Papaya, also called tree melon or pawpaw, is a popular tropical fruit, cultivated in the warmer parts of America and shipped to supermarkets all over the country.

3 papayas
4 tablespoons mayonnaise
4 tablespoons sour cream
1–2 tablespoons Tabasco sauce, to taste
2 tablespoons lime juice

Scant teaspoon sugar
¼ teaspoon salt
3 tablespoons chopped fresh chives
1 pound crabmeat (flesh only)
3 stalks celery, chopped
A few large lettuce leaves

Using a potato peeler, carefully remove the skin from the papayas; halve them and scoop out the seeds and some of the flesh with a spoon.

In a large bowl, mix the mayonnaise, sour cream, Tabasco sauce, lime juice, sugar, salt, and 2 tablespoons chives. Blend and add more salt or sugar if desired. Add the crabmeat and celery and mix well. Arrange the papaya halves on a large dish lined with lettuce leaves. Fill each with the crab mixture and sprinkle a few chopped chives on top. Chill until ready to serve.

175

## SHRIMP AND PAPAYA SALAD

*Serves 6*

5–6 tablespoons mayonnaise
2–3 tablespoons sour cream
1 teaspoon curry powder
Juice of ½ lime
Salt and freshly ground pepper
3–4 stalks celery, chopped

⅓ cup slivered almonds, toasted
   golden brown
1 pound cooked jumbo shrimp,
   chopped into 1-inch pieces
3 papayas
½ lime cut into 4–6 thin slices

In a large bowl, blend the mayonnaise, sour cream, curry powder, and lime juice. Season with salt and pepper. Add the celery, toasted almonds, and shrimp, and mix well.

Fill papaya halves (as described in preceding recipe) and garnish with a slice of lime.

## VINIGRET OLIVIER

*Serves 6–8*

A seafood variation of the basic well-known Russian vinigret.

1 small cucumber
Salt
6 medium-size potatoes, peeled
   and boiled
2 medium-size cooked beets
¼ pound button mushrooms
1 pound fresh or frozen green peas,
   boiled or steamed *al dente*
1 pound green beans, trimmed,
   halved, and boiled *al dente*

5 scallions, chopped, including 2
   inches of green stem
½ pound crabmeat or 1 large can
   salmon, drained
6 tablespoons mayonnaise
1 tablespoon lemon juice
Freshly ground pepper

Peel the cucumber, cut into large dice, and place in a sieve or colander. Salt lightly and allow to drain for half an hour. Dice the potatoes and beets. Clean the mushrooms with a damp paper towel, trim the stalks, and cut into quarters.

In a large bowl, mix all the vegetables and the crabmeat or salmon. Gently fold in the mayonnaise. Add the lemon juice and season to taste with salt and pepper. Chill for at least an hour before serving.

## CRAB SALAD LOUIS

*Serves 4*

This is a San Francisco favorite, said to have originated at Solari's restaurant. The quantities given here are for an appetizer. Always use fresh crabmeat if available.

The dressing can be poured over the crabmeat just before serving or brought to the table in a sauceboat for the portions to be dressed individually.

Lettuce leaves
1 pound crabmeat
Lemon wedges
2 hard-boiled eggs, quartered
Sprigs of parsley
8 tablespoons mayonnaise
4 tablespoons heavy cream, lightly whipped

1 tablespoon paprika (or, for extra spicy dressing, 1 tablespoon Tabasco sauce)
1 teaspoon Worcestershire sauce
5 scallions, chopped, including 2 inches of green stem
2 tablespoons lemon juice

Line a large platter with the lettuce leaves and pile the crabmeat on top. Decorate with lemon wedges, quartered eggs, and parsley. Prepare the dressing by mixing all the remaining ingredients, stirring until thoroughly blended. Chill for at least an hour before using and serve in one of the ways described above.

## INSALATA DI FRUTTI DI MARE

### ITALIAN SEAFOOD SALAD

This delicious salad, a standard appetizer in most Italian restaurants, should be made with the best-quality olive oil, a generous amount of crushed garlic, freshly ground pepper, a sprinkling of lemon juice, and fresh chopped parsley.

The selection and proportions of seafood can vary, but count on ¼ to ½ pound per person; see what is available from your fish store, but use as many fresh ingredients as possible. Shrimp, scallops, squid, octopus, crabmeat, and mussels are all excellent. Where cooking is required, stew the fish in lightly salted boiling water to which a slice of onion and lemon peel have been added, for about 5 minutes, or until tender.

Drain the seafood and mix in a large bowl with crushed garlic, oil, lemon juice, salt, pepper, and chopped parsley, all to taste. (Use ½ cup dressing for every 2 to 3 cups seafood.) Add a dash of oregano, if desired, and let stand for 1–2 hours, stirring occasionally so that the seafood is well marinated.

# ORIENTAL MUSSEL SALAD

*Serves 6–8*

1 large red pepper
One 8-ounce can bamboo shoots
6 stalks celery
12 black olives
36–48 fresh cooked and shelled
    mussels
2 tablespoons capers

3 tablespoons chopped fresh parsley
2 tablespoons sesame oil
1 tablespoon vegetable oil
1–2 tablespoons lemon juice, to taste
2 teaspoons light soy sauce
½ teaspoon sugar (optional)
Salt and freshly ground pepper

Broil the red pepper until all sides are charred. Cool, skin, and remove the core and seeds. Chop into small dice.

Drain the bamboo shoots and cut into pieces about ½ inch thick. Chop the celery and the black olives, discarding the pits.

Drain the mussels and place them in a large glass bowl with the red peppers, bamboo shoots, celery, olives, capers, and parsley.

To prepare the dressing, mix the oils, lemon juice, and soy sauce. Add sugar if a sweeter dressing is preferred. Pour over the salad, toss well, and season with salt and pepper to taste. Chill for 2–3 hours, stirring occasionally, before serving.

# BOW YEE

### CHINESE ABALONE SALAD

*Serves 2–3*

There are many species of this large univalve mollusk, which is such a popular ingredient in Chinese cookery. Fresh abalone needs tenderizing. The Chinese often purchase it dried and then soak it, but for Westerners approaching abalone for the first time, I recommend the canned, precooked variety, which requires no special preparation.

3-ounce can precooked abalone
5 stalks celery
1 tablespoon peanut oil or sesame oil

1 tablespoon light soy sauce
1 teaspoon sugar
Salt

Drain the abalone and slice very thinly. Wash the celery, dry, and chop it coarsely. Place both ingredients in a serving bowl and add the oil, soy sauce, and sugar. Stir to coat the abalone and season with salt to taste. Chill, stirring occasionally, until ready to serve.

## SHRIMP IN DILL MAYONNAISE

*Serves 3–4*

1 pound jumbo shrimp, cooked and
   peeled
1 small cauliflower
½ cup mayonnaise
1 tablespoon peanut or sesame oil

1–2 tablespoons Dijon mustard
2 tablespoons chopped fresh dill
1 shallot, finely chopped (optional)
Salt and freshly ground pepper

Cut each shrimp into three or four pieces. Divide the cauliflower into small florets and discard the tough core. In a small bowl, blend the mayonnaise with the cream, mustard according to taste, and most of the chopped dill. Add the chopped shallot, if desired. In a large glass salad bowl, mix the shrimp and cauliflower, and toss with the mayonnaise dressing. Season to taste with salt and plenty of freshly ground pepper. Garnish with a sprinkling of the remaining dill.

## YAM KOONG

### THAI SHRIMP SALAD

*Serves 6–8*

1 cup milk
1 cup grated fresh white coconut
2 pounds raw jumbo shrimp
2 teaspoons salt
1 bay leaf
1 tablespoon olive oil
2 cloves garlic, finely chopped

2 shallots, finely chopped
1 large green pepper, seeded and
   coarsely chopped
2 tablespoons light soy sauce
1 green apple, peeled and grated
3 tablespoons chopped peanuts

In a small saucepan, combine the milk and coconut. Bring slowly to the boil, remove from the heat, and let stand for 30 minutes. Pass the mixture through a sieve, pressing out all the milk from the coconut. Discard the pulp and set aside the liquid.

    Devein the shrimp and wash thoroughly. Place them in a saucepan with enough water to cover, salt, and the bay leaf. Bring to a boil and simmer for 5 minutes, or until the shrimp have cooked through. Drain, peel, and split the shrimp in half lengthwise. Chill for 1 hour.

    Heat the olive oil in a large frying pan. Add the garlic and shallots and fry gently for 2 minutes, stirring constantly. Remove from the heat and, when slightly cooled, place in a bowl with the green peppers, soy sauce, apple, and

179

peanuts. Toss thoroughly and add the coconut milk. Chill for at least an hour.

Arrange the shrimp in a shallow dish, pour on the chilled dressing, and serve at once.

# SALADE NIÇOISE

### Serves 6

According to Elizabeth David, there are as many versions of salade niçoise as there are cooks in Provence, but in whatever way it is interpreted, it is always a simple and rather crude country salad. The ingredients should be placed in the bowl with each category kept separate, in large pieces, nicely arranged so that the salad looks colorful and fresh. The dressing is mixed in at the table. There should always be plenty of crusty French bread to accompany a salade niçoise.

½–¾ pound fresh green beans
One 7-ounce can tuna fish
6 anchovy fillets
½ medium-size red onion
1 head romaine lettuce, washed,
   dried, and broken into bite-size
   pieces
½ pound Basic Potato Salad, page 98
3 medium-size firm tomatoes,
   quartered
2 hard-boiled eggs, quartered

12–24 oil-cured black olives,
   preferably French
1–2 tablespoons fresh chopped
   seasonal herbs
8 tablespoons olive oil
2–3 tablespoons wine vinegar or
   lemon juice
1 teaspoon Dijon mustard
1 large clove garlic, crushed
Salt and freshly ground pepper

Cook the beans in lightly salted boiling water for approximately 6–8 minutes, or just until tender.

Drain the tuna fish and anchovy fillets. Peel the onion and slice into thin rounds.

Line a large wooden salad bowl with a bed of lettuce leaves. Place chunks of tuna fish in the center and surround, pinwheel fashion, with alternating groupings of green beans, spoonfuls of potato salad, and tomato wedges. Spread the quartered eggs around the outside to form a border and place strips of anchovies and olives between each quarter. Sprinkle onion rings and freshly chopped herbs across the top.

Prepare a dressing of olive oil, vinegar or lemon juice, mustard, garlic, salt, and plenty of freshly ground pepper. Bring the dressing to the table in a sauceboat, to be poured over the salad just before serving.

# SALADE BERTHAULT

*Serves 6–8*

A very expensive way of preparing a niçoise-style salad—perfect for parties and holiday buffets. Tuna fish is optional.

2 pounds new potatoes
1 pound small fresh green beans
4 hard-boiled eggs
1 can anchovy fillets
12 green olives, pitted
12 black olives, pitted
1 tomato, cut into wedges

1 split chilled dry champagne
2 tablespoons cognac
6 tablespoons light olive oil
1 teaspoon prepared French mustard
Juice of ½ lemon, freshly squeezed
  and strained
Salt and freshly ground pepper

Scrub the potatoes and boil for 15 minutes, or until tender but not mushy. Drain and cool. Peel and slice into thin rounds.

Wash and trim the beans. Cook, uncovered, in lightly salted boiling water for 8–10 minutes, or just until tender. Drain and cool.

Slice the eggs into rounds.

In a large glass bowl, layer the ingredients as follows: potatoes, beans, potatoes, egg slices, and anchovy fillets (reserve one or two for decoration), potatoes, olives (reserve 4–5 for garnish), potatoes. Decorate the top with anchovy fillets, olives and tomato wedges.

Pour the champagne over the salad and chill for several hours.

Just before serving, drain off most of the liquid, sprinkle with cognac and pour on a dressing made from the oil, mustard, lemon juice, salt and pepper.

# INSALATA DI PATATE COL TONNO

### ITALIAN-STYLE TUNA FISH SALAD

*Serves 2*

2 medium-size potatoes
Salt and freshly ground pepper
1 small onion
3 tablespoons olive oil

Wine vinegar
One 7-ounce can tuna fish, drained
1 tablespoon chopped fresh parsley
1 tablespoon capers

Boil the potatoes in their skins until tender. Drain, peel, and cut into chunks while still warm. Season with salt and pepper to taste. Slice the onion into thin rounds and mix with the potatoes. Add the olive oil and a sprinkling of vinegar. Stir and allow to stand for about an hour. When ready to serve, place the potato salad in a shallow serving dish and flake the tuna fish on top. Garnish with chopped parsley and capers.

## TUNA FISH SALAD

*Serves 6*

One of the mainstays of the American home lunch, coffee shop, drugstore counter, and picnic basket.

Canned tuna is the base, and a variety of different ingredients—from chopped fresh vegetables such as peppers or onions, to pickles, olives, or even pieces of bacon—are added and blended with mayonnaise, and sometimes also sour cream, as in this recipe.

| | |
|---|---|
| Two 7-ounce cans tuna, drained and flaked | 2 tablespoons sour cream |
| 2 tablespoons lemon juice | Dash of cayenne pepper |
| 1 green pepper, cored, seeded, and finely chopped | Salt and freshly ground pepper to taste |
| 2 stalks celery, chopped | A few large lettuce leaves |
| 3 scallions, chopped, including 2 inches of green stem | 1 tomato, quartered |
| 2 tablespoons mayonnaise | 2 tablespoons capers |
| | Sprigs of parsley |

In a large bowl, mix the tuna, lemon juice, green pepper, celery, and scallions. Add the mayonnaise and sour cream, stirring constantly to blend thoroughly. (For a creamier consistency, add more mayonnaise and sour cream.) Season with cayenne, salt, and pepper. Turn the mixture onto a large serving dish lined with lettuce leaves. Garnish with tomato wedges, capers, and a few parsley sprigs.

## SARDINE SALAD

*Serves 2*

| | |
|---|---|
| 1 can sardines in oil | 1 small dill pickle, chopped |
| 2 tablespoons lemon juice | Salt and freshly ground pepper |
| 2 hard-boiled eggs, finely chopped | A few large lettuce leaves |
| 1 scallion, chopped, including 2 inches of green stem | Radishes |
| 2 teaspoons chopped fresh parsley | Tomato wedges |

Drain the sardines, reserving 1 tablespoon oil. Place them in a bowl and mash; gradually blend in the lemon juice and reserved oil. Add the chopped eggs, scallion, parsley, and pickle. Season to taste with salt and pepper and place on a serving dish lined with lettuce leaves. Decorate with radishes and tomato wedges.

# HERRING SALAD I

*Serves 4–6*

A favorite with Eastern Europeans and Scandinavians, herring makes a delicious luncheon salad. This version is dressed with vinaigrette.

1 medium-size cucumber
Salt
2 salted herring fillets
2 medium-size potatoes, cooked and
    peeled
2 medium-size cooked beets
1 large eating apple

2 scallions
2 hard-boiled eggs
1 teaspoon Dijon mustard
4 tablespoons olive oil
2 tablespoons wine vinegar
Freshly ground pepper
1 tablespoon chopped fresh dill

Peel the cucumber, slice into ½-inch slices, and halve each slice. Place, lightly salted, in a sieve or colander and allow to drain for half an hour. Rinse and drain again. Chop the herring fillets into pieces about 1 inch long. Slice the potatoes into ½-inch pieces and halve each slice. (They should be roughly the same size as the cucumber.)

Peel the beets and cut into large dice; peel and core the apple, and dice. Chop the scallions, including 2 inches of green stem. Place all these salad ingredients in a large bowl, reserving 2 tablespoons chopped beets for garnish.

Mash the hard-boiled egg yolks and separately crumble the whites. To the egg yolk, add mustard and salt (a pinch or two to start). Gradually blend in the oil, followed by the vinegar, and season with freshly ground pepper. Pour over the salad ingredients and mix well. Turn onto a large serving dish and garnish with chopped dill, beets, and egg white.

Chill before serving.

## HERRING SALAD II

*Serves 4–5*

This herring salad is dressed with a creamy sauce.

2 jars herrings pickled in vinegar
1 large beet, cooked
1 medium-size onion
1 tablespoon vinegar
2–3 tablespoons mayonnaise
2–3 tablespoons sour cream

1 medium-size dill pickle, chopped
Salt and freshly ground pepper
1 teaspoon fresh chopped dill
  (optional)
Chopped hard-boiled egg
Chopped fresh parsley

Drain the herring and chop into 1-inch pieces. Peel and chop the beet into coarse chunks. Peel the onion and slice into thin rounds. Place these ingredients in a large bowl and sprinkle with vinegar. Add the mayonnaise, sour cream, dill pickle, salt, and plenty of freshly ground pepper; mix well. If desired, flavor with dill. Garnish with chopped egg and parsley. Chill before serving.

## ENSALADA À BILBAINITA

### SPANISH CODFISH SALAD

*Serves 6*

Hot garlic bread goes wonderfully well with this salad.

1 smoked cod (approximately 1½
  pounds)
Milk
1 head chicory
1 large green pepper, chopped
8 large Spanish olives stuffed with
  almonds or pimientos
2 hard-boiled eggs, coarsely chopped

6 tablespoons Spanish olive oil
2 tablespoons wine vinegar
1 clove garlic, crushed
Dash of cayenne pepper
Salt and freshly ground pepper
4–6 anchovy fillets, drained and
  chopped
1 pimiento, thinly sliced

Soak the codfish overnight (or for at least 8 hours) in milk. Drain and place in a saucepan with enough milk and water, in equal proportions, to cover. Simmer until tender (the fish should separate easily). Drain, remove any bones, and flake. Set aside and chill.

Separate the chicory leaves and wash carefully; drain and dry.

In a large bowl, mix the green pepper, olives, eggs, chicory, and cod.

Make a dressing from the olive oil, vinegar, garlic, and cayenne. Blend and

season with salt and pepper to taste. When ready to serve, pour the dressing over the salad mixture and toss well to coat all the ingredients. Sprinkle the top with chopped anchovies and arrange the pimiento strips, pinwheel fashion, around the center of the bowl.

## I 'A OTA

### TAHITIAN FISH SALAD

#### *Serves 4*

This raw fish salad is actually anything but raw—the fish completely "cooks" in the acid of the lime juice. In Tahiti, it is appreciated as an antidote "for the man who has looked too long upon the flowing bowl the night before."

2 pounds raw fish, boned and filleted, such as bluefish, mackerel, tuna, swordfish
1 cup freshly squeezed lime or lemon juice
6 tablespoons vegetable oil
2 tablespoons vinegar

Salt and freshly ground pepper
2 medium-size onions, thinly sliced
1 tablespoon chopped fresh parsley
1 tablespoon chopped red pepper or 1 teaspoon chopped red chili pepper (see page 95)

Cut the fish into pieces about 1 inch square and ½ inch thick. Place in a large, deep bowl and add the lime or lemon juice. Toss gently to thoroughly cover the fish and let marinate for about 1½ hours.

Drain off all the juices and dress the fish with a mixture of oil and vinegar, seasoned to taste with salt and freshly ground pepper. Toss well, add the onions, and turn the salad onto a large platter. Garnish with chopped parsley and chopped red pepper or chili.

## JAPANESE RAW FISH SALAD

#### *Serves 4*

Salt
1 pound mackerel, filleted
½ pound cucumber
1 cup plus 5 tablespoons vinegar
2 tablespoons light soy sauce

2–3 teaspoons sugar
4 teaspoons *mirin* or dry sherry
1 tablespoon freshly grated *wasabi* (see note)

185

Salt the fish fillets, making sure to thoroughly cover the skin side. Allow to rest, skin side up, for 20 minutes, or until the salt has dissolved and the skin is wet.

In the meantime, wash and scrub the cucumber but do not peel. Cut into julienne strips, place in a sieve or colander, and sprinkle with salt. Allow to stand for 20 minutes, then drain on paper towels or a dish towel.

Place the fish in a shallow bowl and cover with 1 cup vinegar. Turn and leave for another 20 minutes. When ready, the fish will be firm. Peel off the skin and cut into bite-size pieces.

Prepare the dressing by mixing together 5 tablespoons vinegar, soy sauce, sugar to taste, and *mirin* or sherry.

Arrange the fish around the outside of a shallow serving dish; place the cucumber in the center and pour the dressing over the whole salad. Garnish with very small dollops of *wasabi*.

*Note:* *Wasabi* is Japanese horseradish, which is much stronger than the European variety. It can also be made from a powder that is blended with water to a mustardlike consistency.

# FRUIT AND NUT SALADS

ALTHOUGH THE FRUIT COCKTAIL is a popular appetizer in our country, in most others a fruit salad falls into the side-salad or dessert-salad category. As side salads, fruits are often combined with nuts and cheeses—grated hard cheese, cream cheese, and cottage cheese—and with certain vegetables to which they seem to have a natural affinity, for instance, grapefruit and avocado, orange and chicory, apple and celery. Dessert salads made with assorted fruits—fresh, dried, or canned in syrup—are usually dressed with a sweetened vinaigrette, fruit juices, or some creamy concoction made from yogurt, sour cream, or fresh whipped cream (there are several suggestions in the chapter on dressings). Fruits can be turned into luxurious after-dinner salads by macerating them in liqueurs such as kirsch, cassis, port, or sauterne wine; and the addition of a few drops of essence, such as orange-flower water or rose water, creates an exotically perfumed delicacy.

# NOTES ON PREPARING FRUITS

REFRIGERATION ARRESTS the ripening process of fruit. Thin-skinned fruits like peaches, plums, and nectarines ripen most quickly and are therefore most perishable. Tough-skinned fruits, such as apples, pineapples, and oranges, will last longer.

The natural sugars released when fruits are cut can cause the flesh to turn brown. A sprinkling of lemon juice will retard this process.

Fruits can be decoratively cut with special equipment such as apple slicers, melon ballers, and zigzag cutters.

Garnish fruit salads in contrasting colors with sprigs of fresh mint or parsley, fresh bay leaves, rose petals, strips of orange or lemon rind and zest, pomegranate and sesame seeds, bits of dried fruit, crystallized fruit, a sprinkling of chopped nuts or dried coconut.

# APPLES

## GOLDEN APPLE SALAD

*Serves 6*

This recipe originates from the kitchens of West Virginia, where the Golden Grime apple was first cultivated. Golden Delicious may be used with equal success. The hickory nut is related to the walnut family, so if hickory nuts or pecans are not available, substitute walnuts. This salad goes well with cold duck or goose.

| | |
|---|---|
| 1 pound yellow apples | ½ cup heavy cream, whipped to peaks |
| Juice of ½ lemon | 4 tablespoons orange marmalade |
| ½ cup pitted dates, quartered | Lettuce leaves |
| ¼ cup shelled hickory nuts or pecans | 1 tablespoon grated orange rind |
| ½ cup mayonnaise | |

Core the apples, but do not peel. Cut into large dice. Place in a large bowl and sprinkle with lemon juice. Add the dates and nuts and toss.

In a separate bowl, blend the mayonnaise and whipped cream, then fold in the marmalade. Add this mixture to the salad and combine well.

Line a platter with lettuce leaves, heap the apple salad on top, and garnish with grated orange rind. Chill before serving.

## WALDORF SALAD

*Serves 4–5*

Apple, celery, and nuts mixed with mayonnaise are the basic components of this well-known American salad invented by Oscar Tschirky for the very first banquet in 1893 at New York's famous Waldorf Astoria Hotel. Raisins, sultanas, or grapes are frequently added; celeriac, parboiled and diced, can be substituted for celery; and the dressing can be blended with whipped cream if you like.

1 head fresh, crisp celery
1 large crisp apple
½–¾ cup walnuts, coarsely chopped
½ pound seedless green grapes,
   halved, or ¼ pound raisins
Juice of ½ lemon, freshly squeezed
   and strained

4–6 tablespoons mayonnaise
2 tablespoons whipped cream
   (optional)
Salt and freshly ground pepper
Chopped fresh parsley
A few chopped celery leaves

Wash the celery, trim the stalks, and cut into ½-inch pieces. Peel the apple, core, and dice.

In a large bowl, combine the celery, apple, walnuts, and grapes or raisins. Sprinkle with lemon juice and stir. Gradually add the mayonnaise and the whipped cream, if desired, stirring constantly to blend all ingredients. Season with salt and plenty of pepper.

Chill until ready to serve and garnish with chopped parsley and celery leaves.

# BANANAS

## PLANTATION BANANA SALAD

*Serves 6*

So common and popular are bananas today that we easily forget it was as recently as 1870 that the first major shipload of this fruit arrived in Boston Harbor. This salad has other ingredients—rum, brown sugar, and lime—which were also originally brought to these shores from our tropical neighbors.

7 large bananas
1 cup sour cream
2 tablespoons dark rum
2 tablespoons light-brown sugar
1 tablespoon finely chopped candied
    ginger
¼ teaspoon salt

2–3 teaspoons lime juice
6 large romaine lettuce leaves
2 large ripe peaches, cut into sixths
2 cups fresh strawberries, stemmed
    and hulled
6 sprigs of mint

Mash one of the bananas with a fork and gradually blend in the sour cream, rum, brown sugar, ginger, salt, and lime juice to taste. Chill.

Place one romaine leaf on each of six individual serving plates. Peel and slice the remaining bananas lengthwise. Place one on each plate, with two peach sections and a helping of strawberries. Spoon the chilled dressing over all and garnish with a sprig of mint.

## KELAKA RAITA

### INDIAN BANANAS IN YOGURT

*Serves 4–5*

Raita, a popular Indian relish, is a blend of well-seasoned yogurt, served as a side dish to refresh the palate between mouthfuls of hot curries. The "seasonings" are often chopped fruits and vegetables.

2 cups thick yogurt
Salt and freshly ground pepper
1 green chili pepper, finely chopped
    (see page 95)

3 large bananas, thinly sliced
2 tablespoons finely chopped fresh
    coriander leaves

Season the yogurt with salt and pepper. Add the chopped chili and bananas, and mix to thoroughly blend. Chill and garnish with chopped coriander.

## BANANAS WITH CHOPPED WALNUTS

*Serves 4*

1 bunch watercress
4 large firm bananas
Juice of ½ lemon, freshly squeezed
    and strained
3 tablespoons mayonnaise
3 tablespoons sour cream

3 tablespoons finely chopped fresh
    parsley
2 ounces coarsely chopped walnuts
Sugar or salt
Paprika

Wash the watercress and remove any damaged leaves and stems. Drain thoroughly. Peel and slice the bananas into thin rounds. Place them in a large bowl with the lemon juice. Toss gently to moisten all the pieces.

In a separate bowl, blend the mayonnaise, sour cream, and parsley. Add this to the bananas, along with the walnuts, and stir. Season to taste with salt for a savory salad, or sugar for a sweet salad.

Make a bed of watercress on a large dish. Spoon the banana mixture on top. Chill for at least an hour and serve garnished with a sprinkling of paprika.

# CHERRIES

## CHERRIES WITH CUCUMBER

*Serves 3*

This simple salad has a stunning contrast of colors. It should be well chilled before serving and is the perfect accompaniment to cold cooked meats, poultry, and sausages.

½ pound very ripe cherries  
1 large cucumber, peeled  
Salt  

Basic Vinaigrette, page 18  
A few large lettuce leaves  
2 teaspoons chopped fresh dill  

Wash and pit the cherries (special gadgets are available for pitting cherries and olives). Cut the cucumber into thin slices, sprinkle with salt, and place in a sieve or colander to drain for 15–20 minutes. Mix the cherries, cucumber, and vinaigrette in a bowl and turn onto a shallow dish lined with lettuce leaves. Garnish with a sprinkling of chopped dill.

# GRAPEFRUIT

## NHEAM KRAUCH THLONG

### CAMBODIAN GRAPEFRUIT SALAD

*Serves 4*

Serve as a first course to grapefruit lovers. The garnishes add a savory flavor to this popular citrus fruit. Canned dried shrimp can be bought at Chinese grocers.

3 strips bacon
2 large grapefruit
4 jumbo shrimp, peeled and chopped

4 tablespoons grated and toasted
coconut
2 tablespoons dried shrimp

Fry the bacon until very crisp. Drain on paper towels. Peel the grapefruit, re-move the pith and membrane, and cut the flesh into sections. Place in a bowl and squeeze any remaining juice onto the fruit. Add the shrimp and coconut and toss. Crumble the bacon and dried shrimp into the salad and chill. Just before serving, toss again. No dressing is required.

# MANGOES

MANGOES ARE A FRUIT native to Asia and popular in tropical regions all over the world. They can be purchased in most parts of the United States, with best supplies available between May and August.

The kidney-shaped mango has green skin when unripe, changing to deep rose as it ripens. The flesh is yellow or yellow-orange, and each fruit weighs about half a pound.

Test for ripeness as you would an avocado; the fruit should be firm but yielding. To remove the large, flat pit, run a knife around the edge of the mango, cutting through to the pit. Insert a large kitchen spoon through the in-cision and carefully push the spoon's curve around the pit, nudging the flesh up and away. Turn the mango over and repeat this process. Peel and slice.

## YAM CHOMPHU

### THAI MANGO SALAD

*Serves 3–4*

3 firm green mangoes
1–2 teaspoons salt
2 tablespoons peanut or other
vegetable oil
1 tablespoon minced garlic
2 tablespoons finely chopped shallots
3 ounces lean pork, thinly sliced
2 tablespoons soy sauce
1/2 teaspoon anchovy paste

1 teaspoon light-brown sugar
2 tablespoons crumbled dried salted
shrimp (see note)
2 tablespoons peanuts, roasted and
coarsely chopped
Freshly ground pepper
1 red chili pepper, finely chopped
(see page 95)

Peel the mangoes and grate into long strips. Place in a bowl and sprinkle with salt. Use your hands to mix the fruit, making sure the salt is widely distributed. This helps remove some of the sour taste. Rinse under a cold tap, squeeze gently, and place in a sieve or colander to drain.

In the meantime, heat the oil in a frying pan and add the garlic. Remove when crisp and golden brown; next, fry the shallots until soft and translucent, about 3–4 minutes. Set both aside and, in the same oil, fry the pork over medium heat, stirring constantly. After 2 minutes, add the soy sauce, anchovy paste, brown sugar, dried shrimp, and chopped nuts. Stir and cook for another minute or so. Remove from the heat.

Place the fruit in a large bowl and pour in the mixture from the frying pan, along with the garlic and shallots. Toss well and season to taste with salt and pepper. Serve at room temperature in the Thai manner—with a sprinkling of chopped red chili across the top.

*Note:* Dried salted shrimp is available in Chinese grocery stores.

# MELON

MELONS ARE A WONDERFULLY versatile fruit. Prices fluctuate throughout the year and in different parts of the country, but, in general, summer is the best time for bargains and flavor.

Popular varieties of melon include the muskmelon, or rough-skinned cantaloupe, probably our most popular melon, cheapest in August and September, having a juicy, orange flesh; crenshaw, a hybrid muskmelon weighing 7–9 pounds, with a yellow-green rind and pink or bright salmon-colored flesh, generally in the supermarkets between July and October; the pumpkin-shaped casaba, a delicate, pale-fleshed melon, available from July through November; the honeydew, a large (average weight 4–6 pounds), smooth, and pale-green-skinned melon with lovely, juicy green flesh, generally available from February through October; and Persian melon, resembling an oversized cantaloupe, with slightly smoother rind and a more fragrant bouquet. In a class by itself is the watermelon. Its crisp red flesh literally melts in the mouth, but because of its very high water content, it is not an ideal fruit for salads: it tends to lose its crispness very quickly while adding excessive water to the salad.

With their rainbow range of pastel-colored flesh, different melons blend wonderfully together. Scooped into balls and served in chilled glasses, garnished with sprigs of mint, lime zest, fresh blueberries, or a scoop of sherbert, they make one of the most refreshing of all fruit salads. Melon balls also blend well with many other fruits. Try mangoes, papayas, bananas, and berries. Grapes and cherries are also a decorative addition to a bowl of melon balls.

## ISRAELI MELON SALAD

*Serves 3–4*

Galia is a lovely sweet melon with pale-green flesh grown in Israel. A small ripe honeydew melon can be substituted in this recipe.

| | |
|---|---|
| 1 large navel orange | Orange-flower water (optional) |
| ¼ pound dates, pitted and chopped | 1 Galia or small honeydew melon |
| Juice of 1 orange | ½ pound Chinese cabbage, finely |
| Cinnamon | shredded |
| Nutmeg | ½ tablespoon light vegetable oil |

Peel the orange and remove all the white membrane and pith. Carefully remove each section and place in a large bowl, along with the dates and orange juice. Sprinkle with cinnamon and nutmeg, and add orange-flower water, if desired. Stir to blend. Cut the melon in half and scoop out the seeds. Cut out melon balls with a melon cutter and add to the orange. Stir to mix all ingredients.

Toss the shredded cabbage with the oil and arrange on a large platter or shallow bowl. Pile the fruit mixture on top and chill until ready to serve.

## FESTIVE MELON AND GRAPE SALAD

*Serves 4*

| | |
|---|---|
| 1 medium-size honeydew melon or | Juice of 1 lime |
| other green melon | Juice of 1 lemon |
| ½ pound seedless green grapes | Juice of 1 orange |
| 2 tablespoons crème de menthe or | Lettuce leaves |
| kirsch | 6 sprigs mint |

Halve the melon, remove the seeds, and scoop out as much flesh as possible with a melon cutter. Using a sharp knife, trim any remaining flesh from the shell so that neat hollow remains.

Cut the grapes in half. In a large bowl, mix the melon balls, grapes, liqueur, and fruit juices. Toss and chill for several hours, turning occasionally to macerate all the fruit.

When ready to serve, line a large serving dish with lettuce leaves and place the melon shells on top. Fill with fruit salad, garnish with mint, and pour some of the fruit juice over the top.

# ORANGES

SINCE COLUMBUS PLANTED the first orange seeds in the New World in 1493, the United States has become the chief orange-producing country in the world. Many varieties of oranges (as well as tangerines and tangelos) are available throughout the year.

## THE EMIR'S PEARLS

*Serves 4–6*

The dramatic contrasts of orange, black, and white, reminiscent of kingly jewels, probably gave this salad its name. It was introduced to Europe by Anatole France.

4 large navel oranges
2 large sweet onions, thinly sliced
2 ounces black olives, pitted and
    coarsely chopped

Olive oil
Lemon juice

Peel the oranges and cut away the white membrane and pith from the flesh. Slice crosswise and place in a large shallow dish. Place a thin slice of onion on top of each orange and sprinkle with chopped olives. Chill for at least 2 hours, and just before serving, trickle the oil and lemon juice over the salad.

## MOROCCAN ORANGES WITH DATES AND ALMONDS

*Serves 6–8*

6 large navel oranges
8 dates, pitted and chopped
¼ cup blanched and slivered almonds
Juice of ½ lemon

1 tablespoon orange-flower water
1 teaspoon confectioners' sugar
Powdered cinnamon

Peel the oranges and cut away the white membrane and pith from the flesh. Cut into crosswise slices and place in a shallow bowl with the dates and almonds.

    In a small separate bowl, blend the lemon juice, orange-flower water, and sugar. Pour this over the oranges and chill for at least 2 hours. Just before serving, sprinkle with cinnamon.

## ORANGE SALAD WITH SESAME SEEDS

*Serves 4–6*

A delicious accompaniment for cold turkey, duck, or lamb.

1 bunch of watercress
4 large navel oranges
1 ounce toasted sesame seeds (see
  Oriental Salad Dressing, page 31)
1 tablespoon lemon juice, freshly
  squeezed and strained

3 tablespoons corn or safflower oil
¼ teaspoon sugar
¼ teaspoon dry mustard
Salt and freshly ground pepper

Wash the watercress, removing any damaged leaves and stems. Drain and dry thoroughly.

Peel the oranges and cut away the pith and white membrane from the flesh. Cut into sections.

In a large shallow bowl, make a bed of watercress leaves. Add a layer of oranges, and sprinkle with sesame seeds. Repeat until all the ingredients have been used.

Place the lemon juice, oil, sugar, and dry mustard in a small jar. Cover and shake. Season with salt and pepper, and pour over the salad. Chill for an hour before serving.

## SOUTH AFRICAN ORANGE AND GUAVA SALAD

*Serves 4–5*

Guavas are a subtropical fruit, small and sweet, with a slightly mealy flesh, varying in color from white to pale pink. Cultivated to a small extent in Florida, they are available fresh mainly in gourmet food stores. They can, however, be bought in cans from many large supermarkets.

Serve this salad as a dessert or as an accompaniment to venison or roast beef.

2 large navel oranges
3 fresh guavas or one 14-ounce can
½ cup sherry

¼ cup Cointreau or brandy
Confectioners' sugar
Large romaine lettuce leaves

Peel the oranges and remove the pith and white membrane from the flesh. Slice crosswise and set aside in a large bowl.

Peel the guavas if fresh; drain if canned. Slice into sections and add to the oranges. Pour on the sherry, Cointreau or brandy, and a sprinkling of sugar.

Toss and refrigerate for several hours, turning the fruits occasionally to ensure that all pieces are well macerated.

Arrange on a large platter lined with lettuce leaves and spoon on some of the liquid.

# PINEAPPLE

## RUSSIAN PINEAPPLE AND CELERY SALAD

*Serves 4*

Excellent with cold pork, veal, or poultry.

½ fresh pineapple
3 stalks celery
1 medium-size cooked beet
3 tablespoons olive oil
1 tablespoon cider vinegar

½ teaspoon sugar
Salt and freshly ground pepper
8 large romaine lettuce leaves
Sprigs of parsley

Remove the skin from the pineapple and cut away the tough woody core. Cut the flesh into pieces 1 inch square.

Wash and dry the celery; cut crosswise into ½-inch slices. Peel the beet and cut into ½-inch dice.

Prepare the dressing by combining the oil, vinegar, and sugar. Season to taste with salt and pepper.

In a mixing bowl blend the celery and pineapple with the dressing. Toss and turn onto a large platter lined with romaine leaves, leaving a space in the center. Fill the space with the beets.

Chill until ready to serve, garnished with a few parsley sprigs.

# MIXED-FRUIT SALADS

## TROPICAL FRUIT SALAD

*Serves 4–6*

On discovering papaya, a fruit native to tropical America, Columbus wrote in his journal: "The Natives here are very strong and live largely on a tree

197

melon called 'the fruit of the angels.' " Papayas can usually be found in small amounts throughout the year, though for peak quantities, May or June is best. The fruits vary in size from 6 to 12 inches, and the color, too, varies from green-skinned when unripe to deep yellow or orange at maturity.

This salad may be served as a dessert (enhanced by the addition of a little kirsch) or as a light lunch, accompanied by cottage cheese or yogurt.

2 ripe papayas
½ fresh pineapple
2 large bananas
¼ pound green seedless grapes
3 tangerines
Juice of 1 orange

Juice of 1 lemon
2 sprigs fresh mint, coarsely chopped
2 tablespoons kirsch (optional)
1 ounce shredded coconut (preferably fresh)

Cut the papayas in half, scoop out the seeds, and cut away the skin with a paring knife or potato peeler. Cut them into large dice, about 1 inch square, and place in a large bowl.

Cut away the stem and skin of the pineapple, as well as the tough woody core. Cut into pieces 1 inch square and add to the papayas.

Peel the bananas and cut into thin slices. Halve the grapes. Add both fruits to the salad bowl.

Peel the tangerines and remove the white membrane. Separate into sections and add to the other fruits. Pour in the orange and lemon juices, add the mint, and toss well. (If kirsch is to be added, do so now.) Chill for several hours and garnish, just before serving, with shredded coconut.

## GAY NINETIES SALAD

### Serves 8

A rich summer dessert salad, made with fresh fruits and rose-perfumed port wine and cream. Because the fruits need time to macerate, begin preparation well in advance.

1 cup port wine
2 cups freshly picked rose petals, rinsed clean
1 cup heavy cream
2 pints fresh strawberries, hulled
½ pound fresh black cherries, halved and pitted

2 large ripe peaches, pitted and cut into eighths
½ cup granulated sugar
1 tablespoon confectioners' sugar
Mint sprigs

Pour the port into a bowl, add half the rose petals, and stir. Pour the cream into another bowl and add to it the remaining rose petals. Place both bowls in the refrigerator for at least 2 hours. Into another large bowl, place the strawberries, cherries, and peaches. Sprinkle, while stirring, with the granulated sugar. Make sure all the fruits are well covered with sugar, then place in the refrigerator for 2 hours.

Strain the rose petals from the port and pour the liquid into the fruit. Stir gently but thoroughly to moisten all ingredients. Return the fruits to the refrigerator for another hour.

Just before serving, strain the rose petals from the cream. Whip the cream until stiff, adding the confectioners' sugar toward the end. Serve in a sauceboat with the fruit garnished with mint.

## SUMMER MIXED BERRY SALAD

*Serves 4–5*

Throughout the summer different kinds of berries are available. Experiment with both variety and quantity.

1 cup raspberries
1 cup blackberries or boysenberries
1 cup blueberries
1 cup red currants

1 cup light red wine
⅓ cup sugar
Fresh mint
Sour cream or yogurt

Mix the berries in a large bowl with the wine and sugar. Toss gently and chill for several hours.

Serve garnished with mint and with a sauceboat of sour cream or yogurt.

## NEW ZEALAND KIWI SALAD

*Serves 6–8*

The kiwi is a strange-looking fruit, about the size of a lime, with fuzzy brown skin, emerald-green flesh, and a center of tiny, edible black seeds. Originally an exotic import from New Zealand and China (and sometimes known as the Chinese gooseberry), it is now being grown in the United States. Sliced in half, the kiwi can be eaten whole with a small spoon; or, peeled and sliced, it makes a delicious vitamin C–rich addition to a fruit salad, like the one below.

½ large pineapple, peeled and cut
  into chunks
2 medium-size bananas, peeled and
  sliced
2 navel oranges, peeled and sectioned

Juice of 2 lemons
1 cup fresh strawberries, stemmed
  and halved
3 kiwi fruit, peeled and sliced
1 tablespoon honey

Place the pineapple chunks, sliced bananas, and orange sections in a large glass bowl. Squeeze the lemon juice over the fruit and toss. Add the strawberries and kiwi fruit, and mix again. Boil the honey with ¾ cup of water; cool and pour over the salad. Gently toss and refrigerate for several hours.

# ISRAELI POMEGRANATE PYRAMID

*Serves 6–8*

The pomegranate is an ancient Semitic symbol for life and fertility. The seeds were used as seasoning by the early Greeks, as they are still today throughout much of eastern Europe and Asia.

Under the tough, pale-red skin, which can be peeled away with the fingers, is a myriad of bright, translucent little seeds that yield a deliciously tart juice. Pomegranates can usually be bought here throughout the autumn and early winter.

This beautiful salad is served in Israel to celebrate the autumn harvest holiday, Succoth.

2 large grapefruits, peeled and
  sectioned
3 navel oranges, peeled and sectioned
2 tangerines, peeled and sectioned

Seeds of 1 pomegranate
2–3 tablespoons honey
Juice of 1 lemon
A few fresh dates

On a large, round plate make a ring of fanned-out grapefruit sections. Top with a ring of orange sections. Fill the center with tangerine sections and chill for several hours. Mix the pomegranate seeds gently with a dressing made from the honey and lemon juice. Pour the pomegranate mixture over the top of the tangerines, decorate with fresh dates, and serve.

# DRIED FRUIT AND NUT SALADS

## MAIWA KACHUMAR

### INDIAN FRUIT AND NUT SALAD

*Serves 4*

2–3 tablespoons raisins
1 tablespoon ghee (clarified butter),
   melted
2 cups walnuts, chopped
4 dried figs, coarsely chopped
6 dates, pitted and quartered
6 sprigs watercress, coarsely chopped
¼ cup fresh shredded coconut

1 large green apple, peeled, cored,
   and coarsely grated
3 tablespoons olive oil
1 tablespoon white wine vinegar
Salt and freshly ground pepper
A few large lettuce leaves
1 large tomato, cut into wedges
A few sprigs of coriander

Soak the raisins in very hot water for 15 minutes. Drain.

Place the melted ghee in a large bowl and add the walnuts, figs, dates, raisins, watercress, coconut, and apple. Mix well.

In a small separate bowl, prepare a dressing of oil, vinegar, salt, and pepper to taste. Pour over the salad and toss carefully, but thoroughly, to cover all ingredients.

Turn onto a large serving dish lined with lettuce leaves and garnish with tomato wedges and coriander leaves.

## KHOSHAF

*Serves 6–8*

This wonderful salad of macerated fruits was traditionally made with only apricots, raisins, and mixed nuts. Of the many variations, I like this particular combination. *Khoshaf* should be prepared well ahead, so that the bouquet has time to fully permeate the fruit.

¼ pound dried apricots
¼ pound dried figs
¼ pound dried prunes
2 ounces raisins
3 ounces blanched almonds
2 ounces pine nuts
2 ounces unsalted, shelled pistachios

2–3 tablespoons Hymettus honey
1 tablespoon orange-flower water
Orange juice
2 tablespoons pomegranate seeds
   (optional)
Yogurt or sour cream (optional)

201

Wash the dried fruit and soak overnight in cold water. Drain and place in a large mixing bowl. Add the nuts and stir.

In a small, separate bowl, blend the honey with the orange-flower water and several tablespoons of orange juice. Pour this over the salad and toss gently to cover all ingredients. Cover and chill for several hours.

As a dessert, serve garnished with a sprinkling of pomegranate seeds and a bowl of yogurt or sour cream, if desired. *Khoshaf* is also delicious served with roasted meats or as an exotic accompaniment to stews and casseroles seasoned with savory Middle Eastern herbs and spices.

# SALADE AUX NOISETTES

### HAZELNUT SALAD

*Serves 6*

½ pound dried white beans
Salt
1 pound green beans, washed and
   trimmed
2 stalks celery, cleaned and chopped

¼ pound roasted hazelnuts
6 tablespoons Basic Vinaigrette,
   page 18
Pinch of nutmeg

Soak the white beans for 2 hours, then cook in plenty of boiling water, over medium-low heat, for about 45 minutes, or until tender but still whole. Add salt about 10 minutes before cooking is completed. Drain and cool.

Cook the green beans in a little lightly salted boiling water for approximately 8 minutes, or until just tender. Drain, refresh with cold water, and drain again.

In a large bowl, mix the two beans with the celery and nuts. Add the vinaigrette and nutmeg, and toss to thoroughly blend. Serve at once.

# PECAN AND POMEGRANATE SALAD

*Serves 5–6*

The pecan is a truly American nut. Even its name is derived from the Cree Indian word *paccan,* meaning "nut having a hard shell to crack." This salad makes an unusual accompaniment for roasted game.

3–4 hard sweet apples (approximately 1 pound)
2 tablespoons lemon juice
½ pound shelled pecans
2 tablespoons dark rum

4 tablespoons olive oil
Salt and freshly ground pepper
½ teaspoon sugar (optional)
A few large lettuce leaves
4 tablespoons pomegranate seeds

Peel and core the apples and cut into thin wedges. Sprinkle with 1 tablespoon of the lemon juice. Place in a large bowl with the pecans and stir in the rum. Make a dressing from oil, remaining tablespoon lemon juice, salt, pepper, and sugar, if desired. Pour over the apples and pecans and toss gently, but thoroughly, to blend all ingredients. Turn onto a serving dish lined with lettuce leaves and sprinkle all over with pomegranate seeds. Chill for an hour before serving.

# NOUGADA

### ALMOND SALAD

*Serves 4*

References to the almond are numerous in early records. It is mentioned many times in the Bible, and the Greek philosopher Theophrastus described its singular quality of producing blossoms before leaves. The Hebrews called it *shakod* ("the awakening"), for it blooms in Palestine as early as May.

This Middle Eastern salad of ground almonds is an excellent accompaniment to poultry, or as part of a vegetarian supper.

2 cups coarsely ground almonds
3 tablespoons chopped fresh parsley
1 teaspoon superfine sugar
Salt and white pepper
1 clove garlic, crushed

6 tablespoons olive oil
Juice of 1 large lemon, freshly squeezed and strained
Slivered almonds
A few sprigs of parsley

Put the ground almonds and chopped parsley into a bowl. Add the sugar, a sprinkling of salt, and a pinch of white pepper. Stir, then add the garlic. Gradually add the oil and lemon juice, in alternating trickles, while mixing constantly with a fork. Correct the seasoning with additional salt and pepper, and turn the mixture onto a shallow serving dish. Garnish with slivered almonds and parsley sprigs.

# INDEX

205

INDEX